TWO YEAR OLDS OF 1995

11th Edition

STEVE TAPLIN

This Edition First Published in 1995
by
Pride of Place (UK) Ltd
Specialist Sports Publishers

10987654321

All rights reserved. No part of this publication may be reproduced, stored in a retieval system, or transmitted, in any form or by any means without the prior written permission of the publisher, nor be otherwise circulated in any form of binding or cover other than that in which it is published and without a similar condition being imposed on the subsequent purchase

British Library Cataloguing in Publication Data.
A catalogue record for this book is available
from the British Library.

ISBN 1 874645 54-X

Copyright PRIDE OF PLACE (UK) LTD

Printed by
Redwood Books

PRIDE OF PLACE (UK) LTD
UNIT 22, CBTC,
EUXTON LANE, CHORLEY
LANCASHIRE PR7 6TE

CONTENTS

Introduction   5

2 Year Olds of 1995   7

100 to Follow   89

Stallions   111

Racing Trends   132

Index   141

INTRODUCTION

This book aims to provide the reader with the names and trainers of the finest bred young European racehorses of 1995. The bulk of them have been chosen for their excellent bloodlines, with particular emphasis being given to the female side of the pedigree, though as the best broodmares are invariably bred to the top stallions anyway, there is a preponderance of the dominant sire lines of Europe and America. For instance, the pedigrees of no less than forty four colts or fillies by the great sire Sadlers Wells are examined in detail, whilst other sires with large numbers of representatives are Green Desert (21), Nashwan (18), Mr Prospector (15), Kris (14), Danzig (12), Woodman (12), Rainbow Quest (11) and Dayjur (11).

As these equine blue-bloods are most often trained with their three-year-old careers very much in mind, I have added another section to the book this year for two-year-olds from those stables noted for the precocity of their young horses. With the help of such trainers as Jack Berry, Mick Channon, Geoff Lewis and Michael Bell, the two-year-olds in this extra section have been chosen because they are expected to perform especially well this season.

Apart from this exciting new development, the book retains its successful format and is divided into four distinct parts -

a) The premier section of the book, listing Europe's best-bred two-year olds under their trainers.

b) The new section for primarily precocious juveniles.

c) The stallion reference, detailing the racing and stud careers of each sire in part (a).

d) Two-year-old race trends, a statistical analysis which focuses on those races which regularly provide pointers towards future classic events.

All the top training establishments of Britain, France and Ireland are represented - those with the most selections being Henry Cecil - from whose yard at Warren Place I have chosen forty four 2-y-o's - Michael Stoute (30), Andre Fabre (26), John Gosden (22) and Peter Chapple-Hyam (18).

This year I have included many more two-year-olds - over 450 - than ever before, in an even greater effort to uncover the cream of the 1993 crop of foals. Four of the last eight Derby winners and six of the last eight King George VI and Queen Elizabeth Diamond Stakes winners had previously appeared in editions of this book. Regular readers will need no introduction to them, or indeed to the scores of other top class racehorses that were first given a mention in the 'Two-Year-Olds' book. They include such equine heroes as Barathea, Commander in Chief, Dayjur, Ezzoud, Generous, Marling, Mtoto, Musical Bliss, Nashwan, Old Vic, Opera House, Reference Point, Royal Academy, Salsabil, Snow Bride, Warning - the list is as impressive as it is almost endless! Over the past two years this illustrious company has been joined by the likes of Carnegie, Distant View, East of the Moon, Foyer, King's Theatre, La Confederation, Maroof (66-1 winner of the Queen Elizabeth II Stakes!) and numerous 1995 classic contenders including Aqaarid, Diffident, Eltish, Gay Gallanta, Macoumba, Moonshell, Myself and Red Carnival.

This year's selections include the full brothers or sisters to seventeen Group or Grade one winners, notably the Derby winner Quest For Fame, the Oaks winner Diminuendo, the champion European 2-y-o Hector Protector, the Breeders Cup Sprint winner Sheikh Albadou and the dual Juddmonte International Stakes winner Ezzoud.

You will also find the half-brothers or half-sisters to well over a hundred Group or Grade one winners. Among the best of them are the Derby winners Commander in Chief, Dr Devious and Erhaab, the 'King George' winners Belmez, King's Theatre and Opera House, the 'Arc' winners Dancing Brave, Saumarez and Subotica, six Breeders Cup winners - notably Miesque, seven Champion Two Year Olds including Arazi and Celtic Swing, and other favourites such as Lochsong and Rodrigo de Triano. Finally there are the first foals of the high class racemares Chimes of Freedom, In the Groove, Jet Ski Lady, Kartajana and Shadayid. Truly a menu to sharpen any racing fan's appetite!

NOTES

The AEI quoted for American sires in the stallion reference is the Average Earnings Index. This indicates how much prize money the progeny of a sire has earned, on average, in relation to the average earnings of all runners in the same years. The average earnings of all runners in any year is represented by an index of 1.00. Thus a sire with an AEI of 3.00 can be said to have sired the winners of three times the amount of prize money than average.

Steve Taplin. May '95.

TWO YEAR OLDS OF 1995

Robert Armstrong

1 - ALHALAL
Chestnut colt. Cadeaux Genereux - Vaguely (Bold Lad, Ire).
March 4. 95,000 gns.
Half-brother to the high class Shady Heights (by Shirley Heights), winner of 7 races from 6f to 10.5f, notably York's Group 1 International Stakes (on the disqualification of Persian Heights), and 2nd in both the Eclipse Stakes and Phoenix Champion Stakes, to the very useful 3-y-o 8f and 10f winner Dimmer (by Kalaglow), the useful 3-y-o 7f and 8f winner Jdaayel (by Ajdal), the useful 2-y-o 6f winner Top Ruler (by High Top), the minor Irish 3-y-o winner Classic Memory (by Sadlers Wells) and the minor 1994 3-y-o 8f winner Imprecise (by Polish Precedent). The dam, a fairly useful filly, won over 8f at 2 yrs and 10f at 3 yrs. 2nd dam, Vaguely Mine (by Silly Season), won over 12f at 3 yrs and is a half-sister to the St Leger winner Provoke. Robert told me that **Alhalal** is a very good looking horse that has grown a lot and will take a little time but should be out around September, probably making his debut over 7f. (Hamdan Al-Maktoum).
Optimum 3-y-o distance: 7f.

2 - MAWWAL (USA)
Chestnut colt. Elmaamul - Dish Dash (Bustino).
February 13.
Half-brother to the 1994 Group 1 8f Queen Elizabeth II Stakes winner Maroof (by Danzig), the quite useful 1993 2-y-o 6f winner Fawaakeh, the fair 1992 3-y-o 10f winner Mayaasa (both by Lyphard), the minor French winner White Mantle (by Nureyev) and the useful 1987 2-y-o 7f winner Arrasas (by Irish River). The dam, a smart filly, won once over 6f at 2 yrs and over 8f and 12f at 3, the latter event being the Group 2 Ribblesdale Stakes at Royal Ascot. She is a half-sister to 6 winners including Feliciano, Canterbury Tale, Silk and Satin and Smuggly - all at least very useful. 2nd dam, Loose Cover (by Venture VII), was a useful miler and a winner of 4 races. Robert describes **Mawwal** as "a typical 2-y-o type who looks like he's finishing growing upwards and will now start strengthening. He's done a bit of work, I'm pleased with his progress and he should be out by 2,000 gns day. Eventually I feel he'll be best at around a mile." (Hamdan Al-Maktoum).
Optimum 3-y-o distance: 10-12f.

Ian Balding

3 - BALLET HIGH (IRE)
Bay colt. Sadlers Wells - Marie d'Argonne (Jefferson).
April 9. 5th foal.
Closely related to the high class Group 1 Ladbroke Sprint Cup, Group 2 8f Juddmonte Lockinge Stakes and Group 3 8f Prix Edmond Blanc winner Polar Falcon (by Nureyev) and to the quite useful 2-y-o 5f and 3-y-o 7.3f winner La Dama Bonita (by El Gran Senor) and half-brother to the 1995 3-y-o Mokuti (by Green Desert). The dam won over 10f in France, was 3 rd in the Group 3 10.5f Prix Penelope and was also a stakes winner in the USA. She is a half-sister to the Group 2 Prix de Pomone winner Marie de Litz out of the unraced Mohair (by Blue Tom), herself a half-sister to the dam of the Prix Vermeille winner Paysanne. Ian explained to me that **Ballet High** had met with an accident and had been pin-fired. As a result, he felt it unlikely that he

would have more than one run at the back-end. (Watership Down Stud).
Optimum 3-y-o distance: 10f.

4 - DELTA DANCER
Bay colt. Caerleon - Sharp Castan (Sharpen Up).
May 17.
Half-brother to the 1995 3-y-o Royal Solo (by Sadlers Wells), to the smart 2-y-o Group 1 7f Dewhurst Stakes, Group 1 7f National Stakes and 3-y-o Group 1 12f Gran Premio d'Italia winner Dashing Blade (by Elegant Air), the useful 2-y-o dual 7f and subsequent French 6-8f winner Navarzato (by Dominion), the useful 4-y-o dual 7f winner Powerful Edge (by Primo Dominie), the quite useful 3-y-o 12f winner Belle Enfant (by Beldale Flutter) and to minor winners by Chief Singer and Young Generation. The dam, a useful 5f winner at 2 yrs and 3rd in the Hoover Fillies Mile, is a half-sister to the smart miler General Vole. 2nd dam, Sultry One (by Tropique), only ran twice. "A medium-sized, nice shaped colt, though a bit nervous, **Delta Dancer** should be out around mid-June." said Ian. (Mr J. C. Smith).
Optimum 3-y-o distance: 10-12f.

5 - LOCHSPRING
Bay filly. Precocious - Peckitts Well (Lochnager).
March 13. 5th foal.
Half-sister to the champion sprinter Lochsong (by Song), winner of the Prix de l'Abbaye (twice), Kings Stand Stand Stakes, Keeneland Nunthorpe Stakes, King George Stakes (twice) etc., to the fairly useful 1994 2-y-o 7f winner Dashing Water (by Dashing Blade) and the fair 1994 3-y-o 10.2f winner Lochbelle (by Robellino). The dam was a fairly useful winner of five races at 2 and 3 yrs from 5-6f. 2nd dam, Great Grey Niece (by Great Nephew), was placed over 5f at 2 yrs. "**Lochspring** has a lovely temperament and is a nice mover, but is very big and backward and probably won't run as a 2-y-o." (Mr. J. C. Smith).
Optimum 3-y-o distance: 5-7f.

6 - REGAL EAGLE
Bay colt. Shirley Heights - On the Tiles (Thatch).
May 2. 5th foal.
Closely related to the smart 1990 Group 1 10f Prix Saint-Alary winner Air de Rien (by Elegant Air) and half-brother to the very useful 1994 2-y-o 7f winner and Royal Lodge Stakes 2nd Stiletto Blade (by Dashing Blade). The dam won over 10f in Ireland at 3 yrs and is a half-sister to 5 winners out of the placed Afasheen (by Sheshoon), herself a half-sister to the dams of Blushing Groom, Zabarella (Premio Lydia Tesio) and Maroun (Prix Jean Prat). "A big, strong, lovely-natured horse **Regal Eagle** should be suited by 7f as a 2-y-o and is a very nice horse", the trainer tells me. (Mr. J. C. Smith).
Optimum 3-y-o distance: 10-12f.

7 - SILVER BORDER
Chestnut colt. Kris - Silver Fling (The Minstrel).
January 21. 3rd foal.
Brother to the fair 1994 8f to 10.4f placed 3-y-o Sundin and half-brother to the 1995 3-y-o Silver Sting (by Nashwan), unplaced on his only outing at 2 yrs. The dam, a very smart sprinter, won the Group 1 Prix de l'Abbaye and the Group 3 King George Stakes and was placed in the William Hill Sprint Championship at York and the Vernons Sprint Cup (twice). She is a sister to the high class filly Silverdip, winner of the Salisbury 1,000 gns Trial, the Strensall Stakes and the Montrose Handicap before an injury curtailed her career, and half-sister to the German Group 3 stakes winner Imperial Fling and the minor U.S. stakes winner Imperial Dilemma. 2nd dam, Royal Dilemma (by Buckpasser), was a stakes-placed winner at up to 6f out of the champion U.S. 2-y-o filly Queen Empress. Ian tells me that **Silver Border** is a "nice, big, strong colt and a fine mover. He'll probably want 7f as a 2-y-o." (Mr George Strawbridge).
Optimum 3-y-o distance: 8-10f.

8 - SKILLINGTON (USA)
Bay colt. Danzig - Annie Edge (Nebbiolo).
March 19.

Half-brother to the top class miler Selkirk, winner of the Group 1 Queen Elizabeth II Stakes, the Group 2 Beefeater Gin Celebration Mile, the Group 2 Juddmonte Lockinge Stakes and the Group 2 Challenge Stakes, to the minor 3-y-o dual 2 mile winner Casual Flash (both by Sharpen Up), the 1994 3-y-o 8f winner Rory Creek (by Silver Hawk) and the 5-6f winner Vailmont (by Diesis) - both quite useful. The dam, a useful 5f winner at 2 yrs, was a smart winner of the 3-y-o 7f Kiveton Park Stakes before winning two Graded stakes races on turf in the USA at 8f and 10f. 2nd dam, Friendly Court (by Be Friendly), was a fairly useful Irish 2-y-o 5f winner. "A nice colt and one of our best prospects, **Skillington** is medium-sized, round and compact. He should be out by the end of May." (Mr George Strawbridge).
Optimum 3-y-o distance: 8f.

Pascal Bary

9 - GREEN PLANET
Bay colt. Green Desert - Interval (Habitat).
April 10. 5th foal.
Half-brother to the French trained 3-y-o Krisia, the fair 1992 3-y-o 10f winner Intent (both by Kris) and the 1994 French 3-y-o 8f listed stakes winner Cheyenne Dream (by Dancing Brave). The dam was a high class sprinting winner of four races from 5f to 8f including the Group 2 Prix Maurice de Gheest, was 3rd in the 1,000 gns to Miesque and is a half-sister to the very useful 1994 3-y-o 8f and 10f winner Interim and to the unraced Welcome Break, herself dam of the Hoover Fillies Mile winner Invited Guest. 2nd dam, Intermission (by Stage Door Johnny), won the Cambridgeshire Handicap and is a half-sister to 7 winners including the high class middle distance colts Peacetime and Quiet Fling. One notable example of a son of Green Desert out of a Habitat mare is the very useful sprinter Midhish. (Khaled Abdulla).
Optimum 3-y-o distance: 5-7f.

10 - GUEST OF ANCHOR
Bay filly. Slip Anchor - Intimate Guest (Be My Guest).
February 6. 3rd foal.
Closely related to the fair 1994 Irish 3-y-o 6f winner Welcome Guest (by Shirley Heights) and half-sister to the quite useful 1993 3-y-o 8f winner Golden Guest (by Rainbow Quest). The dam, a very useful winner of 4 races including the Group 3 8f May Hill Stakes, was 2nd in the Pretty Polly Stakes, the Sir Charles Clore Memorial Stakes and the Waterford Candelabra Stakes. 2nd dam, As You Desire Me (by Kalamoun), a very useful winner of 3 races at around 8f, was a half-sister to the Irish Derby and St Leger 3rd Classic Example and to the smart middle-distance performer Illustrious Prince. (I. M. Fares).
Optimum 3-y-o distance: 10f.

Michael Bell

11 - ALYSHADEED (USA)
Bay colt. Shadeed - Bialy (Alydar).
April 15. 4th foal.
Brother to the American colt Alydeed, winner of the Grade 1 7f Carter Handicap and Grade 1 Queen's Plate, and 2nd in Preakness Stakes, and half-brother to the minor American winners Imotar (by Icecapade) and Alybro (by Danzig Connection). The dam is an unraced half-sister to 3 stakes winners including the good sire Clever Trick and to Clever Miss - dam of two Graded stakes winners. 2nd dam, Kankakee Miss (by Better Bee), a winner of 4 races at up to 8f and stakes-placed, is a half-sister to Bambee T.T. - herself dam of four good horses in Ascot Knight, Bounding Away, Overreaction and Petit Loup. When I spoke to Michael at the end of May, he had yet to receive **Alyshadeed** in his yard. (Maktoum Al-Maktoum).
Optimum 3-y-o distance: 7-10f.

12 - ANTONELLA BIN (IRE)
Grey filly. Sadlers Wells - Lady Capulet (Sir Ivor).

May 10. 50,000 Ir gns.
Sister to the very smart 1991 Irish 2-y-o El Prado, winner of 4 races including the Group 1 National Stakes and Group 2 Beresford Stakes, to the 1992 Irish 2-y-o 7f and 3-y-o 14f winner Portrait Gallery, the 1993 Japanese 2-y-o winner Pia Tiara and the 1994 2-y-o Royal College (unplaced on his only outing), and half-brother to the high class 8f Desmond Stakes winner and Irish Derby, Irish 2,000 gns and Phoenix Champion Stakes placed Entitled (by Mill Reef). The dam won the 1977 Irish 1,000 gns on the first of her 3 outings, is a sister to the Royal Lodge Stakes winner Sir Wimborne and a half-sister to the good American sire Drone. 2nd dam, Cap and Bells (by Tom Fool), was a stakes-placed winner in the USA. (Mr. L. Gaucci).
Quite apart from the aforementioned El Prado, another good example of this Sadlers Wells - Sir Ivor cross is the useful Ribblesdale Stakes 2nd Ivrea. Michael explained that **Antonella Bin** had been turned out for several months and, now looking a picture, was just about to enter training in late April. (Mr L. Gaucci).
Optimum 3-y-o distance: 10-12f.

Jim Bolger

13 - CATALYST (IRE)
Bay filly. Sadlers Wells - Welsh Love (Ela Mana Mou).
March 6. 3rd foal. 210,000 Ir gns.
Half-sister to the fairly useful 1994 2-y-o 7f and 8f winner Ihtiram (by Royal Academy) and to the moderate 1994 10f placed 3-y-o Bird's Wing (by Bluebird). The dam, a minor Irish 3-y-o 12f winner, is a half-sister to the Coronation Stakes winner Flame of Tara - dam of the Group 1 winners Salsabil and Marju - and to the Lupe Stakes 2nd Fruition - dam of the high class stayer Kneller. 2nd dam, Welsh Flame (by Welsh Pageant), was a useful 3-y-o winner of 4 races at around 8f and is a half-sister to the Musidora Stakes 2nd Sofala - dam of the Doncaster Cup 2nd Bourbon Boy. A notable example of this Sadlers Wells - Ela Mana Mou cross is the smart King Edward VII Stakes winner Foyer.
Optimum 3-y-o distance: 10-12f.

14 - DREAM BAY (USA)
Bay colt. Mr Prospector - Nazoo (Nijinsky).
April 28. 1st foal.
The dam won all four of her 2-y-o races, from 6-7f, and was a very useful filly. She is a sister to 3 winners by Nijinsky, namely the useful Irish 2-y-o 6f and subsequent French 8f winner Lake Como, the fairly useful Irish 6-8f winner Single Combat and the minor American winner La Confidence, herself dam of the multiple U.S. Grade 1 winning filly Flawlessly. She is also a half-sister to 4 winners including the U.S. 5 time winner and Grade 2 9f Round Table Handicap 2nd Magloire (by Exceller), the useful Irish 2-y-o 6f winner Miznah and the useful 3-y-o 7f winner Lacotte. 2nd dam, La Dame du Lac (by Round Table), is an unraced half-sister to 9 winners including the Grade 1 winner and champion sire Halo, the top class filly Tosmah, the stakes winners Fathers Image and Maribeau, and the minor winner Queen Sucree (herself dam of the Kentucky Derby winner Cannonade and grandam of two Grade 1 winners). Like **Dream Bay**, the very useful winners Jade Robbery, Gold Seam and Numerous are all by Mr Prospector and out of Nijinsky mares. (Maktoum Al-Maktoum).
Optimum 3-y-o distance: 8f.

15 - DURRAH GREEN
Bay filly. Green Desert - Durrah (Nijinsky).
May 13. 4th foal.
Half-sister to the 1994 2-y-o 8.2f winner High Standard (by Kris), the 1994 3-y-o 10f winner Mowlaie (by Nashwan) - both fairly useful - and the 1992 Irish 2-y-o 6f winner Short Visit (by Private Account). The dam, a fairly useful French 2-y-o 8f winner, is a sister to the Grade 2 stakes winner Number (dam of the very smart 1989 2-y-o Jade Robbery), closely related to the top class sire Nureyev and a half-sister to Fairy Bridge (dam of Sadlers Wells, Fairy King and Tate Gallery), and Kilavea (dam of Kiliniski). 2nd dam, Special (by Forli), was an unplaced

sister to Thatch. (Maktoum Al-Maktoum).
Optimum 3-y-o distance: 8f.

16 - HIGH PRIORITY (IRE)
Bay colt. Marju - Blinding (High Top).
March 23. 1st foal. 80,000 Ir gns.
The dam, unplaced on both her efforts at 3 yrs, is a half-sister to the Group 3 7.3f Hungerford Stakes, Group 3 7f Kiveton Park Stakes and Group 3 7f Beeswing Stakes winner Hadeer. 2nd dam, Glinting (by Crepello), won over 6f at 2 yrs, was placed in the Nell Gwyn Stakes, and is a half-sister to the dams and grandams of numerous good winners including Bassenthwaite, Braashee, Ghariba and Keen Hunter.
Optimum 3-y-o distance: 8-10f.

17 - SOVIET DREAMER
April 3.
Half-brother to the 1994 5f and 6f placed 2-y-o Mystic Lure (by Green Desert), to the top class miler Thrill Show (by Northern Baby), winner of the Grade 1 9f Hollywood Derby and 2nd in the Prix du Moulin to Sonic Lady, the good 1986 U.S. 2-y-o colt David's Bird (by Storm Bird), the useful 1991 3-y-o 10f listed stakes winner Walim (by Nijinsky) and the fairly useful 2-y-o 7f winner Miss Fancy That (by The Minstrel). The dam won 7 races at up to 8f. 2nd dam, Coccinea (by Jaipur), won three races and is a half-sister to the dam of Affirmed. (Maktoum Al-Maktoum).
Optimum 3-y-o distance: 8f.

18 - VICE PRESIDENT
Bay filly. Polish Precedent - Don't Rush (Alleged).
April 2. 3rd foal.
Closely related to the fair 1994 3-y-o King of Show (by Green Desert) - placed six times from 7-8f, and half-sister to the fairly useful 1993 3-y-o 8.3f winner Reine de Neige (by Kris). The dam, a fairly useful 3-y-o dual 12f winner, is a half-sister to four good winners in Seaside Attraction (Grade 1 Kentucky Oaks), Gorgeous (Grade 1 Hollywood Oaks and Grade 1 Ashland Stakes), the dual Canadian Grade 3 winner Key to the Moon and the Group 3 6f Princess Margaret Stakes winner Hiamm - herself dam of two winners. 2nd dam, Kamar (by Key to the Mint), was a champion Canadian 3-y-o filly and a sister to the Grade 1 winner Love Smitten. (Maktoum Al-Maktoum).
Optimum 3-y-o distance: 8f.

Clive Brittain

19 - AMFORTAS (IRE)
Bay colt. Caerleon - High Spirited (Shirley Heights).
February 24. 2nd foal.
Half-brother to the 1995 3-y-o Motakabber (by Sadlers Wells) - previously a 460,000 gns yearling. The dam, a quite useful filly, won two of her seven races over 14f and 16f at 3 yrs and is a sister to the Premio Roma, Ribblesdale Stakes and Park Hill Stakes winner High Hawk - herself dam of the Breeders Cup Turf winner In the Wings, and a half-sister to the 8f winner Seriema - dam of the Rothmans International winner Infamy. 2nd dam, Sunbittern (by High Hawk II), was a very useful 2-y-o 6f and 7f winner. "**Amfortas** has got very good limbs and is very well balanced. He will win as a 2-y-o but also has plenty of potential." Clive told me. (Mr B. H. Voak).
Optimum 3-y-o distance: 12f.

20 - FLAMANDA
Bay filly. Niniski - Nemesia (Mill Reef).
February 11. 2nd foal.
The dam was a very useful 3-y-o 10.2f and 4-y-o 13.4f listed stakes winner, is a sister to the very useful 2-y-o 5f and 3-y-o 7f winner Fairy Tern and is closely related to the smart Horris Hill

Stakes, Andy Capp Handicap and Westbury Stakes winner Elegant Air. 2nd dam, Elegant Tern (by Sea Bird II), won 3 times at around a mile and was 3rd in the Ribblesdale Stakes. "Very much a nice filly, **Flamanda** is fairly big and probably won't see the racecourse until August, but she could well be one to follow" the trainer informs me. (Exors of the late Dowager Lady Beaverbrook). Optimum 3-y-o distance: 12f.

21 - MAGELLAN (USA)
Bay colt. Hansel - Dabaweyaa (Shareef Dancer).
April 4. 4th foal.
Half-brother to the very useful 1994 2-y-o 6f winner and Group 1 7f Prix de la Salamandre 2nd Bin Nashwan (by Nashwan), to the very useful 1994 3-y-o 6f winner and Group 3 7f Supreme Stakes 2nd Alanees (by Cadeaux Genereux) and the quite useful 1993 3-y-o 8f winner Aneesati (by Kris). The dam was a smart winner of the 8f Atalanta Stakes and was placed in the 1,000 gns and the Kiveton Park Stakes. She is a half-sister to the Group 3 winning sprinter Bruckner, the 12f Galtres Stakes winner Ma Femme and the smart Hoover Fillies Mile and Nassau Stakes winner Acclimatise. 2nd dam, Habituee (by Habitat), won over 8f in France and was 2nd in the Prix d'Aumale. "**Magellan** is a good-looking colt with good limbs and he shows a bit of speed. He should be out around June-July time". (Mr Mohammed Obaida).
Optimum 3-y-o distance: 8f.

22 - NORTH CYCLONE (USA)
Bay colt. Gulch - Dubian (High Line).
April 21. 5th foal.
Half-brother to the 1995 3-y-o Razgee (by Green Desert), to the top class filly Sayyedati, winner of the Cheveley Park Stakes and Moyglare Stud Stakes at 2 yrs and the 1,000 gns and Prix Jacques le Marois at 3 yrs, to the 1990 2-y-o 6f winner Shihama (both by Shadeed) and the fair 7-8f placed 3-y-o Tigwa (by Cadeaux Genereux). The dam, a smart filly, won over 7f at 2 yrs, 12f at 3 yrs and the Group 1 12f Premio Lydia Tesio at 4 yrs. She was also placed in the Epsom Oaks and Irish Oaks, and is a half-sister to the triple champion hurdler See You Then. 2nd dam, Melodina (by Tudor Melody), won the 5f Seaton Delaval Stakes at 2 yrs, a 10f event at 3 yrs when she was placed in the Ribblesdale Stakes and the Musidora Stakes, and was a half-sister to the Irish Oaks winner Celina. "A very easy-moving type of colt and, like Sayyedati, quite light framed, **North Cyclone** is a very nice mover", Clive tells me. (Mr Mohammed Obaida).
Optimum 3-y-o distance: 8f.

Henry Candy

23 - GENEROSA
Bay filly. Generous - Hotel Street (Alleged).
April 25. 6th foal.
Half-sister to the 1995 3-y-o City of Angels (by Woodman), to the useful 1990 2-y-o 7f and 3-y-o 11f winner Widyan (by Fappiano), the fair 2-y-o 7f winner Providence, the 8f placed 2-y-o La Delitzia (both by Diesis) and the fair 8-10f placed Lyphard Street (by Lyphard). The dam, a fairly useful 12f winner at 3 yrs, is a half-sister to the Grade 1 Florida Derby winner Royal and Regal, to the Grade 3 winner Regal and Royal and to the dams of the Group/Graded stakes winners Dowsing (Group 1Vernons Sprint Cup), Ayman, Perfect Parade and Seekers Gold. 2nd dam, Native Street (by Native Dancer), won 8 races at up to 8.5f including the Grade 1 Sorority Stakes. (Fahd Salman).
Optimum 3-y-o distance: 10-12f.

Henry Cecil

24 - ALLIED FORCES (USA)
Chestnut colt. Miswaki - Mangala (Sharpen Up).
March 23. 3rd foal.
Half-brother to 2 winners including Barraq (by Crystal Glitters), a winner of 6 minor races in

France and the USA. The dam, a winner of 2 races in France, is a half-sister to 3 winners including the French listed stakes winner Nureyev's Best and the Park Hill Stakes 3rd Allegedly Blue - herself dam of the listed winner Hawait Al Barr. 2nd dam, Meadow Blue (by Raise a Native), is an unraced sister to the champion 2-y-o Crowned Prince and the Kentucky Derby winner Majestic Prince and a half-sister to the dam of the French Derby winner Caracolero. Henry is quite adamant that this colt is his best 2-y-o at this early stage. This colt is at the top of Henry Cecil's list, and not just alphabetically! He tells me that "**Allied Forces** will make up into a really nice 2-y-o and will probably be introduced over 6f. He could well be an Ascot colt, is very active and I like him very much". (Buckram Oak Holdings).
Optimum 3-y-o distance: 8f.

25 - ARABESKI
Bay filly. Sadlers Wells - Scimitarra (Kris).
January 12. 4th foal.
Half-sister to the quite useful 2-y-o 7f and 3-y-o 8.2f winner Deserve (by Green Desert). The dam, a very useful filly, won over 6f and 7.2f at 2 yrs prior to winning the Lupe Stakes at 3 yrs. On her only subsequent outing she was favourite for the Epsom Oaks and took the lead two furlongs out only to break a cannon bone. Almost certainly she would have finished 2nd to the eventual winner Unite. Scimitarra is a half-sister to the top class sprinter Double Form and to the very useful 5-8f winner Gradiva. 2nd dam, Fanghorn (by Crocket), was placed in the French 1,000 gns. "**Arabeski** is a very nice filly and goes about her work well - don't forget about her!" says her trainer. (Sheikh Mohammed).
Optimum 3-y-o distance: 10-12f.

26 - BALLADUR (USA)
Bay colt. Nureyev - Ballinderry (Irish River).
May 3.
Brother to the very useful 1994 3-y-o listed 10f winner and Group 2 12f King Edward VII Stakes 3rd Opera Score and half-brother to the top class middle distance colt Sanglamore (by Sharpen Up), winner of the Prix du Jockey Club, Prix d'Ispahan and William Hill Dante Stakes and 2nd in the King George VI and Queen Elizabeth Diamond Stakes. The dam won the Group 2 12f Ribblesdale Stakes, was 3rd in the Yorkshire Oaks and is a half-sister to the French Derby and French 2,000 gns placed Sharpman, the Prix Hocquart winner Mot d'Or, the Gran Premio de Milano and Grosser Preis von Berlin winner Lydian, the very useful miler Pride of Araby and the listed Prix de Saint-Cyr winner Miss Summer (herself dam of the useful French 2-y-o Most Precious). 2nd dam, Miss Manon, (by Bon Mot III), was a good winner of 3 races at around 10f. This colt had yet to arrive at Warren Place by mid-April. (Khaled Abdulla).
Optimum 3-y-o distance: 10-12f.

27 - BIRDLIP
Chestnut filly. Sanglamore - Seven Springs (Irish River).
May 19.
Half-sister to the 1995 3-y-o Severn Bridge (by Zilzal) and to 3 winners, namely the champion European 3-y-o colt of 1994 Distant View (by Mr Prospector), winner of the Group 1 Sussex Stakes and 2nd in the St James's Palace Stakes, the minor American winner Springal and the 11 race Swedish winner Gypsy River (both by Alydar). The dam was a very useful French filly and winner of the Group 1 5.5f Prix Robert Papin and Group 1 6f Prix Morny as a 2-y-o in 1984. She is a sister to the subsequent year's Prix Morny winner Regal State and to the useful 1989 French 2-y-o filly Spendomania, a winner over 7f and 2nd in the Prix de Cabourg. 2nd dam, La Trinite (by Lyphard) was a very useful 2-y-o winner of two races at around 6f, was placed in the French 1,000 gns and is out of a half-sister to the Oaks winner Pia. (Khaled Abdulla).
Optimum 3-y-o distance: 8-10f.

28 - BOSRA SHAM (USA)
Chestnut filly. Woodman - Korveya (Riverman).
February 28. 6th foal.
Sister to the champion European 2-y-o and 1991 French 2,000 gns and Prix Jacques le Marois winner Hector Protector, closely related to the 1992 French 2,000 gns winner Shanghai (by Procida) and half-sister to the minor French winner Gioconda (by Nijinsky). The dam was a

useful winner of the 9f Prix Chloe and is a half-sister to the high class 6-7f filly Proskona. 2nd dam, Konafa (by Damascus), was 2nd in the 1,000gns and is a half-sister to the good U.S. colt Akureyri and the Yorkshire Oaks winner Awaasif - herself dam of the Oaks winner Snow Bride. "Quite a big filly, but **Bosra Sham** has lots of scope and I like her very much," said Henry. (Mr Wafic Said).
Optimum 3-y-o distance: 8f.

29 - BRIGHT WATER
Bay colt. Caerleon - Shining Water (Kalaglow).
January 8. 5th foal.
Brother to the high class 1992 2-y-o Group 1 8f Ciga Grand Criterium and 3-y-o Group 2 10.4f Dante Stakes winner Tenby and half-brother to the very useful 1993 2-y-o 7f winner and Group 1 8f Racing Post Trophy 2nd Bude (by Dancing Brave), to the quite useful 1993 4-y-o 9f and 10f winner Reflecting (by Ahonoora) and the 1995 3-y-o Water Quest (by Rainbow Quest). The dam was a very useful winner of the Group 3 7f Solario Stakes and was placed in the Group 2 Park Hill Stakes. 2nd dam, Idle Waters (by Mill Reef), was a smart winner of 3 races including the Park Hill Stakes. "A nice horse with a bit of scope, **Bright Water** will take time but I do like him", said Henry. (Khaled Abdulla).
Optimum 3-y-o distance: 10-12f.

30 - CAXTON STAR
Chestnut colt. Soviet Star - Fiesta Fun (Welsh Pageant).
April 28.
Half-brother to the promising 1994 2-y-o 8.2f winner Balliol Boy (by Nashwan), to the top class 1990 Prix de l'Arc de Triomphe, Grand Prix de Paris and Prix du Prince d'Orange winner Saumarez (by Rainbow Quest), the 1987 2-y-o 5f and 6f winner Vivienda (by Known Fact) and the 1989 3-y-o 8f winner Carnival Spirit (by Kris) - both fairly useful. The dam, a sister to the dam of the Gordon Stakes winner John French and a half-sister to the smart 6f and 7f winner Derrylin, was a useful winner of 3 races over 10f at 3 yrs and was 3rd in the Group 1 Yorkshire Oaks. 2nd dam, Antigua (by Hyperion), was a useful winner of 3 races over 10f at 3 yrs and was 3rd in the 12f Galtres Stakes. (Famestar Ltd).
Optimum 3-y-o distance: 8-10f.

31 - CENSOR
Bay colt. Kris - Mixed Applause (Nijinsky).
April 15.
Brother to the 1995 3-y-o Claque - unplaced on both his starts at 2, to the high class St James's Palace Stakes and Beefeater Gin Celebration Mile winner Shavian, the fairly useful 3-y-o 10f winner Tempering and the minor 3-y-o 10f winner Khandjar, and half-brother to the high class Ascot Gold Cup winner Paean (by Bustino), the 1993 3-y-o dual 6f winner Press Gallery (by Carmelite House) and the 2-y-o 6f and 3-y-o 8f winner Grand Tier (by Habitat) - both fairly useful. The dam, a useful winner of the 2-y-o 6f Sweet Solera Stakes, is a half-sister to the dam of the champion 2-y-o Be My Chief. 2nd dam, My Advantage (by Princely Gift), a fairly useful sprinter, is a half-sister to Lady Seymour, the dam of Marwell. **Censor** is "rather backward at this stage, but he should be quite nice one day." (Lord Howard de Walden).
Optimum 3-y-o distance: 8-10f.

32 - CLEVER CLICHE'
Bay colt. Danehill - Beacon Hill (Bustino).
February 8. 78,000 gns (Newmarket Highflyer).
Closely related to the fair 10-16f winner High Summer (by Green Desert) and half-brother to the quite useful 15.5f and 17f winner Rhodes (by Pharly) and the fair 3-y-o 14f winner Mountain Ballet (by Shareef Dancer). The dam was placed at 3 yrs over 10f and is a sister to the Group 2 Princess of Wales's Stakes winner and top class broodmare Height of Fashion (dam of Nashwan and Unfuwain), is closely related to Burghclere (dam of the Oaks 2nd Wind in Her Hair) and a half-sister to the Princess of Wales's Stakes winner Milford. 2nd dam, Highclere (by Queen's Hussar), won the 1,000 gns and the French Oaks. According to his trainer, **Clever Cliche'** is "a well-bred horse and definitely one to follow later in the season". (Ivan Allan).
Optimum 3-y-o distance: 10f.

33 - DECRESCENDO (IRE)
Chestnut filly. Polish Precedent - Diminuendo (Diesis).
Closely related to the disappointing 3-y-o maidens Carpathian and Thunder Strike (both by Danzig) and half-sister to the French trained 1995 3-y-o Dimity (by Soviet Star). The dam, a top class, game and genuine filly, won all four of her juvenile races from 6-8f including the Hoover Fillies Mile and Cherry Hinton Stakes. As a 3-y-o she won the Epsom Oaks, Irish Oaks (in a dead-heat), Yorkshire Oaks and the Musidora Stakes and was officially rated the top racehorse of her generation in the 11f+ category - above such notables as Assatis, Carroll House, Kahyasi and Unfuwain. 2nd dam, Cacti (by Tom Rolfe), won at around 8f in the USA at 3 yrs and is out of the 8.5f Vanity Handicap winner Desert Love. (Sheikh Mohammed).
Optimum 3-y-o distance: 10f.

34 - DISTANT OASIS (USA)
Bay filly. Green Desert - Just You Wait (Nonoalco).
May 2.
Sister to the fair 6f to 8f placed Just a Mirage, closely related to the useful 2-y-o 7.6f winner and middle-distance placed 3-y-o Waiting (by Polish Precedent) and half-sister to the 1995 3-y-o All the Time (by Dancing Brave), the very smart Group 2, 9.7f Prix Dollar winner Wiorno (by Wassl), the very smart Trusthouse Forte Mile, Gimcrack Stakes and Earl of Sefton Stakes winner Reprimand (by Mummy's Pet), and to the minor winning sprinter Another Rhythm (by Music Boy). The dam is an unraced half-sister to the good broodmares Little Loch Broom (dam of the very useful Fawzi and the Group 3 Prix de la Jonchere winner Soft Currency) and Kristana (dam of the Group 1 Prix Robert Papin winner Ozone Friendly). 2nd dam, Sleat (by Santa Claus), won the Sun Chariot Stakes and is a half-sister to the St Leger winner Athens Wood.
Optimum 3-y-o distance: 8f.

35 - DIVINE QUEST
Chestnut filly. Kris - Dance Quest (Green Dancer).
April 14. 6th foal.
Sister to the 1994 7f placed 2-y-o (on her only start), Divine Pursuit and to the smart French filly Divine Danse, winner of 5 races at 5f and 6f including the Prix d'Arenburg, Prix de Ris-Oranges and Prix du Gros Chene, and half-sister to the high class colt Pursuit of Love (by Groom Dancer), winner of the 7f Free Handicap, 6.5f Prix Maurice de Gheest and 7f Kiveton Park Stakes and placed in the 2,000 gns and July Cup. The dam was a smart French 2-y-o sprinter and a half-sister to the high class 2-y-o Noblequest, winner of the Prix de la Salamandre. 2nd dam, Polyponder (by Barbizon), won from 5-8f including four Group 3 events in France and seemed best at 5f. I took a glance at **Divine Quest** in the yard, was very taken with her and consequently very interested in Henry's comments - "Not over big, but **Divine Quest** will certainly make a 2-y-o as she's a very active filly." (Lady Howard de Walden).
Optimum 3-y-o distance: 6-8f.

36 - DOSTHILL (USA)
Bay filly. Diesis - Dolka (Shergar).
April 21. 6th foal.
Half-sister to the 1995 3-y-o Zeerover (by Bering) and to the 1993 French 3-y-o 8f winner Dourbadakan (by Riverman). The dam was a very useful winner over 6f at 2 yrs and the 8f Venus Fillies Stakes at 3 yrs and is a half-sister to the 2,000 gns winner Doyoun, the Hungerford Stakes winner Dalsaan and the Cork and Orrery Stakes winner Dafayna. 2nd dam, Dumka (by Kashmir II), won the French 1,000 gns in 1974. "A quite attractive, tall and leggy filly, **Dosthill** has grown a lot but she's a decent filly, is doing well now and could be very nice one day." (Sheikh Mohammed).
Optimum 3-y-o distance: 8-10f.

37 - DOUBLE NINER (USA)
Bay or brown colt. Forty Niner - Sure Locked (Lyphard).
January 28. 4th foal.
Closely related to the fair 1992 3-y-o 8f and 8.3f winner Lahoob (by Miswaki) and half-brother to the moderate 1993 14f winner Keylock (by Diesis). The dam, a French 2-y-o 8f listed stakes winner, is a half-sister to the high class St James's Palace Stakes and Queen Elizabeth II Stakes

winner Sure Blade, to the very useful Group 3 Earl of Sefton Stakes winner Sure Sharp and to the 8-10f winner and subsequent South African Group 3 winner Only a Pound. 2nd dam, Double Lock (by Home Guard), a useful 10f winner, was 3rd in the Nassau Stakes. (Mr. S. Khaled).
Optimum 3-y-o distance: 8-10f.

38 - FLAMINEO
Bay colt. Machiavellian - Shojoon (Danzig).
March 13. 1st foal.
The dam, a minor winner in France, is closely related to the high class Group 2 12f Hardwicke Stakes winner Assatis, the smart Group 3 12f Gordon Stakes winner Warrshan and the very useful 10f Predominate Stakes winner Razeen. 2nd dam, Secret Asset (by Graustark), is an unraced half-sister to the Group 1 winners Dance Number (herself dam of the top class U.S. colt Rhythm) and Private Account (a high class American sire). (Sheikh Mohammed).
Optimum 3-y-o distance: 8-10f.

39 - DUSHYAMTOR (USA)
Bay colt. Sadlers Wells - Slightly Dangerous (Roberto).
April 11.
Half-brother to the 1993 Epsom Derby and Irish Derby winner Commander in Chief, to the fairly useful 1993 3-y-o 14f winner Totality (both by Dancing Brave), the champion 1987 2-y-o and champion miler Warning (by Known Fact), the high class 10.6f and 12f winner and Irish Derby 2nd Deploy, the useful 3-y-o 11.8f winner and Park Hill Stakes 4th Shirley Valentine (both by Shirley Heights) and the very useful middle distance colt Timefighter (by Star Appeal). The dam, a very smart filly, won the 7.3f Fred Darling Stakes, was 2nd in the Oaks to Time Charter and is a half-sister to the dams of the Arc winner and top class sire Rainbow Quest and the Dewhurst Stakes dead-heater Scenic. 2nd dam, Where You Lead (by Raise a Native), was a smart winner of the Musidora Stakes and was 2nd in the Oaks behind Mysterious. 3rd dam, the top class filly Noblesse (by Mossborough), won the 1963 Oaks. "An active horse, he'll make a 2-y-o later on and is far more like Warning than Commander in Chief, being a slightly earlier horse. Certainly one to watch closely," Henry suggests. (Khaled Abdulla).
Optimum 3-y-o distance: 12f.

40 - FLAMING JUNE (USA)
Chestnut filly. Storm Bird - Affirmative Fable (Affirmed).
February 6. 5th foal. $250,000 (Keeneland July).
Half-sister to the moderate 1994 3-y-o 9.4f all-weather winner Lyphard's Fable, to the useful 1990 2-y-o Group 3 8f May Hill Stakes winner Majmu (both by Al Nasr) and the minor American winner of 5 races, Granlund (by Procida). The dam, a minor winner in America at 4 yrs at around 8f, is a half-sister to the U.S. Grade 3 winner Northern Fable - herself dam of the very useful 2-y-o Haiati. 2nd dam, Fairway Fable (by Never Bend), was a stakes winner in the USA, a sister to the Grade 3 winner Torsion and a half-sister to the Grade 2 winner Fairway Flyer. "An attractive, chestnut filly, **Flaming June** will make her mark as a 2-y-o later on in the season" confirmed Henry. She is bred on the same lines - by Storm Bird out of an Affirmed mare - as the top class 1994 filly Balanchine. (Sir Andrew Lloyd Webber).
Optimum 3-y-o distance: 8-10f.

41 - GRACE AND GLORY
Bay filly. Sadlers Wells - Grace Note (Top Ville).
March 24. 6th foal to live.
Sister to the 1995 3-y-o Chalk Circle and closely related to the top class 1990 3-y-o King George VI and Queen Elizabeth Diamond Stakes, Great Voltigeur Stakes and Chester Vase winner Belmez (by El Gran Senor) and the useful 1991 Irish 3-y-o 13.5f and 4-y-o 10f winner Dowland (by Sovereign Dancer). The dam, a fairly useful 10f Chepstow winner and 2nd in the Group 3 12f Lingfield Oaks Trial, is a half-sister to the dams of the high class Prix de Diane winner Lypharita and the very useful winners Arousal and In Focus. 2nd dam, Val de Grace (by Val de Loir), won over 10f and is out of a half-sister to another Prix de Diane winner in Fine Pearl. **Grace and Glory** had not arrived at Warren Place by mid-April, as she'd had a slight setback. However, Henry did say that she was reputedly a nice looking filly. (Sheikh Mohammed).
Optimum 3-y-o distance: 12f.

42 - GREEN CHARTER
Bay filly. Green Desert - By Charter (Shirley Heights).
May 5. 2nd foal.
Half-sister to the quite useful 1994 2-y-o 7f all-weather winner Magna Carta (by Royal Academy). The dam, a useful 2-y-o 7f winner, is a sister to the very useful Jockey Club Stakes winner Zinaad. 2nd dam, Time Charter (by Saritamer), was one of the best and most popular fillies of the Eighties. She won the Oaks, the King George, the Champion Stakes, the Coronation Cup, the Prix Foy and the Sun Chariot Stakes. **Green Charter** is a filly Henry Cecil likes very much and he expects her to do well. (Mr. E. Hinojosa).
Optimum 3-y-o distance: 8-10f.

43 - HELICON (IRE)
Bay colt. Nashwan - Hebba (Nureyev).
March 19. 2nd foal.
The dam, a quite useful 2-y-o 6f winner, was placed over 8f and 8.5f at 3 yrs, is a half-sister to the top class American colt Creme Fraiche and to the Grade 1 Monmouth Oaks winner Dream Deal. 2nd dam, Likely Exchange (by Terrible Tiger), won 23 races including the Grade 1 10f Delaware Handicap. 3rd dam, Likely Swap, was a stakes winner of 15 races. Henry observed that **Helicon** is "not very big, being out of a Nureyev mare, but he's an active sort and I quite like him. One to follow I should think." (Sheikh Mohammed).
Optimum 3-y-o distance: 8-10f.

44 - KERENZA
Chestnut filly. Seattle Dancer - Home Love (Vaguely Noble).
February 6.
Half-sister to the very smart 1989 3-y-o Group 1 9.2f Prix Jean Prat winner Local Talent (by Northern Dancer), the high class 1984 2-y-o Group 2 6f Mill Reef Stakes winner Local Suitor (by Blushing Groom) and minor winners by Conquistador Cielo, Mr Prospector, Plugged Nickle and Soy Numero Uno. The dam is an unraced half-sister to 2 good American horses in Sportin' Life (sire of the Belmont Stakes winner Bet Twice) and Folk Art (both by Nijinsky). 2nd dam, Homespun (by Round Table), a stakes-placed winner at 2 and 3 yrs in the USA, is a sister to the U.S. stakes winner Sphere and to the Ulster Harp Derby winner Dumbwaiter. (Sheikh Mohammed).
Optimum 3-y-o distance: 8-10f.

45 - KING'S ACADEMY (IRE)
Bay colt. Royal Academy - Regal Beauty (Princely Native).
May 3. 6th foal.
Brother to the 1995 3-y-o Regal Portrait and half-brother to the top class colt King's Theatre (by Sadlers Wells), winner of the Group 1 Racing Post Trophy at 2 yrs and the Group 1 King George VI and Queen Elizabeth Stakes at 3 yrs and 2nd in both the Epsom Derby and Irish Derby, to the champion 2-y-o colt High Estate (by Shirley Heights) and to the dual 1991 2-y-o 8f winner and smart 3-y-o 10f winner King's Loch (by Salmon Leap). The dam was unplaced in two starts and is a half-sister to 8 minor winners. 2nd dam, Dennis Belle (by Crafty Admiral) won 6 races at up to 8f in the USA. "**King's Academy** is a lovely, active horse with plenty of scope and a touch of class," Henry tells me, "certainly one for the notebook." (Mr. M. Poland).
Optimum 3-y-o distance: 10f.

46 - KINLOCHEWE
Bay filly. Old Vic - Reuval (Sharpen Up).
March 20.
Half-sister to the 1995 3-y-o Pitcroy (by Unfuwain) - 2nd over 7f on her only outing at 2yrs, to the very useful 1994 Group 3 7f Jersey Stakes winner Ardkinglass (by Green Desert) and the useful 3-y-o dual 10f winner Jura (by Rousillon). The dam, a useful winner of 2 races over 8f at 3 yrs, is closely related to Kristana (dam of the Prix Robert Papin winner Ozone Friendly) and a half-sister to Just You Wait (dam of the Group 2 winners Reprimand and Wiorno) and Little Loch Broom (dam of the very useful colts Fawzi and Soft Currency). 2nd dam, Sleat (by Santa Claus), won the Sun Chariot Stakes and is a half-sister to the St Leger winner Athens Wood. (Sir

David Wills).
Optimum 3-y-o distance: 10f.

47 - MODERN DAY (USA)
Brown colt. Dayjur - Modena (Roberto).
March 27.
Half-brother to the high class 1990 3-y-o Group 1 10f Coral Eclipse Stakes and Group 1 10f Phoenix Champion Stakes winner Elmaamul (by Diesis), to the 1995 3-y-o A La Mode, placed 3rd over 8f on her only start at 2 yrs, the very useful 7f (at 2 yrs) and 8.5f winner Modernise, subsequently a Grade 3 8.5f winner in the USA (both by Known Fact) and to Modesto (by Al Nasr), a winner of 8 minor events from 10-12f. The dam is an unraced half-sister to the smart 2-y-o 7f winner and Queen Elizabeth II Stakes 3rd Zaizafon - herself dam of Zafonic. 2nd dam, Mofida (by Right Tack), won 8 races at up to 7f and was placed in the Duke of York Stakes. **Modern Day** "is a colt that should make up into a nice 2-y-o later on." (Khaled Abdulla). Optimum 3-y-o distance: 7-9f.

48 - OMARA (USA)
Brown filly. Storm Cat - Alamosa (Alydar).
April 26. 1st foal.
The dam is an unraced half-sister to the minor French 3-y-o winner Starstruck. 2nd dam, Love Smitten (by Key to the Mint), won 9 races including the Grade 1 Apple Blossom Handicap and the Grade 2 Santa Maria Handicap and is a half-sister to 5 winners including the Graded stakes winner Stellarette (herself dam of the Grade 1 winner Cuddles) and the champion Canadian filly Kamar (herself dam of the Grade 1 winners Gorgeous and Seaside Attraction). "We bought **Omara** in America." Henry told me "She'll be quite early - probably May time - and is one to take note of!" By Storm Bird and out of an Alydar mare, she is bred in similar fashion to the Grade 1 Test Stakes and Grade 1 Alabama Stakes winner November Snow.
(Mr. F. Hinojosa).
Optimum 3-y-o distance: 6-8f.

49 - PAPAHA (FR)
Bay filly. Green Desert - Turban (Glint of Gold).
April 2. 4th foal.
Sister to the fairly useful 1993 2-y-o 6f winner and 3-y-o 7f placed Tricorne and half-sister to the useful 1993 3-y-o 8f and 8.5f winner Barboukh and the 1995 3-y-o Lovely Lyca (both by Night Shift). The dam, a fair 10f and 11.7f winner at 3 yrs, is a half-sister to the top class French and Irish Derby winner Old Vic and the smart Group 3 Prix Foy winner Splash of Colour. 2nd dam, Cockade (by Derring Do), won over 8f at 3 yrs and is a sister to the 2,000 gns winner and high class sire High Top. Another filly Henry thought I should certainly include, **Papaha** is an active sort that should make up into a nice 2-y-o. (Mr. T. Harris).
Optimum 3-y-o distance: 7-8f.

50 - PHANTOM QUEST
Bay colt. Rainbow Quest - Illusory (Kings Lake).
March 19. 2nd foal.
Half-brother to the quite useful 1994 2-y-o 5.7f winner Painted Desert (by Green Desert). The dam, a quite useful 3-y-o 6f winner, is a sister to the Lowther Stakes winner Kingscote (dam of the smart Rainbow Corner) and a half-sister to 5 winners. 2nd dam, Bold Fantasy (by Bold Lad, Ire), won the Group 3 Mulcahy Stakes and was 2nd in the Irish 1,000 gns and the Cork and Orrery Stakes. This colt, very closely related to the aforementioned Rainbow Corner, was the subject of a pleasing report from his trainer. "He has just split a pastern but he's a very nice colt and will make a useful back end 2-y-o and a lovely 3-y-o. He's a very active, well-made horse and a good colour - a good bright bay - I like him." (Khaled Abdulla).
Optimum 3-y-o distance: 8-10f.

51 - PLACE DE L'OPERA
Bay filly. Sadlers Wells - Madame Dubois (Legend of France).
February 27. 2nd foal.
Half-sister to the 1994 3-y-o Richelieu (by Kris). The dam, a very smart filly, won five of her

seven starts at 3 yrs from 9f to 14.6f including the Group 2 Park Hill Stakes, the Group 2 Prix de Royallieu and the Galtres Stakes. 2nd dam, Shadywood (by Habitat), a useful 10f winner, was 2nd in the Lancashire Oaks and is a half-sister to the very useful fillies Kashmir Lass and Mill on the Floss (dam of the useful winners Hatta's Mill, Milly Ha Ha and Yeltsin). **Place de L'Opera** is "certainly a nice filly but stoutly bred and will take time." (Cliveden Stud).
Optimum 3-y-o distance: 12f.

52 - PRICKET (USA)
Chestnut filly. Diesis - Cacti (Tom Rolfe).
February 15.
Sister to the top class filly Diminuendo, winner of the Epsom Oaks, Irish Oaks (in a dead-heat), Yorkshire Oaks, Hoover Fillies Mile, Cherry Hinton Stakes and Musidora Stakes etc., and to the fairly useful 10f and 10.3f winner Bayaireg and half-sister to the fairly useful 3-y-o 10f winner Cascassi (by Nijinsky) and to minor winners in the USA by Effervescing and Wild Again. The dam, a winner at around 8f in the USA at 3 yrs, is out of the Grade 1 8.5f Vanity Handicap and Grade 1 8.5f Santa Susana Stakes winner Desert Love (by Amerigo), herself a half-sister to the Grade 1 San Capistrano Handicap, Grade 1 San Luis Rey Stakes and Grade 1 Century Handicap winner Astray. "A different type to her sister Diminuendo, **Pricket** is longer and scopier. She's a nice filly and a good mover. One to follow," assures Henry. (Sheikh Mohammed).
Optimum 3-y-o distance: 10-12f.

53 - PRIVATE AUDIENCE (USA)
Bay colt. Private Account - Monroe (Sir Ivor).
April 8.
Half-brother to the Group 3 8f Prix Quincey winner Masterclass (by The Minstrel), the Group 3 10.5f Prix Corrida winner Diese (by Diesis) - both very useful, the useful triple 6f winner Didicoy (by Danzig), the useful 4-y-o 8f and 10.4f winner Esquire (by High Line), the French 3-y-o 5f winner Victoriana (by Storm Bird) and the fair Wolverhampton 5f winner Danthonia (by Northern Dancer). The dam, a useful Irish 5f and 6f winner, is a sister to the good 2-y-o Gielgud and to the very smart Malinowski, and a half-sister to the dual Grade 1 winner Blush With Pride and to Sex Appeal - the dam of El Gran Senor and Try My Best. 2nd dam, Best in Show (by Traffic Judge), was a very useful stakes winner of 5 races at up to 7f. (Khaled Abdulla).
Optimum 3-y-o distance: 6-8f.

54 - QUESTONIA
Bay filly. Rainbow Quest - Danthonia (Northern Dancer).
March 14. 2nd foal.
Half-sister to the 3-y-o Dantean (by Warning). The dam, a quite useful 2-y-o 5f winner, is closely related to the Group 3 8f Prix Quincey winner Masterclass (by The Minstrel), the useful triple 6f winner Didicoy (by Danzig) and the French 3-y-o 5f winner Victoriana (by Storm Bird) and a half-sister to the Group 3 10.5f Prix Corrida winner Diese (by Diesis) and the useful 4-y-o 8f and 10.4f winner Esquire (by High Line). 2nd dam, Monroe (by Sir Ivor), a useful Irish 5f and 6f winner, is a sister to the good 2-y-o Gielgud and to the very smart Malinowski, and a half-sister to the dual Grade 1 winner Blush With Pride and to Sex Appeal - the dam of El Gran Senor and Try My Best. Another nice filly of Prince Khaled's, Henry didn't hesitate to put **Questonia** in his list of 2-y-o's to follow. Her Rainbow Quest - Northern Dancer cross is the same as the Group 1 Racing Post Trophy winner Armiger's, who was also trained by Henry Cecil. (Khaled Abdulla).
Optimum 3-y-o distance: 8-10f.

55 - QUOTA
Bay filly. Rainbow Quest - Armeria (Northern Dancer).
January 15. 3rd foal.
Brother to the top class 1992 2-y-o Group 1 8f Racing Post Trophy winner Armiger, (a somewhat disappointing 3-y-o when winner of the Chester Vase and 2nd in the Prix Lupin and St Leger). The dam, a fair 3-y-o 10f winner at Windsor, is a half-sister to the Park Hill Stakes winner I Want to Be. 2nd dam, Frontonian (by Buckpasser), was placed 3rd once over 10f in France and is a half-sister to Diomedia (dam of Media Starguest), Crown Treasure (dam of Glint

of Gold and Diamond Shoal) and Carefully Hidden (dam of Ensconse). "Very active and well made" according to her trainer, "this is a very nice filly though she'll take a bit of time - look out for her!" (Khaled Abdulla).
Optimum 3-y-o distance: 12f.

56- SANDY FLOSS (IRE)
Bay colt. Green Desert - Mill on the Floss (Mill Reef).
May 5. 6th foal.
Brother to the 1995 3-y-o Desert Harvest, 2nd over 7f on his only start at 2 yrs and to the useful 1992 3-y-o 10.2f winner Hatta's Mill, and half-brother to the very useful 1994 3-y-o 10f winner Milly Ha Ha (by Dancing Brave), the useful 7f (at 2 yrs) and 10.3f winner Yeltsin (by Soviet Star) and the fairly useful 10.2f and 12f winner Top Mill (by High Top). The dam, a winner over 7f at 2 yrs and the Group 3 12f Lingfield Oaks Trial at 3 yrs, was also 2nd in both the Ribblesdale and Princess Royal Stakes, is closely related to the useful Queen Alexandra Stakes winner Overdrive and a half-sister to the very useful Sun Chariot Stakes 2nd Kashmir Lass and to the dam of the smart Park Hill Stakes winner Madame Dubois. 2nd dam, Milly Moss (by Crepello), won the Cheshire Oaks and is a sister to the very smart Park Hill Stakes winner Mil's Bomb. (Cliveden Stud).
Optimum 3-y-o distance: 8-10f.

57 - SHADY WELLS (IRE)
Bay colt. Sadlers Wells - Shadywood (Habitat).
April 19.
Closely related to Sun and Shade (by Ajdal), winner of an Ascot maiden over 8f at 2yrs on her only start, and half-brother to the 1994 8.2f placed 2-y-o Dacha (by Soviet Star) and to the very smart Group 2 Park Hill Stakes and Group 2 Prix de Royallieu winner Madame Dubois (by Legend of France). The dam was a useful 10f winner, was 2nd in the Lancashire Oaks and is a half-sister to the smart filly Kashmir Lass, the Lingfield Oaks Trial winner Mill on the Floss and the very useful middle distance stayer Overdrive. 2nd dam, Milly Moss (by Crepello), won the Cheshire Oaks and is a sister to the very smart Park Hill Stakes winner Mil's Bomb. (Cliveden Stud). Habitat mares have already bred Barathea, Batshoof and Alnasr Alwasheek to Sadlers Wells. (Cliveden Stud).
Optimum 3-y-o distance: 12f.

58 - STORM CARD
Chestnut filly. Zalazl - Trikymia (Final Straw).
February 11. 5th foal.
Sister to the extremely promising 1994 2-y-o 6f winner (on only start) Epagris, and half-sister to the 3-y-o 10f winner Graegos (by Shareef Dancer) and the 5.8f to 8f winner (from 2 to 4 yrs) Wave Hill (by Sizzling Melody) - both quite useful. The was placed 3rd over 5f at 2 yrs on her only outing and is a half-sister to the Irish Derby winner Tyrnavos, the champion 2-y-o Tromos, the Coronation Stakes winner Tolmi and the Middle Park Stakes winner Tachypous. 2nd dam, the celebrated broodmare Stilvi (by Derring Do), won the 5f King George Stakes and the 6f Duke of York Stakes. Henry describes **Storm Card** as "a well-made and lovely filly- definitely one to watch out for." (Mr. L. Marinopoulos).
Optimum 3-y-o distance: 8-10f.

59 - STORM SHELTER (USA)
Brown filly. Storm Bird - Dockage (Riverman).
February 18. 5th foal.
Sister to the very useful 1992 2-y-o Group 3 6f July Stakes and 3-y-o listed 9f winner Wharf and half-sister to the promising 1994 2-y-o 7f winner Shapely and the fairly useful 1993 2-y-o 8f winner Colza (both by Alleged). The dam, a winner over 8f and 9f in France, is out of Golden Alibi (by Empery), a three-parts sister to the brilliant mare Dahlia. (Khaled Abdulla).
Optimum 3-y-o distance: 8-10f.

60 - STORM TROOPER (USA)
Bay colt. Diesis - Stormette (Assert).
February 17. 4th foal. 67,000 gns.

Brother to the very useful 1992 2-y-o Group 3 8f May Hill Stakes and 3-y-o Group 3 10.4f Musidora Stakes winner Marillette. The dam, a winner over 12f in Ireland at 3 yrs, is a half-sister to the champion 2-y-o Storm Bird, to the Canadian stakes winner Ocean's Answer - dam of the Prix Robert Papin winner Didyme and to the high class filly Northernette - herself dam of the Grade 1 winner Scoot and of the Group 2 winner Gold Crest. 2nd dam, South Ocean (by New Providence), won the Canadian Oaks. "**Storm Trooper** is a really active, scopey colt and he'll make a nice 2-y-o as the season progresses, probably over 6f or further," the trainer reports. (Fahd Salman).
Optimum 3-y-o distance: 10-12f.

61 - SUBTERFUGE
Brown filly. Machiavellian - Sandy Island (Mill Reef).
March 18.
Half-sister to the promising 1995 3-y-o winner Sebastian (by Sadlers Wells), to the very useful 10f Newmarket Pretty Polly Stakes winner Sardegna (by Pharly) and to 4 disappointing animals by Pharly, Dancing Brave, Shareef Dancer and Green Desert. The dam, a very useful filly, won the Group 3 12f Lancashire Oaks and the 10f Pretty Polly Stakes. She is closely related to Slip Anchor and a half-sister to the German 2,000 gns winner Swazi. 2nd dam, Sayonara (by Birkhahn), won 5 races at up to 10.5f and was 2nd in the German Oaks. "**Subterfuge** is a nice filly, though she will take time to come to hand." (Lord Howard de Walden).
Optimum 3-y-o distance: 10-12f.

62 - UNREAL CITY
Bay colt. Rock City - Tolmi (Great Nephew).
March 25.
Half-brother to the fairly useful 1994 3-y-o dual 12f winner Double Dagger (by Reference Point), to the fair 3-y-o 8f winner Nile Delta (by Green Desert) and to Zorkos (by Niniski) - a winner of 8 minor races in Europe. The dam, a very smart winner of the Coronation Stakes and Princess Margaret Stakes, was 2nd in the 1,000 gns and is a half-sister to the Irish Derby winner Tyrnavos, the champion 2-y-o Tromos, the Middle Park Stakes winner Tachypous and to the placed Trykimia - herself dam of the very promising filly Epagris. 2nd dam, the great broodmare Stilvi (by Derring Do), won the King George Stakes and the Duke of York Stakes. Henry advises me that **Unreal City** is "a big, quite heavy colt, quite laid back and active. He'll make a good 2-y-o over 6f or more." (Mr. L. Marinopoulos).
Optimum 3-y-o distance: 8f.

63 - VILAYET
Chestnut colt. Machiavellian - Vilikaia (Nureyev).
April 22.
Half-brother to the 1995 3-y-o Villakin (by Nashwan) and to the 1989 2-y-o 5f winner and useful 3-y-o 7f and 8f winner Villeroi (by Kris). The dam won 3 races at 7f and 8f including the listed Prix Imprudence, was 2nd in the Irish 1,000 gns and Prix de l'Abbaye and 4th in the English 1,000 gns. She is a sister to the listed Prix des Lilas winner Navratilovna and a half-sister to the good filly Maximova, herself dam of the Group 1 winners Septieme Ciel and Macoumba. 2nd dam, Baracala (by Swaps), is a half-sister to the top class 2,000 gns winner Nonoalco and the smart Whitehall Stakes winner Stradavinsky. "**Vilayet** is a really nice colt and certainly one of those I like best at this stage," says his trainer. (Sheikh Mohammed).
Optimum 3-y-o distance: 8f.

64 - WELCOME PARADE
Bay colt. Generous - Jubilee Trail (Shareef Dancer).
February 18. 2nd foal.
Half-brother to the very promising 1994 2-y-o 7f winner Peace Envoy (by Warning). The dam, a quite useful 3-y-o 10.4f winner, is a sister to the fairly useful 8-10f winner Green Turban and a half-sister to 7 winners including the very useful middle distance performer Colorific and the Park Hill Stakes winner Rejuvenate. 2nd dam, Miss Petard (by Petingo), won the Ribblesdale Stakes. "**Welcome Parade** has split a pastern, so he'll be off for a little bit, but he's going to be a very nice horse!" Henry assures me. (Khaled Abdulla).
Optimum 3-y-o distance: 10-12f.

65 - YAMUNA (USA)
Bay filly. Forty Niner - Nimble Feet (Danzig).
January 26. 4th foal.
Half-sister to the very smart 1994 2-y-o colt Eltish (by Cox's Ridge), winner of the 7f Lanson Champagne Stakes and 8f Royal Lodge Stakes and runner-up to Timber Country in the 8.5f Breeders Cup Juvenile, to the useful 5f and 6f winner Forest Gazelle (by Green Forest) and to the French 3-y-o listed 10f winner Souplesse (by Majestic Light). The dam, a quite useful 2-y-o 5f winner, is a sister to the Grade 1 Washington Lassie Stakes winner Contredance and to the listed Roses Stakes winner Old Alliance and is a half-sister to the Group winners Shotiche and Skimble. 2nd dam, Nimble Folly (by Cyane), is an unraced sister to the very useful Group 3 winner and Group 1 3rd Misgivings. Henry was quite positive about the fortunes of **Yamuna**. "She's an active filly who is certainly going to make a nice 2-y-o." (Khaled Abdulla).
Optimum 3-y-o distance: 8-10f.

66 - NOT NAMED
Chestnut colt. Green Forest - Perlee (Margouillat).
March 4.
Brother to the fairly useful 1992 3-y-o 7f winner Forest Tiger and half-brother to the 1989 French 1,000 gns winner Pearl Bracelet, the very useful Fench 2-y-o 6f winner Sugar Wells (both by Lyphard) and the French 3-y-o 7.5f winner Million Stories (by Exclusive Native). The dam was a very smart winner of the Group 3 12f Prix de Minerve and was 3rd in the Group 1 Prix Saint-Alary. 2nd dam, Zirconia (by Charlottesville), was a useful 6f and 8f winner and was 5th in the 1,000 gns. (Buckram Oak Holdings).
Optimum 3-y-o distance: 7-10f.

67 - NOT NAMED
Bay colt. Silver Hawk - Pink Topaze (Djakao).
February 24.
Half-brother to the high class French 2,000 gns and Prix Lupin winner Fast Topaze (by Far North), to the very useful French 8f winner Peak Value (by Blushing Groom) and the minor 6f (at 2 yrs) to 10f placed Instant Desire (by Northern Dancer). The dam is an unplaced half-sister to the French 2,000 gns winner Blue Tom, the top class sprinter Amber Rama and the French Derby 2nd Timmy My Boy. 2nd dam, Pink Silk (by Spy Song), was a half-sister to the good stakes winner Pink Velvet. Henry explained that this colt is "a big, backward horse that will take a long time, but I do like him and he should be one to watch out for later in the season." (Buckram Oak Holdings).
Optimum 3-y-o distance: 8-10f.

Julie Cecil

68 - CALLALOO
Bay colt. Mtoto - Catawba (Mill Reef).
February 21. 4th foal.
Half-brother to the 1995 3-y-o Web of Intrigue (by Machiavellian), placed 4th once over 7f at 2 yrs, to the 1993 3-y-o 10-12f winner Licorne (by Sadlers Wells) and the 1994 3-y-o 12f winner Isle of Pines (by Kris) - both fairly useful. The dam, a useful 3-y-o 10.5f winner, is a half-sister to the useful 12f winner Kenanga and to Strigida - winner of the Ribblesdale Stakes - a race also won by the second dam, Catalpa (by Reform), and the third dam Ostrya. (Lord Howard de Walden).
Optimum 3-y-o distance: 10-12f.

Peter Chapple-Hyam

69 - AILESBURY HILL (USA)
Chestnut filly. Woodman - Golden Oriole (Northern Dancer).
April 18. $225,000.

Sister to the 1995 3-y-o Silvicolous, unplaced on his only start at 2 yrs, and half-sister to the quite useful 8f and 10f winner Gold Law (by Law Society) and the fair 3-y-o 12f winner Funoon (by Kris). The dam, a 3-y-o 6f winner at the Curragh, is a sister to the Irish Derby and exceptional 2,000 gns winner El Gran Senor and to the Dewhurst Stakes winner Try My Best and a half-sister to the dual Group 3 winner Solar. 2nd dam, Sex Appeal (by Buckpasser), is an unraced half-sister to the Group or Graded stakes winners Gielgud, Malinowski, Blush With Pride and Monroe (herself dam of the useful 6f filly Didicoy and the Group 3 winners Diese and Masterclass). "**Ailesbury Hill** is a nice enough filly, though she needs a bit of time," says her trainer. (Mr. R. Sangster).
Optimum 3-y-o distance: 8-10f.

70 - CHALAMONT (IRE)
Chestnut filly. Kris - Durtal (Lyphard).
April 11.
Half-sister to the dual Ascot Gold Cup winner Gildoran (by Rheingold), the useful 1991 3-y-o 8f winner River Defences, the French 7f and 8f winner Lady Isis (both by Riverman), the fairly useful 8f Royal Hunt Cup winner True Panache (by Mr Prospector) and the fairly useful but disappointing 3-y-o 10.4f winner Regimental Arms (by Sir Ivor). The dam won 4 races including the Cheveley Park Stakes and is a half-sister to the Arc winner Detroit, herself dam of the 1994 Arc winner Carnegie. 2nd dam, Derna II (by Sunny Boy III), was placed from 10f to 13f. Peter told me that **Chalamont** is "a filly with plenty of speed, considering her pedigree. She's a smallish filly and will be introduced at around 6f." The Prix de la Salamandre winner and useful sire Common Grounds is, like **Chalamont**, by Kris and out of a Lyphard mare. (Mr R. Sangster).
Optimum 3-y-o distance: 8-10f.

71 - CHIEF CONTENDER (USA)
Bay colt. Sadlers Wells - Minnie Hauk (Sir Ivor).
March 30. $385,000.
Brother to the fair 1992 3-y-o 10f winner Tafrah and closely related to the very useful Group 1 5f Heinz 57 Phoenix Stakes winner Aviance (by Northfields and herself dam of the good filly Chimes of Freedom) and half-brother to minor winners by Lomond (in Germany), Kings Lake and Chief's Crown (both in the USA). The dam, a winner over 7f and 8f, is a sister to the smart winners Gielgud, Malinowski and Monroe (herself dam of the Group 3 winners Diese and Masterclass) and a half-sister to the dual U.S. Grade 1 winner Blush With Pride and the top class broodmare Sex Appeal - dam of El Gran Senor and Try My Best. 2nd dam, Best in Show (by Traffic Judge), was a very useful stakes winner at up to 7f. "A big horse that is just cantering at the moment (late April), **Chief Contender** is a colt that will take a long time to come to hand." He is bred on the same Sadlers Wells - Sir Ivor cross as the very useful winners El Prado and Ivrea. (Mr. R. Sangster).
Optimum 3-y-o distance: 10-12f.

72 - ELMSWOOD (USA)
Bay filly. Woodman - Lilian Bayliss (Sadlers Wells).
March 29. 1st foal.
The dam, a useful 2-y-o 7f and 3-y-o 9f winner, was 3rd in the Nell Gwyn Stakes and is a sister to the very useful French 2-y-o 6f winner Ernani, the minor 3-y-o 8f winner Legendary and the Japanese 3-y-o winner Ravissement, is closely related to the high class 6-8f winner Phydilla (by Lyphard) and a half-sister to the Irish Derby 2nd but ultimately disappointing Observation Post, the minor 1993 3-y-o 7f winner Kosata (both by Shirley Heights), the useful middle-distance colt Colchis (by Golden Fleece), the fair 1994 2-y-o dual 6f winner Sayl (by Danehill), and to minor winners by Kings Lake, Rheingold, Top Ville and Try My Best. 2nd dam, Godzilla (by Gyr), a useful half-sister to 7 winners, won 7 races in Italy at up to 7.5f. "Elmswood is a filly with speed, though she may need some cut in the ground. I'll introduce her at 6f," Peter told me. (Mr. R. Sangster).
Optimum 3-y-o distance: 8-10f.

73 - HIGH BAROQUE (IRE)
Bay colt. High Estate - Alpine Symphony (Northern Dancer).
April 7. 6th foal. 52,000 gns.

Brother to the 1995 3-y-o Berliese, unplaced on her only outing at 2 yrs, and to the quite useful 1993 3-y-o 10f winner Dancing Heights. The dam is an unraced half-sister to the Irish 2,000 gns winner Nikoli, the Waterford Crystal Mile winner Captain James and the Coronation Stakes winner Sutton Place. 2nd dam, Aliceva (by Alcide), won a 10f maiden and is a half-sister to the dam of Le Moss and Levmoss. "A nice horse that has grown quite a lot, **High Baroque** will want 6 or 7 furlongs this year." (Mr. M. Tabor).
Optimum 3-y-o distance: 10f.

74 - JOHNNY JONES (USA)
Bay colt. Mr Prospector - Fantastic Look (Green Dancer).
March 19. 1st foal. $350,000.
The dam won 7 races including the Grade 1 8.5f Fantasy Stakes and the Grade 2 9f Silver Belles Handicap in the USA and was placed in three other Grade 1 events. She is closely related to the stakes winners Bravo Fox (7f Barronstown Stud Stakes) and Majestic Style and a half-sister to the stakes winner Fantastic Ways. 2nd dam, Fantastic Girl (by Riva Ridge), won 7 races including a stakes event and is out of a half-sister to the Sussex Stakes winner Ace of Aces. Peter tells me that **Johnny Jones** is "a colt with a lot of speed. He'll start at 6f but I think he'll get 7f this year." He is bred on the same lines, by Mr Prospector out of a Green Dancer mare, as the smart 1994 2-y-o filly Macoumba. (Mr. R. Sangster).
Optimum 3-y-o distance: 8f.

75 - LA PELLEGRINA (IRE)
Bay filly. Be My Guest - Spanish Habit (Habitat).
February 2. 150,000 Ir gns.
Closely related to the smart 1994 1,000 gns winner and Irish 1,000 gns 2nd Las Meninas, to the Irish 2-y-o winner Head of the Abbey (both by Glenstal) - subsequently a winner of 6 races in the USA, and half-sister to the Scandinavian winners Spanish Run (by Commanche Run) and Schiefalora (by Mas Media). The dam is an unraced half-sister to 5 winners. 2nd dam, Donna Cressida (by Don), won 4 races including the Group 2 Player-Wills Stakes. "**La Pellegrina** looks like being a nice 2-y-o. She pleased me with her first piece of work the other day when she went well," said Peter. By Be My Guest and out of a Habitat mare, she is bred on the same lines as the top class colt Most Welcome. (Mr. R. Sangster).
Optimum 3-y-o distance: 8-10f.

76 - LOTHLORIAN
Chestnut filly. Woodman - Fairy Dancer (Nijinsky).
January 30. 5th foal. $250,000.
Half-sister to the fair 1993 3-y-o 10.3f winner Fair Shirley (by Shirley Heights), the Irish 1990 7f and 9f winner Adjudicate (by Law Society), the minor 1992 3-y-o 14f winner Wand and the Japanese winner Osumi Napoleon (both by Reference Point). The dam, a winner over 6f in Ireland at 2 yrs, is closely related to 4 winners by Northern Dancer, notably the top class racehorse and sire Sadlers Wells, the very useful sire Fairy King and the 2-y-o Group 1 winner Tate Gallery. 2nd dam, Fairy Bridge (by Bold Reason), was a good 2-y-o 5f and 6f winner and a half-sister to Nureyev. Peter explained that **Lothlorian** would not be rushed and would need 7f this term. (Mr. R. Sangster).
Optimum 3-y-o distance: 8-10f.

77 - MAZUREK
Bay colt. Sadlers Wells - Maria Waleska (Filiberto).
May 3. 100,000 Ir gns.
Closely related to the high class sprinter Polish Patriot, a winner of five races over 6f, notably the Group 1 July Cup and the Group 3 Cork and Orrery Stakes, to the minor Italian 3-y-o 7.5f winner Polish Princess and the minor U.S. 2-y-o winner Big Show (all three by Danzig), and half-brother to the 1994 Italian 2-y-o 9f winner Grand Cayman (by Slip Anchor) and to 2 other minor winners in America by Alydar and Mr Prospector. The dam won 6 races including the Group 1, 11f Italian Oaks and the Group 1 12f Gran Premio d'Italia. 2nd dam, Miss Protege (by Successor), a minor winner at 3 yrs in the USA, is a sister to Sound of Success, herself dam of both the Benson and Hedges Gold Cup winner Hawaiian Sound and the 1992 St Leger 2nd Sonus. "One of the last to come in to the yard, **Mazurek** is a nice horse that is cantering at the

moment and would want 7f this year." (Mr. R. Sangster).
Optimum 3-y-o distance: 10-12f.

78 - MERIBEL (IRE)
Bay filly. Nashwan - Dark Lomond (Lomond).
April 18. 4th foal.
Sister to the very useful 2-y-o 6f winner and Group 1 8f Prix Marcel Boussac, Group 1 12f Irish Oaks and Group 2 12f Ribblesdale Stakes placed Gothic Dream, and half-sister to the Japanese 3-y-o winner St Jones (by Shirley Heights) and the 1995 3-y-o Machikane Kagairibi (by Lomond). The dam, a very smart filly, won the Irish St Leger and the Curragh Pretty Polly Stakes and is a half-sister to the 12f Blandford Stakes winner South Atlantic. 2nd dam, Arkadina (by Ribot), was placed in the Epsom Oaks, Irish Oaks and Irish 1,000 gns, is a sister to the high class stayer Blood Royal and a half-sister to Mazaca - herself dam of 3 good winners in Gypsy Talk, Itsamaza and Trove. Peter is very pleased with **Meribel**. Although she's only cantering at the moment, he expects her to be a nice filly later in the season.
Optimum 3-y-o distance: 10-12f.

79 - MUSICK HOUSE (IRE)
Bay colt. Sadlers Wells - Hot Princess (Hot Spark).
February 6. 5th foal.
Closely related to the top class colt Rodrigo de Triano (by El Gran Senor), winner of the Group 1 6f Middle Park Stakes and Group 2 7f Laurent-Perrier Champagne Stakes at 2 yrs and the 2,000 gns, Irish 2,000 gns, Juddmonte International Stakes and Dubai Champion Stakes (all Group 1 events from 8-10.4f) at 3 yrs, and to the fair 1990 2-y-o 7f winner Cedrila (by Assert) - subsequently a winner in Malaysia. The dam was a useful winner over 5f and 6f at 2 yrs, the 7f Ballycorus Stakes at 3 yrs and three races in the USA from 8.5f to 9f as a four year old. 2nd dam, Aspara (by Crimson Satan), was placed over 5f in Britain and Ireland. "**Musick House** shows a lot of speed for a Sadlers Wells 2-y-o. He's going very well and will be introduced at either 6 or 7 furlongs," the trainer informs me. (Mr. R. Sangster).
Optimum 3-y-o distance: 8-10f.

80 - NAMOUNA (IRE)
Bay filly. Sadlers Wells - Amaranda (Bold Lad, Ire).
February 2.
Sister to the very useful 1993 4-y-o 8f Royal Hunt Cup winner Imperial Ballet - previously a winner over 10f at 3 yrs, closely related to the minor 8.5f winner Town Square (by The Minstrel) and half-sister to 4 winners including the very useful 3-y-o 7f winner Bold Citadel (by Caerleon),the fairly useful 3-y-o 8f winner Mount Holyoke (by Golden Fleece) - herself dam of the Italian Group 2 winner Wooton Rivers and the fair 2-y-o 5f winner Port St Mary (by Seattle Slew). The dam was a very useful winner of 4 races at 5f including the Queen Mary Stakes and is a half-sister to the Nell Gwyn Stakes winner and 1,000 gns 2nd Favoridge. 2nd dam, Favoletta (by Baldric II), won the Irish 1,000 gns and is a half-sister to the dams of Ashayer, Braiswick, Give Thanks, Old Country, Percy's Lass, Teenoso and Topsy. "**Namouna** is a bit like the colt **Musick House** in that she's showing plenty of speed and will probably need 7 furlongs this year," says Peter. (Mr. R. Sangster).
Optimum 3-y-o distance: 8f.

81 - NASH HOUSE (IRE)
Bay colt. Nashwan - River Dancer (Irish River).
May 14. 6th foal.
Closely related to the 1995 Irish 2,000 gns winner Spectrum (by Rainbow Quest) and half-brother to the 1993 3-y-o dual 5f winner Ballet Shoes (by Ela Mana Mou) and the 1991 3-y-o 10f winner Snow Plough (by Niniski) - both quite useful. The dam was a smart French filly, winning over 5f at 2 yrs, the 8f Prix de la Calonne at 3 and was 3rd in the French 1,000 gns. 2nd dam, Dancing Shadow (by Dancer's Image), was a smart winner from 8-10f including the Sean Graham Fillies Stakes and is a half-sister to the Oaks, St Leger and Yorkshire Oaks winner Sun Princess - herself dam of the smart colt Prince of Dance, to the high class middle distance colt Saddlers Hall and to the dam of the Italian Group 1 winner Poliuto. "**Nash House** is a colt that

will need time. He may have a run at the back-end." (Lord Weinstock).
Optimum 3-y-o distance: 8-10f.

82 - ROYAL COURT (IRE)
Bay colt. Sadlers Wells - Rose of Jericho (Alleged).
April 12. 6th foal.
Closely related to a 3-y-o in Japan by Fairy King and half-brother to the top class Epsom Derby, Irish Champion Stakes and Dewhurst Stakes winner Dr Devious (by Ahonoora) and to the very useful 6f Greenlands Stakes winner Archway (by Thatching). The dam is an unraced daughter of Rose Red (by Northern Dancer), a minor Irish 2-y-o 6f winner and herself a half-sister to the high class middle distance colt Critique and to Cambretta - (dam of the smart French 8-10f winner Pluralisme and of the very useful winners Singletta and Classic Tale). "**Royal Court** is cantering and moving well at the moment, though he's more backward than Dr Devious was at this stage and will require 7 furlongs as a 2-y-o," Peter told me.
Optimum 3-y-o distance: 12f.

83 - STATE THEATRE (IRE)
Bay colt. Sadlers Wells - Fruition (Rheingold).
May 17. 150,000 Ir gns.
Brother to the 1995 3-y-o Charente River and the smart Group 3 14f Prix du Lys and 15f Prix Hubert de Chaudenay winner Northern Spur, closely related to the high class Doncaster Cup, Jockey Club Gold Cup and Tote Ebor Handicap winner Kneller (by Lomond) and the 1993 Irish 3-y-o 10f and 11f and 4-y-o German listed winner Oenothera (by Night Shift), and half-brother to the smart Jockey Club Gold Cup winner Great Marquis (by Touching Wood) and to McCoist (by Dunbeath), a winner in Switzerland. The dam, a quite useful maiden, was 2nd in the 12f Lupe Stakes and 4th in the Lingfield Oaks Trial. She is a half-sister to 6 winners including the brilliant broodmare Flame of Tara, dam of the Oaks, Irish Derby and 1,000 gns winner Salsabil and of the St James's Palace Stakes winner Marju. 2nd dam, Welsh Flame (by Welsh Pageant), won 4 races at up to 8f and is a half-sister to the dams of the Group 3 winners Bourbon Boy and Tanwi. "Physically, **State Theatre** is looking one of the best in the yard, but though he's doing very well, he's another one for the back-end of the season." (Mr. R. Sangster).
Optimum 3-y-o distance: 12f+

84 - TILLYARD (IRE)
Bay filly. Caerleon - Royal Heroine (Lypheor).
February 15.
Half-sister to the useful 6f and 7f winner and 8.5f Diomed Stakes 3rd Regal Sabre (by Sharpen Up). The dam won 10 races in England, France and the USA, including the 6f Princess Margaret Stakes at 2 yrs, followed by the Group 2 9.2f Prix de l'Opera, Group 3 8f Child Stakes and, in America, the 9f Hollywood Derby, 9f Matriarch Stakes and the Breeders Cup Mile (all Grade 1 events). She is a half-sister to the U.S. stakes winner Fahdi and to the useful sprinter Betsy Red. 2nd dam, My Sierra Leone (by Relko), ran unplaced twice. "Rather backward at the moment, **Tillyard** will want 7 furlongs this year." (Mr. R. Sangster).
Optimum 3-y-o distance: 8-10f.

85 - UPPER GALLERY (IRE)
Bay colt. Sadlers Wells - Elevate (Ela Mana Mou).
April 8. 4th foal.
Closely related to the 1993 French 3-y-o winner and Group 3 12f Prix de Royaumont 3rd Elite Guest and to the 1995 Japanese 3-y-o Admire Lupis (both by Be My Guest) and half-brother to the fair 8f placed 3-y-o Hoist (by Bluebird). The dam, a fairly useful dual 3-y-o 12f winner was listed placed and is a half-sister to the top class Sun Princess and Saddlers Hall. 2nd dam, Sunny Valley (by Val de Loir), won over 10.5f and 12f in France and is a half-sister to the dam of the good miler Then Again. "A nice horse that moves well, **Upper Gallery** will take time to come to hand." Like the Jim Bolger trained 2-y-o Catalyst and the smart colt Foyer, **Upper Gallery** is by Sadlers Wells and out of an Ela Mana Mou mare. (Mr. R. Sangster).
Optimum 3-y-o distance: 12f.

86 - WILD RUMOUR (IRE)
Bay filly. Sadlers Wells - Gossiping (Chati).
April 8.
Closely related to the very useful 6f Cherry Hinton Stakes, 7f Rockfel Stakes and 7.3f Fred Darling Stakes winner Musicale (by The Minstrel) and half-sister to the fairly useful 2-y-o 8.2f winner and 3-y-o listed 11.5f placed Idle Chat (by Assert). The dam, a minor winner over 6f in the USA at 3 yrs, is a half-sister to the high class sprinter Committed. 2nd dam, Minstinguette (by Boldnesian), ran just once but is a half-sister to the Grade 1 Vanity Handicap winner Miss Toshiba - herself dam of 8 winners including the Yorkshire Oaks 2nd Guilty Secret. "A rather nice filly, though backward, **Wild Rumour** is another for the end of the year." (Mr. R. Sangster).
Optimum 3-y-o distance: 10f.

Roger Charlton

87 - AIR QUEST
Bay colt. Rainbow Quest - Aryenne (Green Dancer).
April 10.
Brother to the 1990 Derby winner Quest For Fame, to the very useful 14f winner and 16f Queens Vase 2nd Silver Rainbow and to the 1994 2-y-o Lost Paradise, and half-brother to the smart 1994 3-y-o, 12.5f listed stakes winner and Prix Vermeille 2nd Yenda (by Dancing Brave) and the minor 10f winner In Orbit (by Habitat). The dam was a high class winner of the French 1,000 gns and is a half-sister to Apachee, herself dam of the Group winners Antheus and Alexandrie. (Khaled Abdulla).
Optimum 3-y-o distance: 12f.

88 - DARKNESS AT NOON (USA)
Chestnut filly. Night Shift - Tara's Charmer (Majestic Light).
February 21. 4th foal.
Closely related to the quite useful 1991 2-y-o 6f winner Yafill (by Nureyev) and half-sister to the minor U.S. 3-y-o winner Naughty Notions (by Relaunch). The dam, a winner at 3 and 4 yrs in the USA at up to 7f, is a half-sister to the top class miler Zilzal. 2nd dam, French Charmer (by Le Fabuleux), won 5 races at 3 yrs including the Grade 2 Del Mar Oaks and is a half-sister to the dams of the top class miler Polish Precedent, the French 1,000 gns winner Culture Vulture and the U.S. Grade 1 winner Awe Inspiring. (Mr G. Howard-Spink).
Optimum 3-y-o distance: 8f.

89 - DON VITO
Chestnut colt. Generous - Dance By Night (Northfields).
March 15.
Closely related to the useful 1994 2-y-o dual 7f winner Don Corleone (by Caerleon) and half-brother to the smart Group 1 6f Prix Robert Papin, Group 1 8f French 1,000 gns and Group 1 7f Prix de la Foret winner Danseuse du Soir (by Thatching), the very useful 1993 3-y-o 8-12f winner Dana Springs (by Aragon), the quite useful 2-y-o 6f winner Sarah Georgina (by Persian Bold), the French 2-y-o 7f winner Reveuse du Soir (by Vision) and the French 2-y-o 8f winner Danseuse du Nord (by Kahyasi). The dam was a quite useful 2-y-o dual 7f winner. 2nd dam, Elvina (by Dancers Image), won over 6f and 10f in Ireland at 3 yrs. "A small, neat colt and a good mover, **Don Vito** should be a fairly early 2-y-o," according to Roger. (Wafic Said).
Optimum 3-y-o distance: 10f.

90 - GAIN LINE (USA)
Bay colt. Dayjur - Safe Play (Sham).
January 24.
Half-brother to the smart 1990 3-y-o Grade 1 11f Man O'War Stakes, Group 3 10f Guardian Classic Trial and Group 3 10.6f Burtonwood Brewery Rose of Lancaster Stakes winner Defensive Play (by Fappiano), to the useful 6f and 7f winner Averti (by Known Fact) and the French 11f winner Livry (by Lyphard). The dam, a high class American filly and winner of the Grade 1 9f La Canada Stakes and the Grade 3 8.5f Falls City Handicap, is a half-sister to the

1,000 gns winner Musical Bliss. 2nd dam, Bori (by Quadrangle), is a placed half-sister to the very useful Grade 3 winner Bob's Majesty and the Dewhurst Stakes 2nd Draw the Line. 3rd dam, Lucretia Bori (by Bold Ruler), won 3 races at up to 6f including the Jasmine Stakes and is a half-sister to the champion English miler Romulus. (Khaled Abdulla).
Optimum 3-y-o distance: 6-9f.

91 - HARD NEWS (USA)
Bay colt. Lyphard - Social Column (Vaguely Noble).
May 6.
Brother to the American winner of 5 races Mondanite and half-brother to the very smart 1989 3-y-o Group 2 10f Prince of Wales's Stakes winner Two Timing, the French 4-y-o 10f listed stakes winner Liaison (both by Blushing Groom) and the fairly useful 3-y-o 7f winner Singing (by The Minstrel). The dam was placed over 6f at 3 yrs in the USA and is a half-sister to the dams of Beyton (King Edward VII Stakes winner), Missed the Storm (American Grade 2 winner), Winning Colors (Kentucky Derby winner) and to the grandam of Chief's Crown. 2nd dam, Miss Carmie (by T.V.Lark), was a 2-y-o 6f stakes winner. Vaguely Noble mares, bred to Lyphard, have bred the Grade 1 winners Dahar, Llandaff and Sabin. (Khaled Abdulla).
Optimum 3-y-o distance: 8-10f.

92 - HIGH SUMMER (USA)
Chestnut filly. Nureyev - Miss Summer (Luthier).
April 29.
Sister to the 1987 French 2-y-o listed 8f Prix de Lieurey winner, Group 1 Prix de la Salamandre 2nd and Group 1 Grand Criterium 3rd Most Precious, closely related to Ofanto (by Lyphard), a winner of 3 races in France and 2 races in the USA and half-sister to the 1994 French 3-y-o 10.5f winner Summer Groom (by Blushing Groom) and the 1994 2-y-o 7f winner - on her only start - Private Line (by Private Account). The dam won the listed 8f Prix de Saint-Cyr and is a half-sister to the Group 2 Prix Hocquart winner Mot d'Or, the Group 1 Gran Premio de Milano winner Lydian, the Group 2 Ribblesdale Stakes winner Ballinderry (herself dam of Sanglamore) and the French 2,000 gns 2nd Sharpman. 2nd dam, Miss Manon (by Bon Mot III), was a good winner of 3 races at around 10f and was 4th in the French Oaks. The trainer tells me that **High Summer** is a tall, very big and backward filly that might have just the one run in the autumn. (Khaled Abdulla).
Optimum 3-y-o distance: 8-10f.

93 - INCHYRE
Bay filly. Shirley Heights - Inchmurrin (Lomond).
February 4. 4th foal.
Closely related to the 1995 3-y-o Inchkeith (by Reference Point) and half-sister to the very smart and tough 1993 3-y-o 7f Greenham Stakes, 7f Criterion Stakes and 7.3f Hungerford Stakes (all Group 3 events) winner Inchinor (by Ahonoora) and to the fairly useful 1994 3-y-o 8f listed stakes winner Ingozi (by Warning). The dam was a very useful winner of 3 races at 2 yrs over 5f and 3 races at 3 yrs including the Child Stakes and was 2nd in the Group 1 8f Coronation Stakes. She is closely related to the very useful 8f winner Guest Artiste and a half-sister to the Mill Reef Stakes winner Welney. 2nd dam, On Show (by Welsh Pageant), won over 10f and was 2nd in the November Handicap. "Like the rest of the family, **Inchyre** is neat and attractive. She'll run in mid-summer." (Sir Philip Oppenheimer).
Optimum 3-y-o distance: 8-10f.

94 - KING ALEX
Bay colt. Rainbow Quest - Alexandrie (Val de l'Orne).
April 14. 300,000 Ir gns.
Half-brother to the 1994 2-y-o Group 1 10f Criterium de Saint-Cloud and Group 3 9f Prix de Conde winner Poliglote (by Sadlers Wells), to the very useful 1989 French 3-y-o Group 2 12f Prix de Malleret and Group 3 10f Prix de la Nonette winner and Epsom Oaks 3rd Animatrice (by Alleged), and the minor French 3-y-o winners Green Song (by Green Dancer) and Ring Beaune (by Bering). The dam, a very useful French filly, won the Group 3 10.5f Prix Cleopatre and is a half-sister to the high class French middle distance colt Antheus. 2nd dam, Apachee (by Sir Gaylord), was a very useful half-sister to the French 1,000 gns winner Aryenne(dam of the

Derby winner Quest For Fame) and to the unraced dam of the smart Prix d'Astarte winner Lady Winner. Roger says that **King Alex** is a nice prospect for middle-distances next year and will be introduced around September at 7-8f. (Wafic Said).
Optimum 3-y-o distance: 10-12f.

95 - KISSING GATE (USA)
Chestnut filly. Easy Goer - Love's Reward (Nonoalco).
March 26. 4th foal.
Half-sister to the very smart Group 1 5f Prix de l'Abbaye winner Keen Hunter, the minor 4-y-o 7f winner Shedad (both by Diesis) and the quite useful 3-y-o 14f winner Amoodi (by Forli). The dam is an unplaced half-sister to the Group 1 Middle Park Stakes winner Bassenthwaite and the very useful 2-y-o 5f and 6f winner Glancing. 2nd dam, Splashing (by Petingo), won the Cornwallis Stakes. "A quite well-grown, strong filly, **Kissing Gate** should be a nice filly in the autumn," states the trainer. (The Queen).
Optimum 3-y-o distance: 7f.

96 - MEDSEE
Bay filly. Alzao - Liaison (Blushing Groom).
May 6. 3rd foal.
Half-sister to the 3-y-o Cross Talk (by Darshaan). The dam, a French 10f listed stakes winner, is a sister to the high class Prince of Wales's Stakes winner Two Timing and a half-sister to the fairly useful 3-y-o 7f winner Singing. 2nd dam, Social Column (by Vaguely Noble), was placed over 6f at 3 yrs in the USA and is a half-sister to the top class mares Chris Evert (grandam of Chief's Crown), All Rainbows (dam of Winning Colors), Ann Stuart (dam of the King Edward VII Stakes winner Beyton) and Missed the Wedding (dam of the Astarita Stakes winner Missed the Storm). (Khaled Abdulla).
Optimum 3-y-o distance: 8-10f.

97 - PRIVATE SONG (USA)
Bay colt. Private Account - Queen of Song (His Majesty).
February 15.
Half-brother to the 1995 3-y-o Easy Listening (by Easy Goer) and to 3 winners including the U.S. 2-y-o winner Ladyago (by Northern Dancer). The dam won 14 races in the USA including the Grade 2 8.5f Shuvee Handicap and the Grade 3 8.5f Sixty Sails Handicap (twice), was 3rd in the Grade 1 Apple Blossom Handicap and is a sister to the Grade 1 Jersey Derby winner Cormorant. 2nd dam, Song Sparrow (Tudor Minstrel), was a stakes-placed 2-y-o winner and a half-sister to the Grade 2 Beverly Hills Handicap and Group 3 Diadem Stakes winner Swingtime and to the Grade 2 Kentucky Oaks winner Bag of Tunes (herself grandam of the Cheveley Park Stakes winner Prophecy). (Khaled Abdulla).
Optimum 3-y-o distance: 8-10f.

98 - REVEUSE DE JOUR (IRE)
Bay filly. Sadlers Wells - Magic of Life (Seattle Slew).
March 22. 4th foal.
Half-sister to the 1995 3-y-o Mountains of Mist (by Shirley Heights), to the useful French 3-y-o listed 10f winner From Beyond and the fair French 3-y-o 10.7f winner Circle of Chalk (both by Kris). The dam was smart winner of 3 races from 5f to 8f at 3 yrs including the Group 1 Coronation Stakes. 2nd dam, Larida (by Northern Dancer), won 10 races including the Grade 2 8.5f Orchid Handicap and two Grade 3 stakes events and is a half-sister to Miss Oceana, a winner of six Grade 1 races in the USA. Roger tells me that **Reveuse de Jour** is a small, neat and attractive filly that should be suited by 6f as a 2-y-o. He hopes she'll be on the racecourse by June or July. (S.Niarchos).
Optimum 3-y-o distance: 10f.

Nick Clement

99 - MACHAERA
Bay filly. Machiavellian - Somfas (What a Pleasure).
March 1.
Closely related to the very useful 2-y-o Group 3 9f Prix de Conde winner Cristofori (by Fappiano) and the minor 1987 U.S. 3-y-o 9f winner Brio Cielo (by Conquistador Cielo) and half-sister to the 1995 3-y-o Somreffe (by Polish Precedent), the very useful 1988 2-y-o Group 2 6f Mill Reef Stakes winner Russian Bond, the useful 1991 4-y-o 6f listed stakes winner Snaadee (both by Danzig) and the useful dual 7f winner Adbass (by Northern Dancer). The dam, a stakes-placed winner of 4 races at up to 7f in the USA, is a half-sister to the Canadian Horse of the Year Fanfreluche, herself dam of the good winners L'Enjoleur, Montelimar and Medaille d'Or. 2nd dam, Ciboulette (by Chop Chop), won the 8.5f Maple Leaf Stakes in Canada and also bred the very useful sire Night Shift. (Sheikh Mohammed).
Optimum 3-y-o distance: 8-10f.

100 - TARQUINIA (IRE)
Bay filly. In the Wings - Tarsila (High Top).
March 3.
Half-sister to the 1995 3-y-o Tarnbrook (by Riverman), to the smart Group 2 10.5f Dante Stakes winner Torjoun, the very useful Group 2 10f Pretty Polly Stakes winner Takarouna (both by Green Dancer), the quite useful 2 mile Northumberland Plate winner Tamarpour (by Sir Ivor) and the hurdles winner Torkabar (by Vaguely Noble). The dam, a winner over 8f and (at Longchamp) 9f, is a sister to Top Ville. 2nd dam, Sega Ville (by Charlottown), won the Group 3 10.5f Prix de Flore and is out of the French 1,000 gns winner La Sega. (Sheikh Mohammed).
Optimum 3-y-o distance: 10-12f.

Paul Cole

101 - ALPINE
Bay colt. Alzao - Pine Ridge (High Top).
February 26.
Half-brother to the 1995 3-y-o Creme de Menthe (by Green Desert), to the top class filly In the Groove (by Night Shift), winner of the Champion Stakes, Juddmonte International Stakes, Irish 1,000 gns and Coronation Cup, to the useful 5-8f winner Spanish Pine (by King of Spain), the quite useful 3-y-o 7f winner Awesome Venture (by Formidable), the fair 3-y-o 12f winner Pineapple (by Superlative) and the minor American winner Stripped Pine (by Sharpo). The dam won two minor races at 3 yrs over 12f. 2nd dam, Wounded Knee (by Busted), won two small races over 12f and 14f. **Alpine** is "a small colt, that should be suited by 7f this year," says Paul. (Blandford Thoroughbreds).
Optimum 3-y-o distance: 10f.

102 - DISMISSED (USA)
Bay colt. Dayjur - Bemissed (Nijinsky).
April 24.
Half-brother to the very smart filly Jet Ski Lady (by Vaguely Noble), a winner over 6f, 7f (both at 2 yrs), 10f and notably the Epsom Oaks and 2nd in both the Irish Oaks and Yorkshire Oaks, to the U.S. stakes-placed winner at around 8f Lady Bemissed (by Sir Ivor) and the minor American 3-y-o winner Barmistress (by Alydar). The dam won 5 races including the Grade 1 8.5f Selima Stakes at 2 yrs in the USA, was 3rd in the Kentucky Oaks and is a half-sister to the very useful Group 2 12f Princess of Wales's Stakes winner Desert Team. 2nd dam, Bemis Heights (by Herbager), won 5 races in the USA including the Grade 3 9f Ruthless Stakes and is a half-sister to two Grade 3 winners. "A medium sized, attractive colt and highly regarded by connections, **Dismissed** should be suited by a mile eventually," suggests the trainer. (Fahd Salman).
Optimum 3-y-o distance: 7-9f.

103 - EL OPERA (IRE)
Bay filly. Sadlers Wells - Ridge the Times (Riva Ridge).
January 24. 6th foal.
Closely related to the very useful 1989 Group 1 6f Heinz 57 Phoenix Stakes, Group 3 6f Princess Margaret Stakes and 5f Windsor Castle Stakes winner Pharaoh's Delight and to the fair 1994 6f placed 3-y-o Elfland (both by Fairy King) and half-sister to the quite useful 3-y-o 8f winner Jumby Bay (by Thatching) - subsequently a winner 6 times in Sweden - and to the minor 3-y-o 7.5f and 8.5f winner Kateb (by Pennine Walk) - subsequently a 12f listed winner in Denmark. The dam, a fair 2-y-o 5f winner, is out of the unraced Oath of Allegiance (by Olden Times) - herself a half-sister to the Group 3 Prix de Conde winner French Friend and to the dam of the U.S. fillies triple crown winner Open Mind. **El Opera** is "a big filly and a good mover that should be a nice mid-season 2-y-o." (Faisal Salman).
Optimum 3-y-o distance: 8-10f.

104 - FAIRLIGHT DOWN (USA)
Bay filly. Dayjur - Stresa (Mill Reef).
February 28. $425,000.
Half-sister to the high class colts Mill Native (by Exclusive Native), winner of the Grade 1 10f Arlington Million, and French Stress (by Sham), winner of the Group 3 8f Prix du Chemin de Fer du Nord and Group 3 8f Prix Edmond Blanc, to the very useful Group 3 10.5f Prix de Flore winner Sporades (by Vaguely Noble), the 2-y-o 5f Prix du Bois winner American Stress (by Sham), the minor 3-y-o 10f winner Private Talk (by Damascus) - subsequently a winner of 2 races in the USA, and the promising 1994 French 2-y-o winner Tremplin (by Trempolino). The dam won over 10f at 3 yrs at Deauville and is a half-sister to Terreno and Antrona - both very smart. 2nd dam, Ileana (by Abernant), was a very useful winner of the Ascot 1,000 gns Trial. **Fairlight Down** is a good mover and a medium sized filly that will prefer 6-8 furlongs this year." (Sir. A. Lloyd-Webber).
Optimum 3-y-o distance: 7-9f.

105 - LIKE A HAWK (USA)
Bay filly. Silver Hawk - Like a Train (Great Sun).
February 16.
Sister to the minor American 3-y-o winner Miss Henderson Co. and half-sister to the Grade 1 8.5f Apple Blossom Handicap and Grade 1 9f Milady Handicap winner By Land By Sea (by Sauce Boat), to the U.S. 3-y-o winner of 3 races Club Car (by Private Account) and to a minor winner by Junction. The dam won 3 minor races in the USA, is a sister to the stakes winner Great Boone and a half-sister to 2 other stakes winners. 2nd dam, Boone Tavern (by Jester), was a stakes-placed winner of 9 races in the USA and was a half-sister to the Florida Derby winner Williamston Kid. Paul tells me that **"Like a Hawk** is a small, strong colt that is going well at the moment." (Mr Brereton C. Jones).
Optimum 3-y-o distance: 8-10f.

106 - SUPAMOVA (USA)
Bay filly. Seattle Slew - Maximova (Green Dancer).
February 22.
Sister to the very smart colt Septieme Ciel, winner of the Group 1 7f Prix de la Foret, the Group 3 8f Prix Messidor and, at 2yrs, the Group 3 7.5f Prix Thomas Bryon, and half-sister to the 1994 2-y-o Group 1 8f Prix Marcel Boussac winner Macoumba (by Mr Prospector), the Grade 3 8.5f Fort Marcy Handicap and Grade 3 8.5f Oceanport Handicap winner Maxigroom, the listed 3-y-o 10f Prix d'Automne winner Balchaia (both by Blushing Groom) and the French listed stakes winner Manureva (by Nureyev). The dam, a smart filly, won the Group 1 7f Prix de la Salamandre (in a dead-heat), the Prix de Meautry, Prix du Calvados and Prix de Seine-et-Oise (all Group 3 events) and was placed in the French and Irish 1,000 gns. 2nd dam, Baracala (by Swaps), was a useful 8f winner and a half-sister to Nonoalco, Stradavinsky and Vilikaia. **Supamova** is a big, strong, backward filly that moves well and will appear later on this season." (Mr M. Arbib).
Optimum 3-y-o distance: 8f.

Con Collins

107 - SONHOS (IRE)
Chestnut filly. Machiavellian - Sorbus (Busted).
June 6. 140,000 Ir gns.
Half-sister to the 1991 3-y-o Irish and Italian 12f winner and Irish Oaks 3rd Eileen Jenny (by Kris), the 1992 3-y-o 12f listed stakes winner Kasmayo (by Slip Anchor), the 1985 3-y-o Lingfield Oaks Trial winner Bahamian (by Mill Reef and herself dam of the smart filly Wemyss Bight) - all three very useful, the good Irish miler Captivator (by Artaius), the useful Irish 7f winner Klarifi and the useful middle-distance stayer West China (by Habitat). The dam was disqualified after winning the Irish Oaks and was 2nd in the Irish 1,000 gns, Irish St Leger and Yorkshire Oaks. 2nd dam, Censorship (by Prince John), won over 8f in the USA and is a half-sister to the Santa Anita Derby winner Four-and-Twenty.
Optimum 3-y-o distance: 10-12f.

Luca Cumani

108 - BALALAIKA
Bay filly. Sadlers Wells - Bella Colora (Bellypha).
February 24. 6th foal.
Sister to the high class Group 2 10f Prince of Wales's Stakes and Group 3 10f Brigadier Gerard Stakes winner Stagecraft and to the quite useful 1993 3-y-o 9f winner Bella Ballerina, and half-sister to the very useful dual 3-y-o 8f listed stakes winner Hyabella (by Shirley Heights) and the fairly useful middle-distance maiden Alum Bay (by Reference Point). The dam, from an excellent family, won four races including the Group 2, 9.2f Prix de l'Opera and the Group 3, 7f Waterford Candelabra Stakes and was a very close 3rd in the 1,000 gns. She is a half-sister to the Irish Oaks winner Colorspin, herself dam of the top class middle distance colt Opera House, and to the very useful filly Rappa Tap Tap. 2nd dam, Reprocolor (by Jimmy Reppin), was a very useful winner of the 12f Lingfield Oaks Trial, Lancashire Oaks and Pretty Polly Stakes. Luca told me that **Balalaika** only arrived at Bedford House Stables in February. Although she's a very attractive filly, she's big and very backward and, at best, may have one race at the back-end. (Helena Springfield Ltd).
Optimum 3-y-o distance: 10f.

109 - ELA-YIE-MOU (IRE)
Chestnut colt. Kris - Green Lucia (Green Dancer).
April 13.
Brother to the 3-y-o Korambi and half-brother to the smart 12f colt Luchiroverte, to the fairly useful 3-y-o 11.8f-14.6f winner Acanthus (both by Slip Anchor), the very useful 2-y-o 7f Houghton Stakes winner Muthaiga (by Kalaglow), the minor 4-y-o 10f winner Elhudhud (by Habitat) and the minor Irish 3-y-o 12f and 14f winner Euromill (by Shirley Heights). The dam, a half-sister to the outstanding middle-distance colt Old Vic, won over 6f and 10f,was 2nd in the Group 1 Yorkshire Oaks and 3rd in the Group 1 Irish Oaks. 2nd dam, Cockade (by Derring-Do), won over 8f, is a sister to High Top and Camden Town and has also bred the smart colt Splash of Colour. A good-looking colt that will need time, **Ela-Yie-Mou** should be out around August. (Mr A. Michael).
Optimum 3-y-o distance: 12f.

110 - FLAMANDS (IRE)
Bay filly. Sadlers Wells - Fleur Royale (Mill Reef).
May 9. 5th foal 165,000 Ir gns.
Sister to the Irish trained 1995 3-y-o Heaven's Gable, closely related to the 1992 Irish 2-y-o 7f winner Oiseau de Feu (by Nijinsky) and the 1990 Irish placed 2-y-o African Dance (by El Gran Senor). The dam, a very useful filly, won the Group 2 10f Pretty Polly Stakes and was 2nd in the Irish Oaks. She is a half-sister Sweet Habit, dam of the smart colts Nomrood, Alleging and Monastery. 2nd dam, Sweet Mimosa (by Le Levenstell), was a smart winner of the French Oaks and a sister to the top class colts Levmoss and Le Moss. **"Flamands** is a very backward filly that

will stay well and may just have the one run at the end of the season." (Sultan Al Kabeer).
Optimum 3-y-o distance: 10-12f.

111 - FREEQUENT
Chestnut colt. Rainbow Quest - Free Guest (Be My Guest).
March 6. 5th foal to live.
Half-brother to the very useful filly, Shamshir (by Kris), winner of the Group 1 Brent Walker Fillies Mile and placed in the Oaks, Yorkshire Oaks, Nassau Stakes and Musidora Stakes, to the useful 1992 3-y-o 12f winner and Lupe Stakes 3rd Fern and the fair 1993 12f and 14f placed 3-y-o Firm But Fair (both by Shirley Heights). The dam was a high class winner of 9 races from 2-4 yrs and from 7-12f, notably the Sun Chariot Stakes (twice), the Nassau Stakes and the Princess Royal Stakes. 2nd dam, Fremanche (by Jim French), won over 9f in Italy on her only outing. Another rather backward type, although a good-looking colt, **Freequent** may take until August before he's ready to run. (Fittocks Stud).
Optimum 3-y-o distance: 10-12f.

112 - HEIGHT OF SECRECY
Bay filly. Shirley Heights - Night Secret (Nijinsky).
March 29. 3rd foal.
Half-sister to the 1995 3-y-o Dream Town (by Top Ville) and to the quite useful 1994 Irish 3-y-o 8f winner Night City (by Kris). The dam, a quite useful 1989 3-y-o 10f winner at Beverley, is closely related to the Group 2 Royal Lodge Stakes winner Desert Secret and to the useful Yorkshire Oaks 2nd Bineyah. 2nd dam, Clandestina (by Secretariat), won over 10f at 3 yrs in Ireland and is a half-sister to the great racehorse Seattle Slew and to the 2,000 gns winner Lomond. **Height of Secrecy** has been injured and it is questionable whether he will come into training as a 2-y-o or not. (Sheikh Mohammed).
Optimum 3-y-o distance: 10-12f.

113 - HOUSE OF RICHES
Bay colt. Shirley Heights - Pelf (Al Nasr).
May 1. 5th foal.
Closely related to the fair 1994 13.8f 3-y-o winner Referential (by Reference Point) and half-brother to the 1995 3-y-o Kreef (by Kris). The dam won over 7f at 3 yrs in Italy and was stakes-placed. She is a half-sister to the good broodmares Crown Treasure (dam of Glint of Gold and Diamond Shoal), Carefully Hidden (dam of Enscone) and Frontonian (dam of I Want to Be). 2nd dam, Treasure Chest (by Rough n Tumble) was a very useful stakes winner over 6.5f and 8f. Luca informs me that **House of Riches** is "probably a back-end 2-y-o. He's a medium-sized athletic horse that looks like he'll come together in the autumn." (Sheikh Mohammed).
Optimum 3-y-o distance: 12f.

114 - HOW LONG
Bay colt. Alzao - Fresh (High Top).
February 25.
Half-brother to the useful dual 3-y-o 6f winner Be Fresh (by Be My Guest) and to the minor dual 3-y-o 11f winner Dr Robert (by Commanche Run). The dam, a very useful Italian middle distance winner, is a half-sister to the high class Sun Chariot Stakes and Nassau Stakes winner Free Guest - herself dam of the smart filly Shamshir - and to the smart middle distance filly Royal Ballerina. 2nd dam, Fremanche (by Jim French), won over 9f in Italy on her only start. "**How Long** is a good-looking horse that should have some racing as a 2-y-o and is not quite as backward as some of the other 2-y-o's in the yard," Luca informs me. (Dr. M. Boffa).
Optimum 3-y-o distance: 10f.

115 - KILVINE
Bay colt. Shaadi - Kilavea (Hawaii).
February 3.
Half-brother to the smart 1985 Lingfield Oaks Trial winner and Yorkshire 2nd Kiliniski (by Niniski), to the minor Irish 2-y-o 7f winner Elusive Quest (by Be My Guest) and the minor 7f and 8f winner Puget Sound (by High Top). The dam, a winner over 5f on her only start, is a sister to Nureyev and to the dam of Sadlers Wells and Fairy King. 2nd dam, Special (by Forli), is an

unplaced sister to Thatch. Luca informs me that **Kilvine** is a fairly sharp, attractive colt that should be ready to run in May or June. (Sheikh Mohammed).
Optimum 3-y-o distance: 8f.

116 - MIGWAR
Bay colt. Unfuwain - Pick of the Pops (High Top).
February 12. 3rd foal. 40,000 gns.
Half-brother to the unraced 1994 2-y-o Atlantic Record (by Slip Anchor). The dam, a useful 2-y-o 7f winner and 2nd in the Group 2 Fillies Mile, is out of the very useful listed Blue Seal Stakes winner Rappa Tap Tap (by Tap on Wood), herself a half-sister to Bella Colora (dam of Stagecraft), Colorspin (dam of Opera House) and Sistabelle (dam of Torch Rouge). "A strong sort of horse that I like a lot, we should see **Migwar** on the racecourse about August time," noted Luca. (Umm Qarn Racing).
Optimum 3-y-o distance: 10f.

117 - OLD IRISH
Bay colt.. Old Vic - Dunoof (Shirley Heights).
February 18. 6th foal.
Brother to the 1995 3-y-o Oldenburg, closely related to the fairly useful 1992 3-y-o 10-12f winner Folia (by Sadlers Wells) and half-brother to the minor middle-distance placed Dunnellon (by Shareef Dancer). The dam, a fairly useful 2-y-o 7f winner, became disappointing at 3 yrs. She is a sister to the Premio Roma, Park Hill Stakes and Ribblesdale Stakes winner High Hawk (dam of the high class French colt In the Wings) and to the 8f winner Seriema (dam of the Grade 1 Rothmans International and Group 2 Sun Chariot Stakes winner Infamy). 2nd dam, Sunbittern (by Sea Hawk II), was a very useful 6f and 7f 2-y-o winner. (Sheikh Mohammed).
Optimum 3-y-o distance: 12f.

Ed Dunlop

118 - ABSOLUTE UTOPIA (USA)
Bay colt. Mr Prospector - Magic Gleam (Danzig).
February 2. 2nd foal.
Brother to the 1994 3-y-o Touch a Million, unplaced on his only outing at 2 yrs. The dam was a very smart winner of 2 races, once over 7f and the Group 2 8f Child Stakes, and was placed in the Coronation Stakes, Prix Jacques le Marois and the Juddmonte International - all Group 1 events. She is a half-sister to 3 winners including the South African Grade 1 winner Flying Snowdrop. 2nd dam, All Agleam (by Gleaming), is a half-sister to the top class CCA Oaks winner Davona Dale (herself dam of the good colt Le Voyageur). **Absolute Utopia** "could well be a useful 2-y-o later in the season." (Maktoum Al-Maktoum).
Optimum 3-y-o distance: 8f.

119 - ANGEL FACE
Bay filly. Zilzal - Touching Love (Touching Wood).
January 23. 5th foal.
Half-sister to the Irish 8f winner Leyaali (by Lyphard). The dam won over 7f (at 2 yrs) and 9f in France and was placed in the Group 3 8f Prix d'Aumale. 2nd dam, Loveshine (by Gallant Romeo), won 5 races including a minor stakes in the USA and is a half-sister to 9 winners including the high class American colt Clever Trick and to the dam of the dual Grade 1 winner Alydeed. Trainer Ed Dunlop was particularly keen to mention **Angel Face**, saying that she's a particularly nice filly that he likes very much. He added, however, that she is very hot - or temperamental - just like her sire, in fact. (Maktoum Al-Maktoum).
Optimum 3-y-o distance: 8f.

120 - BASOOD (USA)
Bay filly. Woodman - Basoof (Believe It).
March 21. 6th foal.
Half-sister to the 1995 3-y-o Reaganesque (by Nijinsky) and to the 1993 French 2-y-o 7f winner

and Group 3 8f Prix de Sandringham 2nd Melting Gold (by Cadeaux Genereux). The dam, a fair 3-y-o 9f winner at Ayr, is a half-sister to the 2,000 gns and Queen Elizabeth II Stakes winner Shadeed. 2nd dam, Continual (by Damascus), won twice at up to 7f in the USA and is a sister to the dam of the outstanding Kentucky Derby and Belmont Stakes winner Swale. Discussing **Basood,** Edward Dunlop explained to me that he has her unraced half-brother by Nijinsky (the aforementioned Reaganesque) and that he's a very big horse and so very different from **Barood** who is "a small, black filly that should be a nice 2-y-o." (Maktoum Al-Maktoum).
Optimum 3-y-o distance: 8f.

121 - BRIGHT DESERT
Bay colt. Green Desert - Smarten Up (Sharpen Up).
June 3. 45,000 gns.
Half-brother to the 1995 3-y-o Merlin's Fancy (by Caerleon), unplaced on her only outing at 2 yrs, to the champion sprinter Cadeaux Genereux (by Young Generation), winner of the July Cup, William Hill Sprint Championship, Diadem Stakes etc., the useful 3-y-o 8f winner Military Fashion (by Mill Reef), the 7f to 10.8f winner Dress Sense (by Top Ville), the sprinter La Tuerta (by Hot Spark) - both fairly useful, the fair 5f to 8.5f winner Young Jason (by Star Appeal) and the fair 1991 7-12f placed 3-y-o Mathkoor (by Be My Guest) - subsequently a winner in Macau. The dam, a smart sprinter, was 2nd in the William Hill Sprint Championship and won twice over 5f. She is a half-sister to the very useful sprinters Solar and Walk By. 2nd dam, L'Anguissola (by Soderini), was a useful 2-y-o 6f winner. "Very backward and will need plenty of time, **Bright Desert** may have one or two runs at the end of the year." He is bred on the same lines, by Green Desert out of a Sharpen Up mare, as the very useful Henry Cecil trained colt Ardkinglass. (Maktoum Al-Maktoum).
Optimum 3-y-o distance: 5-7f.

122 - DESERT SERENADE (USA)
Bay filly. Green Desert - Sanctuary (Welsh Pageant).
March 1.
Sister to the top class sprinter Sheikh Albadou, winner of the Keeneland Nunthorpe Stakes, Breeders Cup Sprint, Haydock Park Sprint Cup and Kings Stand Stakes and half-sister to the useful 1994 4-y-o 14f and 16f winner Captain Jack (by Salse), the quite useful 5-6f winner Assignment and the minor Irish 2-y-o 5f winner Sawlah (both by Known Fact). The dam is an unraced half-sister to the good horses Little Wolf (Ascot Gold Cup), Smuggler (Yorkshire Cup), Camouflage (Royal Hunt Cup) and Disguise (Horris Hill Stakes), and to the dam of the Nell Gwyn Stakes winner Niche. 2nd dam, Hiding Place (by Doutelle), was a very useful winner of the Nell Gwyn Stakes and a half-sister to the Sussex Stakes winner Queen's Hussar. The trainer told me that **Desert Serenade** is "a lovely filly but very backward at this stage (mid April), as indeed her brother Sheikh Albadou was. She will hopefully have one or two runs this season." (Maktoum Al-Maktoum).
Optimum 3-y-o distance: 5-7f.

123 - HANBITOOH (USA)
Bay colt. Hansel - Bitooh (Seattle Slew).
January 19. 1st foal.
The dam, a very useful filly, won the Group 2 7f Criterium de Maisons-Laffitte as a two-year-old and 2 listed events over 7f at 3 yrs and is a half-sister to the very useful 6f (at 2 yrs) to 10f winner Monaassabaat and to the U.S. 8f stakes winner Air Dancer. 2nd dam, It's in the Air (by Mr Prospector), a joint champion 2-y-o filly in the USA, is out of a half-sister to the good American racehorse and sire Native Royalty. Edward tells me that **Hanbitooh** is a very nice horse that's had a slight setback and is backward at this stage, but hopefully will make a nice mid-season 2-y-o. (Maktoum Al-Maktoum).
Optimum 3-y-o distance: 7-10f.

124 - DUSTY GEMS (USA)
Bay filly. Danzig - Dusty Dollar (Kris).
February 15. 4th foal.
Sister to the fair 1993 3-y-o dual 10f winner Miss Shagra. The dam was a smart winner of the Group 2 10f Sun Chariot Stakes, was 2nd in both the Child Stakes and Sceptre Stakes, and is a

half-sister to the high class Group 2 Prince of Wales's Stakes winner Kind of Hush. 2nd dam, Sauceboat (by Connaught), won 4 races including the Child Stakes and is out of the Sun Chariot Stakes winner Cranberry Sauce. "Unfortunately **Dusty Gems** only has one eye, is big and backward at this early stage and it is doubtful whether she'll make a 2-y-o. However, she should be alright next year," Ed tells me. (Maktoum Al-Maktoum).
Optimum 3-y-o distance: 10f.

125 - OOD YA ZAMANN
Bay colt. Mtoto - Possessive Dancer (Shareef Dancer).
May 16. 1st foal.
The dam was a smart winner of 5 races from 6f (at 2 yrs) to 12f including the Group 1 Irish Oaks and Group 1 Italian Oaks. She is a half-sister to the moderate 3-y-o dual 8f winner Possessive Lady and to the promising 1994 2-y-o 6f winner Desert Courier. 2nd dam, Possessive (by Posse), is an unraced half-sister to 10 winners including the smart miler Long Row and the Norfolk Stakes winner Colmore Row. 3rd dam, Front Row (by Epaulette), won the Irish 1,000 gns. (Sheikh Ahmed Al-Maktoum).
Optimum 3-y-o distance: 10-12f.

126 - TA RIB (USA)
Chestnut filly. Mr Prospector - Madame Secretary (Secretariat).
April 23. 6th foal.
Half-sister to the useful 2-y-o 6f listed Firth of Clyde Stakes and 3-y-o 8f winner Tabdea (by Topsider), to the fair 2-y-o 8f winner Hawl (by Lyphard) and to the 1995 3-y-o Itab (by Dayjur). The dam won 2 races in America at around 8f including a minor stakes and is a half-sister to 4 winners including the useful stayer Zero Watt and the Stewards Cup winner Green Ruby. 2nd dam, Ruby Tuesday (by T.V.Lark), was placed at 3 yrs and is a half-sister to the very smart French colt Cresta Rider. "**Ta Rib** is certainly one for the notebook, though she's not an early foal and should be out around mid-summer," Edward told me. Secretariat mares, bred to Mr Prospector, have bred the American Grade 1 winners Classic Crown and Gone West and the smart French colt Lion Cavern. (Hamdan Al-Maktoum).
Optimum 3-y-o distance: 8f

127 - WINTER ROMANCE
Chestnut colt. Cadeaux Genereux - Island Wedding (Blushing Groom).
April 28. 2nd foal.
Half-brother to the 3-y-o Dream Wedding (by Soviet Star). The dam, a fairly useful filly, won over 7f and 8.5f at 3 yrs and is a half-sister to 2 minor winners. 2nd dam, South Sea Dancer (by Northern Dancer), won as a 4-y-o and 5-y-o in America and is a sister to Storm Bird and Northernette (dam of Scoot and Gold Crest) and closely related to Stormette (dam of Marillette). "**Winter Romance** is a colt you really ought to mention" said Edward, "He's one I like very much, though again he wasn't an early foal and it will be mid-summer before I run him." (Maktoum Al-Maktoum).
Optimum 3-y-o distance: 7-8f.

John Dunlop

128 - BINT SALSABIL (USA)
Chestnut filly. Nashwan - Salsabil (Sadlers Wells).
February 14. 2nd foal.
Sister to the 1995 3-y-o Firdous - unraced due to an accident. Salsabil won two of her three races as a two-year-old, notably the Group 1 8f Prix Marcel Boussac, and trained on to become a top class 3-y-o, winning the 1,000 gns, Irish Derby, Epsom Oaks and the Prix Vermeille - all Group 1 events. She is a half-sister to the high class colt Marju, winner of the St James's Palace Stakes and the Craven Stakes, and to the very useful Prix de Psyche winner Danse Royale. 2nd dam, Flame of Tara (by Artaius), won the Coronation Stakes and the Curragh's Pretty Polly Stakes and was 2nd in the Champion Stakes. Although the beautifully bred **Bint Salsabil** has a good action, reports her trainer, she is rather big and backward at the moment. (Hamdan Al-

Maktoum).
Optimum 3-y-o distance: 10-12f.

129 - BINT SHADAYID (USA)
Grey filly. Nashwan - Shadayid (Shadeed).
April 5. 1st foal.
The dam, a very smart filly, won the Group 1 8f Prix Marcel Boussac, the Group 1 8f 1,000 gns and the Group 3 7.3f Fred Darling Stakes, and was placed in the Oaks, Coronation Stakes, Queen Elizabeth II Stakes, Sussex Stakes and Ladbroke Sprint Cup. She is a half-sister to the very useful dual 7f winner and Jersey Stakes 3rd Dumaani. 2nd dam, Desirable (by Lord Gayle), won the Group 1 6f Cheveley Park Stakes, was 3rd in the 1,000 gns and is a half-sister to the Irish Oaks and Ribblesdale Stakes winner Alydaress and the Cheveley Park Stakes winner Park Appeal. Clearly very excited about **Bint Shadayid**, her trainer tells that she's a lovely, big filly with a beautiful action. (Hamdan Al-Maktoum).
Optimum 3-y-o distance: 8-10f.

130 - FAATEQ
Bay colt. Caerleon - Treble (Riverman).
March 18. 1st foal.
The dam, a smart winner over 9f at 2 yrs and the Group 1 10f Prix Saint-Alary at 3 yrs, is out of the unraced Trevilla (by Lyphard), herself a half-sister to the outstanding racemare Triptych and to the Group 3 Prix Vanteaux winner Barger (dam of the Group 3 winner Baya). 2nd dam, Trillion (by Hail to Reason), won 9 races including the Group 1 Prix Ganay and is a half-sister to the dam of the Derby winner Generous. This is a colt his trainer expects will prove useful. John tells that **Faateq** is a very strong, close coupled colt that moves well. (Hamdan Al-Maktoum).
Optimum 3-y-o distance: 10-12f.

131 - INSIYABI (USA)
Bay colt. Mr Prospector - Ashayer (Lomond).
January 15. 3rd foal.
Half-brother to the highly promising 1994 2-y-o Group 1 Fillies Mile and 3-y-o Group 3 Fred Darling Stakes winner Aqaarid and the fairly useful 1993 2-y-o 10f and 3-y-o 12f winner Muwafik (both by Nashwan). The dam was a smart winner of 3 races including the Group 1 8f Prix Marcel Boussac and the gr 3 10f Prix de Psyche and was placed in the Hoover Fillies Mile. 2nd dam, Good Lassie (by Moulton), won over 6f at 2 yrs, was a quite useful 8-10f placed 3-y-o and is a half-sister to the good mares Favoletta (dam of Amaranda and Favoridge), Furioso (dam of Teenoso and Topsy), Laughing Girl (dam of Braiswick and Percy's Lass), Little Miss (dam of Old Country) and Parthica (dam of Give Thanks). Trainer John Dunlop told me that **Insiyabi** has had problems with sesamoids and came late into training, but describes him as a fine, big horse that moves well. (Hamdan Al-Maktoum).
Optimum 3-y-o distance: 8-10f.

132 - MANSAB (USA)
Bay colt. Housebuster - Epitome (Summing).
January 28. 3rd foal. $400,000.
Half-brother to Faltaat (by Mr Prospector), a winner of 7 races in Dubai. The dam won 5 races, notably the Grade 1 Breeders Cup Juvenile Fillies Stakes, was the champion 2-y-o filly in America in 1987 and is a half-sister to 4 winners including the fair 1987 3-y-o 8f and 8.2f English winner Farfurr. 2nd dam, Honest and True (by Mr Leader), won 6 races including a stakes event over 8.5f, was third in the Grade 1 Fantasy Stakes and Grade 1 Kentucky Oaks and is half-sister to the champion 2-y-o and miler Green Forest and to the Group 3 Prix Perth winner and French 2,000 gns 2nd Green Paradise. "A medium sized, bay colt, **Mansab** will be relatively early and I expect him to make up into a nice 2-y-o," the trainer tells me. (Hamdan Al-Maktoum).
Optimum 3-y-o distance: 8f.

133 - MUHTADI (IRE)
Bay colt. Marju - Moon Parade (Welsh Pageant).

April 20.
Half-brother to the very useful 1992 3-y-o Rain Rider (by Fools Holme), winner of four races from 14f to 14.8f including the listed March Stakes, to the minor Irish 12f and 13f winner Coronado (by Rainbow Quest) and the Italian 3-y-o winner Internet (by Tender King). The dam, a minor 3-y-o 10.2f winner at Bath, is a half-sister to the high class Coronation Cup, Grand Prix de Saint-Cloud, King Edward VII Stakes and Great Voltigeur winner Sheriff's Star and to the high class St Leger, Grand Prix de Saint-Cloud, Geoffrey Freer Stakes, Cumberland Lodge Stakes and Yorkshire Cup winner Moon Madness. 2nd dam, Castle Moon (by Kalamoun), won from 8-13f, is a sister to the smart middle-distance colt Castle Keep and a half-sister to the Gold Cup winner Ragstone and to the grandam of the outstanding 1994 2-y-o Celtic Swing. John explained to me that **Muhtadi** is a good actioned colt, but also quite big and backward at the moment (mid-April). (Hamdan Al-Maktoum).
Optimum 3-y-o distance: 10-12f.

134 - NAJIYA
Bay filly. Nashwan - The Perfect Life (Try My Best).
January 15. 1st foal.
The dam won the Group 3 5f Prix du Bois and the listed 7f Prix Imprudence and was 2nd in the Group 2 Prix Robert Papin. She is a full sister to the top class colt Last Tycoon, winner of the Grade 1 Breeders Cup Mile, Group 1 Kings Stand Stakes and Group 1 William Hill Sprint Championship, and is closely related to the very useful Group 2 6f Premio Melton and Group 3 6f Goldene Peitsche winner Astronef. 2nd dam, Mill Princess (by Mill Reef), won over 10f at 3 yrs in France and is a half-sister to the Irish Sweeps Derby winner Irish Ball and to the top class broodmare Irish Bird (dam of the classic winners Assert, Bikala and Eurobird).
"Although she's going to take a little time, **Najiya** is a lovely filly and a very good mover," says John Dunlop. (Hamdan Al-Maktoum).
Optimum 3-y-o distance: 8f.

135 - NINOTCHKA (USA)
Bay filly. Nijinsky - Puget Sound (High Top).
March 23.
Closely related to the useful dual 3-y-o 12f winner Middle Kingdom (by Northern Dancer) and the fair 1993 3-y-o 7f winner Dagny Juel (by Danzig). The dam was a fairly useful 3-y-o 7f and 8f winner and is a half-sister to the Lingfield Oaks Trial winner and Yorkshire Oaks 2nd Kiliniski. 2nd dam, Kilavea (by Hawaii), won over 5f on her only start and is a half-sister to Nureyev and to the dam of Sadlers Wells. (Miss K. Rausing).
Optimum 3-y-o distance: 10-12f.

136 - SAMIM (USA)
Bay colt. Nureyev - Histoire (Riverman).
May 27.
Brother to the very useful Group 2 10f Premio Lydia Tesio and Lupe Stakes winner Oumaldaaya and half-brother to the Epsom Derby and Dante Stakes winner Erhaab (by Chief's Crown), the fairly useful French 8f and 9f winner Hispaniola (by Kris), the minor French winner Historique (by Rainbow Quest) and to Hittias (by Touching Wood), a winner in France and the USA and 3rd in the Grade 3 13f Seneca Handicap. The dam won once, in France over 10.5f, and is a half-sister to the Group 3 7f Prix de la Porte Maillot winner Hamanda. 2nd dam, Helvetie (by Klairon), won once in France over 8f. "A small, very late foal, **Samim** will need time to come to hand." (Hamdan Al-Maktoum).
Optimum 3-y-o distance: 10f.

137 - SCARLET PLUME
Bay filly. Warning - Circus Plume (High Top).
February 8. 5th live foal.
Half-sister to the useful 3-y-o 8f and 9f winner Circus Feathers (by Kris), the useful 8.2f to 10.8f winner Circus Light (by Kalaglow) and the fair 1993 3-y-o 10f and 12f winner Circus Colours (by Rainbow Quest). The dam was a high class middle distance winner of 4 races, notably the Epsom Oaks and the Yorkshire Oaks, and was 2nd in the Prix Vermeille. She is a half-sister to 2 winners including the very useful stayer Marriageable. 2nd dam, Golden Fez (by Aureole),

won over 11f in France at 3 yrs and is out of the champion English 2-y-o and 1,000 gns winner Zabara. "A racey, medium-sized filly, **Scarlet Plume** should be a nice 2-y-o," says John. (Mrs Nigel Elwes).
Optimum 3-y-o distance: 8-10f.

138 - SKI FOR GOLD
Bay filly. Shirley Heights - Quest (The Minstrel).
April 16.
Half-sister to the very useful 2-y-o Brighton 6f and subsequent Grade 1 10f Santa Barbara Handicap winner Bequest (by Sharpen Up), the useful 2-y-o 7f winner and 8-12f placed 3-y-o Fitzcarraldo (by Riverman) and the 3-y-o middle distance winners Inquirendo (by Roberto) and Rozinante (by Sir Ivor) - both quite useful. The dam won 3 races from 9-10f at 3 yrs, was 3rd in the Group 3 Queen Mary Stakes, is a sister to the Group 1 Grand Criterium winner Treizieme and a half-sister to the Group 2 Yorkshire Cup winner Eastern Mystic. 2nd dam, Belle Pensee (by Ribot), a winner over 10f, is a sister to the Group 1 stakes winners Junius and Gentle Thoughts. **Ski For Gold** is "a strong, though backward filly at this stage," John tells me. (Windflower Overseas Holdings Inc).
Optimum 3-y-o distance: 12f.

139 - THRACIAN
Bay filly. Green Desert - Triple First (High Top).
May 1.
Half-sister to the 1995 3-y-o Frimaire, to the very useful Group 2 12f Ribblesdale Stakes winner Third Watch (both by Slip Anchor), the high-class Group 2 9f (at 2 yrs) Prix Saint-Roman and Group 3 12f Prix Foy winner Richard of York (by Rainbow Quest), the smart Group 2 8f Premio Dormello (at 2 yrs) and Group 3 12f Lancashire Oaks winner Three Tails (by Blakeney) and the smart Group 3 7f Gainesborough Stud Fred Darling Stakes winner and 1,000 gns and Oaks placed Maysoon (by Shergar). Also to the 1993 French 3-y-o 10.5f listed stakes winner Trefoil, the fair 3-y-o 12f winner Janaat (both by Kris), the useful 8f listed Atalanta Stakes winner Triagonal (by Formidable) and to minor winners by Dance in Time, Formidable and Shareef Dancer. The dam won 7 races including the Group 2 10f Nassau Stakes, Group 2 10f Sun Chariot Stakes and Group 3 10.5f Musidora Stakes. 2nd dam, Field Mouse (by Grey Sovereign), was a useful 5f winner of 6 races at 2 and 3 yrs. A late foal that will need time, but nevertheless John Dunlop reports that **Thracian** is an attractive filly that moves well. (Hesmonds Stud Ltd).
Optimum 3-y-o distance: 8-10f.

140 - TRIA KEMATA
Bay colt. Kris - Third Watch (Slip Anchor).
March 22. 1st foal.
The dam, a 2-y-o 7f and very useful 3-y-o Group 2 12f Ribblesdale Stakes winner, is a half-sister to numerous winners including the high class Prix Foy and Prix Saint-Roman winner Richard of York, the Group 2 Premio Dormello and Group 3 Lancashire Oaks winner Three Tails and the Group 3 Fred Darling Stakes winner Maysoon. 2nd dam, Triple First (by High Top), won 7 races including the Sun Chariot Stakes, Nassau Stakes and Musidora Stakes. Though big, backward and unfurnished at present, John tells me that **Tria Kemata** is also a very good mover and should be a nice sort for the back-end of the season. (Hesmonds Stud).
Optimum 3-y-o distance: 12f.

Andre Fabre

141 - ALAMO BAY (USA)
Bay colt. Nureyev - Albertine (Irish River).
6th foal.
Half-brother to the French 3-y-o Asnieres (by Spend a Buck), to the top class Grade 1 10f Breeders Cup Classic, Group 1 9f Prix d'Ispahan and Group 2 10f Prix Eugene Adam winner Arcangues, the minor French winner Afrique Bleu Azur (both by Sagace), and the very useful 1994 3-y-o Group 3 10f Prix de Psyche winner and French 1,000 gns and Prix de Diane placed

Agathe (by Manila). The dam won twice in France, was 3rd in the Group 2 9.2f Prix de l'Opera and is a half-sister to the high class middle distance stayer Ashmore and the smart middle distance filly Acoma. 2nd dam, Almyre (by Wild Risk), won three races in France including the listed Prix Omnium over 12f and was 2nd in the Prix de Pomone. (Mr. D. Wildenstein).
Optimum 3-y-o distance: 8-10f.

142 - ARUTUA (USA)
Bay filly. Riverman - All Along (Targowice).
Closely related to Along All (by Mill Reef), winner of the Group 3 8f Prix de Chenes at 2 yrs and the Group 2 10.5f Prix Greffulhe at 3 yrs. The dam won the Prix de l'Arc de Triomphe, the Prix Vermeille, the Turf Classic, the Washington D.C. International and the Rothmans International and is a half-sister to the very useful miler Abala. 2nd dam, Agujita (by Vieux Manoir), won the Group 3 10.5f Prix Royaumont. (Mr. D. Wildenstein).
Optimum 3-y-o distance: 12f.

143 - ANASAZI
Bay filly. Sadlers Wells - Navajo Princess (Drone).
January 29.
Closely related to the great Dancing Brave, winner of the Prix de l'Arc de Triomphe, King George VI and Queen Elizabeth Diamond Stakes, 2,000 gns and Eclipse Stakes, to the top class filly Jolypha, winner of the Prix de Diane and Prix Vermeille, and to the quite useful 3-y-o 10f winner Balleta (all by Lyphard). The dam, a good winner of 16 races at up to 8f including the Grade 2 Molly Pitcher Handicap and the Grade 3 Falls City Handicap, is a sister to the stakes winner Passamaquoddy and a half-sister to the Grade 3 winner Soldier Boy. 2nd dam, Olmec (by Pago Pago), was a stakes winner of 5 races. (Khaled Abdulla).
Optimum 3-y-o distance: 10-12f.

144 - FIRST FLAME
Bay colt. Polish Precedent - Fatah Flare (Alydar).
May 25.
Half-brother to the 1995 3-y-o Flaviol (by Sadlers Wells), the useful triple 3-y-o 7f winner Mata Cara (by Storm Bird), the fairly useful 3-y-o 10f winner Refugio (by Reference Point) and the fair 2-y-o 6f winner Fire and Shade (by Shadeed). The dam, a 2-y-o 6f winner, was placed in both the Princess Margaret Stakes and the Waterford Candelabra Stakes before winning the Group 3 10.5f Musidora Stakes at 3 yrs. She is a half-sister to the dual U.S. Grade 1 winner over 9f and 10f, Sabin, and to the useful 2-y-o 6f winner Soughaan. 2nd dam, Beaconaire (by Vaguely Noble), a winner of 3 races at up to 10f in France including a stakes event, is a half-sister to the Grade 2 winner Kittiwake (dam of the multiple Grade 1 winner Miss Oceana, the Grade 2 winner Larida (herself dam of the Coronation Stakes winner Magic of Life) and the 1992 Prix Jean Prat winner Kitwood). (Sheikh Mohammed).
Optimum 3-y-o distance: 8-10f.

145 - FLYING PEGASUS (IRE)
Bay colt. In the Wings - Mill Princess (Mill Reef).
January 3. 340,000 gns.
Closely related to the quite useful 1993 2-y-o 6f winner Flowerdrum (by Sadlers Wells), and half-brother to the top-class colt and good sire Last Tycoon, winner of the Grade 1 Breeders Cup Mile, Group 1 Kings Stand Stakes and Group 1 William Hill Sprint Championship, the useful Group 3 5f Prix du Bois winner The Perfect Life (both by Try My Best), the very useful Group 2 6f Premio Melton and Group 3 6f Goldene Peitsche winner Astronef, the French 4-y-o 6f and 6.5f winner Love Boat (both by Be My Guest) and the minor French winners Save Me the Waltz (by Kings Lake), Forging Ahead (by Lomond) and Zelda (by Caerleon). The dam won over 10f at 2 yrs in France and is a half-sister to the Irish Sweeps Derby winner Irish Ball and the top class broodmare Irish Bird, dam of the classic winners Assert, Bikala and Eurobird. 2nd dam, Irish Lass II (by Sayajirao), won the 12f Prix de Minerve and was a sister to the Irish Oaks, Irish St Leger and Yorkshire Oaks winner Lynchris. (Wafic Said).
Optimum 3-y-o distance: 8-10f.

146 - GRAPE TREE ROAD
Bay colt. Caerleon - One Way Street (Habitat).
February 28. 250,000 Ir gns.
Brother to the fair 1993 3-y-o 16f winner Usk the Way and half-brother to the 1995 3-y-o Wassl Street (by Dancing Brave), the smart Group 2 13.3f Geoffrey Freer Stakes winner Red Route (by Polish Precedent), the useful 1990 2-y-o 8f winner Road to the Isle (by Lomond), the minor Irish 14f winner Street Opera (by Sadlers Wells) and the minor 1994 5-y-o 12f winner Olympic Way (by Ela Mana Mou). The dam, a winner of 4 races including the Group 3 12f Princess Royal Stakes, is a sister to the dual 7f winner Shorthouse (dam of the Hungerford Stakes and May Hill Stakes winner Ever Genial). 2nd dam, Guillotina (by Busted), won the 7f Houghton Stakes at 2 yrs and the 12.5f Prix de Royallieu at 3. (Mr. M. Tabor).
Optimum 3-y-o distance: 12f.

147 - HANDSOME DANCER
Bay colt. Nijinsky - It's in the Air (Mr Prospector).
April 18.
Brother to the quite useful 1993 3-y-o 10f winner Arkaan, closely related to the American 8f stakes winner Air Dancer (by Northern Dancer) and the French trained winners Sous Entendu (by Shadeed) and Try to Catch Me (by Shareef Dancer), and half-brother to the very useful 1994 3-y-o 7.6f and 10f winner Monaassabaat (by Zilzal) and the very useful 1987 2-y-o Group 2 Criterium de Maisons-Laffitte winner Bitooh (by Seattle Slew). The dam, a joint-champion 2-y-o filly in the USA, won from 6f to 10f and is out of the 2-y-o winner A Wind is Rising (by Francis.S), herself a half-sister to the good racehorse and sire Native Royalty. (Maktoum Al-Maktoum).
Optimum 3-y-o distance: 10-12f.

148 - HELSINKI
Brown filly. Machiavellian - Helen Street (Troy).
May 25.
Half-sister to the 1995 3-y-o Varvarka, the French 8f and 12f winner and 10f listed placed 3-y-o Sovetsky (both by Soviet Star), the useful 1994 8.3f -11.6f winner Grecian Slipper (by Sadlers Wells), the 2-y-o 6f winner Mount Helena and the Irish 12-14f placed 3-y-o Helenus (both by Danzig). The dam was a high class 3-y-o filly, winning the Irish Oaks and being placed in the Yorkshire Oaks, Champion Stakes and Washington D.C. International. 2nd dam, Waterway (by Riverman), won twice including the 7f Prix du Calvados (as did Helen Street), was 3rd in the French 1,000 gns and is out of a half-sister to the top class miler Sun Prince. (Sheikh Mohammed).
Optimum 3-y-o distance: 10f.

149 - LAFITTE THE PIRATE
Bay colt. Sadlers Wells - Reprocolor (Jimmy Reppin).
April 26. 270,000 gns.
Closely related to the high class 1994 5-y-o Cezanne (by Ajdal), winner of the Group 1 10f Guinness Champion Stakes and the John Smith's Magnet Cup, and half-brother to the 1995 3-y-o Colour Code (by Polish Precedent), to the Irish Oaks winner Colorspin (by High Top and herself dam of the top class colt Opera House), the Group 2 Prix de l'Opera and Group 3 Waterford Candelabra Stakes winner Bella Colora (by Bellypha and herself dam of the smart colt Stagecraft), the useful 6-8f winner Rappa Tap Tap (by Tap on Wood), the fair 1994 4-y-o 9f winner Colorful Ambition (by Slip Anchor) and the unraced Sistadari (by Bellypha and herself dam of the very useful 1994 3-y-o 7f and 8f winner Torch Rouge). The dam was a very useful winner of the 12f Lingfield Oaks Trial and the 12f Lancashire Oaks. 2nd dam, Blue Queen (by Majority Blue), was an unplaced half-sister to the high class sprinter Sandford Lad.
Optimum 3-y-o distance: 10f.

150 - LEGAL OPINION (IRE)
Bay filly. Polish Precedent - Golden Opinion (Slew O'Gold).
March 4. 3rd foal.
Closely related to the 1995 3-y-o Gold Sand (by Green Desert) and half-sister to the 1993 French 2-y-o 8f winner Sun Music (by Sadlers Wells). The dam, a top class miler, ran only at 3 yrs when

she won four races including the Group 1 Coronation Stakes and the Group 3 Prix du Rond Point, was 2nd in the July Cup to Cadeaux Genereux and 3rd in the French 1,000 gns to Pearl Bracelet. 2nd dam, Optimistic Lass (by Mr Prospector), was a smart winner of the Group 2 10f Nassau Stakes and the Group 3 10.5f Musidora Stakes. (Sheikh Mohammed).
Optimum 3-y-o distance: 8f.

151 - LIPPI (IRE)
Bay colt. Royal Academy - Last Tango (Luthier).
May 23.
Half-brother to the 1994 2-y-o Lexington Star (by Sadlers Wells), to the smart 1993 2-y-o Group 1 8f Grand Criterium winner Lost World (by Last Tycoon), the high-class Group 1 Grand Criterium, Group 1 10f Grand Prix de Paris and Group 2 12f Prix Niel winner Fijar Tango (by In Fijar) and to 3 minor winners by Carwhite, Kenmare and Trepan. The dam is an unraced half-sister to 3 winners. 2nd dam, La Bamba (by Shantung), won the Group 1 8f Prix Jacques le Marois and was 3rd in both the Prix de l'Arc de Triomphe and Epsom Oaks. (Mr. D. Wildenstein).
Optimum 3-y-o distance: 10f.

152 - LUNA WELLS (IRE)
Bay filly. Sadlers Wells - Lunadix (Breton).
March 2.
Half-sister to the high class French 2,000 gns and 2-y-o 8f Prix le Rochette winner Linamix (by Mendez), to the very smart 2-y-o 10f Prix de Conde and 4-y-o 12f Grand Prix d'Evry winner Long Mick (by Gay Mecene), the useful colt (at up to 10f) Moonbeam (by Bolkonski), and the winner of 3 races in France, Lenaquest (by Noblequest). The dam won over 6f at 2 yrs and 8f at 3 yrs, and was placed in the Prix du Calvados and Prix de Sandringham. 2nd dam, Lutine (by Alcide), won a 10f maiden and was 3rd in the Ascot 1,000 gns Trial. (Mr. J. L. Lagardere).
Optimum 3-y-o distance: 10-12f.

153 - LYDENBURG (IRE)
Chestnut colt. Lycius - Whitehaven (Top Ville).
February 25. 2nd foal.
Half-brother to the 1995 3-y-o Cumbrian (by Darshaan). The dam, a smart filly, won the Group 2 13.5f Prix de Pomone at 3 yrs after winning over 8f as a juvenile, is a sister to the Irish 6-12f winner Whitesville and a half-sister to 5 winners including the useful 2-y-o 7f winner Native Wizard. 2nd dam, White Star Line (by Northern Dancer), won 9 races including 3 Grade 1 events from 8.5f to 10f in the USA and is a half-sister to Trick Chick (dam of the high class French filly Northern Trick and the U.S. Grade 1 winner On the Sly), to Day Line (dam of the Coaching Club of America Oaks winner Magazine), to the Prix Morny winner Filiberto and to the U.S. Grade 2 winner and good broodmare Fairway Fun. (Sheikh Mohammed).
Optimum 3-y-o distance: 10f.

154 - POLENT
Bay filly. Polish Precedent - Awaasif (Snow Knight).
April 23.
Half-sister to the 3-y-o Siberian (by Machiavellian), to the high class filly Snow Bride, winner of the Epsom Oaks (awarded race), Musidora Stakes and Princess Royal Stakes and herself dam of the promising 1994 2-y-o winner Lammtarra, to the useful middle-distance winner Habaayib (both by Blushing Groom), the fair 8.2f winner and subsequent U.S. Grade 3 New Orleans Handicap winner Jarraar (by Mr Prospector) and the 2-y-o 7f and subsequent U.S. winner Salaadim (by Seattle Slew). The dam won the Group 1 Yorkshire Oaks and the Group 1 Gran Premio del Jockey Club and is a half-sister to numerous winners including the high class American colt Akureyri, the 1,000 gns 2nd Konafa (herself dam of the high class French 6f and 7f performer Proskona) and the unraced Royal Stance (dam of the very useful 8-10f colt Majuscule and the U.S. Grade 3 winner Royal Cielo). 2nd dam, Royal Statute (by Northern Dancer), a 2-y-o 5f winner, is a sister to the dual Canadian champion handicap horse Dance Act. (Sheikh Mohammed).
Optimum 3-y-o distance: 10f.

155 - PROUD FACT
Bay filly. Known Fact - Proud Lou (Proud Clarion).
March 16.
Half-sister to the very useful French 1,000 gns and Group 3 8f Prix de la Grotte winner and Group 1 Prix Marcel Boussac 2nd Houseproud (by Riverman). The dam won 4 races at 2 yrs in the USA over 6f and 8f including the Grade 1 Frizette Stakes and is a half-sister to 5 winners. 2nd dam, Baby Louise (by Exclusive Native), was a 2-y-o stakes winner in the USA. (Khaled Abdulla).
Optimum 3-y-o distance: 8f.

156 - RESTLESS CARL (IRE)
Bay colt. Caerleon - Resless Kara (Akarad).
March 27. 2nd foal.
Half-brother to the French trained 3-y-o Resless Rain (by Rainbow Quest). The dam, a winner over 7.5f at 2 yrs, was a high class winner of the Group 1 10.5f Prix de Diane at 3 yrs, was 3rd in the Prix Saint-Alary and is a half-sister to the 2-y-o 8f Prix des Reservoirs winner Restiver. 2nd dam, Restless Girl (by Bolkonski), was unraced. (Mr. J. L. Lagardere).
Optimum 3-y-o distance: 10-12f.

157 - SETTING SUN
Chestnut colt. Generous - Suntrap (Roberto).
February 8. 4th foal.
Half-brother to the 1995 3-y-o Hunt the Sun, to the high class Grade 1 12f Rothmans International, Group 1 15.5f Prix Royal-Oak and Group 2 15f Prix Kergorlay winner Raintrap and to the very smart Group 1 10f Criterium de Saint-Cloud and Group 2 12f Prix du Conseil de Paris winner Sunshack (all by Rainbow Quest). The dam, a useful dual 7f winner at 2 yrs and 3rd in the Group 3 Prix d'Aumale, is a half-sister to the Group 2 German winner Non Partisan and to the Grade 3 Canadian stakes winner Jalaajel. 2nd dam, Sunny Bay (by Northern Bay), won 3 stakes events in the USA and was 2nd in the Grade 1 Sorority Stakes. (Khaled Abdulla).
Optimum 3-y-o distance: 12f.

158 - SOURIRE (USA)
Bay colt. Dayjur - Southern Seas (Jim French).
Half-brother to the top class U.S. turf colt Steinlen (by Habitat), winner of the Breeders Cup Mile, the Arlington Million and the Bernard Baruch Handicap - all Grade 1 events, to the Group 2 12f Prix Jean de Chaudennay winner Seurat (by Crimson Beau), the listed 11f Prix Charles Laffitte winner Sophonisbe (by Wollow) and the minor French winners Seconde Bleue (by Glint of Gold) and Sea Symphony (by Faraway Son). The dam won 4 races at 3 yrs over 14f and 16f and is a half-sister to the dam of the Arc winner Sagace. 2nd dam, Schonbrunn (by Pantheon), won the German 1,000 gns and Oaks. (Mr. D. Wildenstein).
Optimum 3-y-o distance: 8f.

159 - TAMATETE
Bay colt. Caerleon - Triple Couronne (Riverman).
2nd foal.
Half-brother to the French 3-y-o Teterboro (by Sadlers Wells). The dam is a sister to the top class filly Triptych and the Group 3 winner Barger (dam of the Group 3 Prix de la Grotte winner Baya). 2nd dam, Trillion (by Hail to Reason), won 9 races including the Prix Ganay and was the champion grass mare in the USA. (Mr. D. Wildenstein).
Optimum 3-y-o distance: 10-12f.

160 - THREE MORE
Chestnut colt. Sanglamore - Tertiary (Vaguely Noble).
February 11.
Half-brother to the very smart 9f Feilden Stakes and 10f Mecca Bookmakers' Classic winner Kefaah (by Blushing Groom), the useful Tote-Ebor Handicap winner Primary (by Green Dancer), the smart 1991 2-y-o 7f Somerville Tattersall Stakes winner and Group 2 Criterium de Maisons Laffitte 2nd Tertian (by Danzig) and the French 2-y-o 8f winner Riverhead (by Riverman). The dam was 2nd over 10.5f in France, is a sister to the Washington D.C.

International and Prix Saint-Alary winner Nobiliary and a half-sister to the Prix de la Foret and Prix Jacques le Marois winner and top class sire Lyphard. 2nd dam, Goofed (by Court Martial), won 4 races including the New York Handicap and the Ladies Handicap in the USA. (Khaled Abdulla).
Optimum 3-y-o distance: 10-12f.

161 - TRUST BALL (FR)
Bay filly. Highest Honor - Terre de Feu (Busted).
June 7. 6th foal. 60,000 gns.
Half-sister to the 1995 3-y-o Mein Ange (by Darshaan) and to the top class colt Subotica (by Pampabird), winner of the Prix de l'Arc de Triomphe, Grand Prix de Paris, Prix Ganay (all Group 1 events) and the Group 2 Prix Niel. The dam won over 8f and 10f at 3 yrs in France and is a half-sister to the listed Prix de Gouvieux winner Force de Frappe. 2nd dam, Ludivine (by Luthier), won one race in France and is a half-sister to the Group 2 Prix Hocquart and Group 2 Prix Dollar winner Margouillat. (Mr. D. Wildenstein).
Optimum 3-y-o distance: 8-10f.

162 - TRYING TIMES (IRE)
Bay colt. Sadlers Wells - Ozone Friendly (Green Forest).
March 4. 2nd foal.
Half brother to the 1995 3-y-o Desert Water (by Green Desert). The dam was a useful 2-y-o winner of the Group 1 5.5f Prix Robert Papin, was 4th in the Group 1 6f Prix Morny but failed to train on as a 3-y-o. She is a half-sister to the U.S. 2-y-o stakes winner Storm Flight. 2nd dam, Kristana (by Kris), a fairly useful 3-y-o 10f winner, was placed in the Group 3 Prix de Royaumont and is a half-sister to the dams of the good winners Ardkinglass, Reprimand, Wiorno and Fawzi. (Maktoum Al-Maktoum).
Optimum 3-y-o distance: 8f.

163 - VIVAT REGINA (IRE)
Chestnut filly. Nashwan - Truly Special (Caerleon).
March 2. 4th foal.
Closely related to the 1995 3-y-o Rain Queen (by Rainbow Quest) and half-sister to the 1993 2-y-o 8f Evry and 3-y-o Grade 2 10f E.P.Taylor Stakes winner Truly a Dream (by Darshaan). The dam was a smart winner of the Group 3 10.5f Prix de Royaumont at 3 yrs after winning over 8f at 2 yrs and is a half-sister to the Group 2 Grand Prix de Deauville winner Modhish. 2nd dam, Arctique Royale (by Royal and Regal), won the Irish 1,000 gns and Moyglare Stud Stakes and is a half-sister to the dam of Ardross. (Sheikh Mohammed).
Optimum 3-y-o distance: 10f.

164 - WATER POET (IRE)
Bay colt. Sadlers Wells - Love Smitten (Key to the Mint).
March 19. 4th live foal.
Half-brother to the French trained 3-y-o Swain (by Nashwan). The dam won 9 races, notably the Grade 1 8.5f Apple Blossom Handicap and Grade 2 8.5f Santa Maria Handicap and is a sister to the Canadian Oaks winner Kamar (herself dam of two Grade 1 winners in Gorgeous and Seaside Attraction) and a half-sister to the Grade 3 Barbara Fritchie Handicap winner Stellarette and the U.S. stakes winner Dancing on a Cloud. 2nd dam, Square Angel (by Quadrangle), won 7 races including the Canadian Oaks and was the Canadian champion 3-y-o of 1973. (Sheikh Mohammed).
Optimum 3-y-o distance: 10-12f.

165 - WILLSTAR (USA)
Chestnut filly. Nureyev - Nijinsky Star (Nijinsky).
February 28.
Sister to the 1993 French 3-y-o 10f listed stakes winner Viviana and half-sister to the French 1990 3-y-o winner and U.S. Grade 2 11f Tidal Handicap winner Revasser (by Riverman) and the U.S. 3-y-o 6f stakes winner Hometown Queen (by Pleasant Colony) - placed in four Grade 1 stakes events including the 9f Kentucky Oaks. The dam is an unraced half-sister to the Meadow Queen Stakes winner Six Crowns - herself dam of the champion 2-y-o colt and high

class sire Chief's Crown and the Grade 1 Frizette Stakes winner Classic Crown. 2nd dam, Chris Evert (by Swoon's Son), a champion 3-y-o filly, is a half-sister to the dams of the Kentucky Derby winner Winning Colors, the Prince of Wales's Stakes winner Two Timing, the Grade 2 Astarita Stakes winner Missed the Storm and the King Edward VII Stakes winner Beyton. Interestingly, this filly is inbred 2x3 to Northern Dancer. (Khaled Abdulla).
Optimum 3-y-o distance: 8-10f.

166 - YAHNI (USA)
Bay colt. Danzig - Razyana (His Majesty).
February 14.
Brother to the top class sprinter and notable young sire Danehill, winner of the Group 1 6f Ladbroke Sprint Cup, the 6f Cork and Orrery Stakes and the 7f Ladbroke European Free Handicap, and to the 1993 French 2-y-o 5f winner Eagle Eyed. The dam, placed over 7f at 2 yrs and 10f at 3 yrs, is out of Spring Adieu (by Buckpasser), a winner of 3 small sprint races at 3 yrs and a half-sister to Northern Dancer. (Khaled Abdulla).
Optimum 3-y-o distance: 6-7f.

James Fanshawe

167 - UNSOLD
Bay colt. Green Desert - Shoot Clear (Bay Express).
April 2. 24,000 Ir gns.
Half-brother to the 1995 3-y-o Clearly Devious (by Machiavellian), to the useful 1989 3-y-o dual 12.3f winner Shoot Ahead (by Shirley Heights), the 1990 3-y-o 10f winner Elmaftun (by Rainbow Quest) and the 1990 2-y-o 7f winner Dance Ahead (by Shareef Dancer) - both quite useful. The dam won 3 races at 2 yrs including the Group 3 7f Waterford Candelabra Stakes, was 4th in the 1,000 gns and is a half-sister to Sally Brown (winner of the Yorkshire Oaks and Ribblesdale Stakes and herself dam of the useful filly Anne Bonny) and to Untold (winner of the Yorkshire Oaks and Hoover Fillies Mile). 2nd dam, Unsuspected (by Above Suspicion), was a fairly useful winner of 8 races from 8f to 14f and a half-sister to 3 winners. (Bottisham Heath Stud).
Optimum 3-y-o distance: 8-10f.

John Gosden

168 - ALTAMURA (USA)
Bay filly. El Gran Senor - Narwala (Darshaan).
January 21. 2nd foal.
The dam was placed over 7f on her only appearance at 2 yrs, then won over 10.2f on her first outing at 3 yrs prior to a smart victory in the Group 3 12f Princess Royal Stakes. She then travelled to the USA for her last outing where she was 2nd in the Grade 2 12f Long Island Handicap. 2nd dam, Noufiyla (by Top Ville), a middle-distance maiden, is a half-sister to the Cherry Hinton Stakes winner Nasseem. John told me that **Altamura**, a weak, light-framed filly, should be seen on the racecourse by July. (Sheikh Mohammed).
Optimum 3-y-o distance: 10-12f.

169 - AMBASSADRESS (USA)
Bay or brown filly. Alleged - Ancient Regime (Olden Times).
April 11. $350,000.
Half-sister to the 1995 French 3-y-o Trois Graces (by Alysheba), to the very smart 5f Prix Yacowlef winner and Group 1 5f Prix de l'Abbaye 2nd La Grande Epoque (by Lyphard and herself dam of the very useful 6-7f winner Matelot), the very useful 6f and 7f winner and Group 2 Queen Anne Stakes 2nd Rami (by Riverman) and the very useful 1990 2-y-o Group 3 6.5f Prix Eclipse winner Crack Regiment (by El Gran Senor). The dam, winner of the Group 1 6f Prix Morny, was the champion French 2-y-o filly of 1980, is a sister to the Group 2 6.5f Prix Maurice de Gheest winner Cricket Ball and the American stakes winner Olden, and a half-sister to the

U.S. Grade 3 winner Mug Punter. 2nd dam, Caterina II (by Princely Gift), won 4 races, notably the 5f Nunthorpe Stakes and was a half-sister to the Eclipse winner Scottish Rifle. John tells me that **Ambassadress** "is a backward filly and as such will take a lot of time to come to hand. Like all her bloodline, she'll require a lot of cut in ground and I wouldn't expect her to run until about September." (Hesmonds Stud).
Optimum 3-y-o distance: 8f.

170 - AMEER JUMAIRAH (IRE)
Chestnut colt. Caerleon - Ameerat Jumaira (Alydar).
March 22. 1st foal.
The dam was placed once over 10.3f at 3 yrs, from 4 starts, is a sister to the Irish 2-y-o 7f and minor U.S. 8f stakes winner Charmante and a half-sister to the top class miler Zilzal. 2nd dam, French Charmer (by Le Fabuleux), won 5 races at 3 yrs including the Grade 2 Del Mar Oaks and is a half-sister to the dams of the Group/Grade 1 winners Awe Inspiring, Culture Vulture and Polish Precedent. (Sheikh Ahmed Al-Maktoum).
Optimum 3-y-o distance: 8-10f.

171 - BRAIDWOOD (USA)
Bay or brown filly. Danzig - Braiswick (King of Spain).
May 5. 2nd foal.
Closely related to the 1995 3-y-o Prickwillow (by Nureyev). The dam was a very smart filly and winner of the Grade 1 10f E.P.Taylor Stakes and Group 2 10f Sun Chariot Stakes and is a half-sister to the Group 3 12f September Stakes winner Percy's Lass. 2nd dam, Laughing Girl (by Sassafras), won the 10f Lupe Stakes, was placed in the Oaks and Park Hill Stakes and is a half-sister to the dams of Teenoso, Topsy, Give Thanks, Favoridge and Old Country. **Braidwood** is "a rather big filly that will take some time. In fact she's the biggest 2-y-o filly in the yard. I would hope to see her out in October," commented John. (Sheikh Mohammed).
Optimum 3-y-o distance: 8-10f.

172 - CANYON CREEK (IRE)
Bay colt. Mr Prospector - River Memories (Riverman).
May 10. 3rd foal.
Half-brother to the 1995 3-y-o Lufira (by Nureyev). The dam was a very smart winner of the Group 1 12f Rothmans International, Group 2 12.5f Prix Maurice de Nieuil, Group 2 10.5f Prix de Royaumont and Group 3 13.5f Prix de Pomone. She is a half-sister to the 2-y-o Group 3 7.5f Prix Thomas Bryon winner Raise a Memory out of the 8-12f placed Le Vague a l'Ame (by Vaguely Noble), herself a half-sister to the top class middle distance colt Celestial Storm. John explained that **Canyon Creek** is "a little light-framed and lacks any real strength at this stage" (mid-April) "and although his pedigree suggests he might be fairly precocious, he's going to take until at least August to reach the racecourse." (Sheikh Mohammed).
Optimum 3-y-o distance: 10-12f.

173 - CHIRICO (USA)
Bay colt. Danzig - Colour Chart (Mr Prospector).
April 9. 1st foal.
The dam was a very smart winner of the Group 2 9.2f Prix de l'Opera, Group 3 10f Prix de la Nonette and Group 3 8f Prix du Muguet and is a half-sister to the very useful stayer Dance Spectrum. 2nd dam, Rainbow Connection (by Halo), was a champion 2-y-o and 3-y-o filly in Canada and a half-sister to three other Canadian Grade 1 winners - Archdeacon, Hangin' on a Star and Mr Macho. John explained that **Chirico** is a similar type to **Canyon Creek**. "He's still weak and leggy and lacks any real strength at this stage. I wouldn't think you'd see him until August or September." By Danzig and out of a Mr Prospector mare, Chirico is bred on the same lines as the outstanding sprinter Dayjur. (Sheikh Mohammed).
Optimum 3-y-o distance: 8f.

174 - DUEL AT DAWN
Chestnut colt. Nashwan - Gayane (Nureyev).
February 28. 4th foal.
Brother to the 1995 3-y-o Galafron. The dam, a very smart winner of the 6f Sandy Lane Stakes

and 7f Oak Tree Stakes, is a half-sister to the Sun Chariot Stakes winner Ristna. 2nd dam, Roussalka (by Habitat), was also a classy filly, winning the Nassau Stakes twice and the Coronation Stakes and is a half-sister to the Fillies Triple Crown winner Oh So Sharp - herself dam of the Prix Saint-Alary winner Rosefinch. **Duel at Dawn** is a "powerful, sprinting type that has had sore shins but should be out on a racecourse soon," according to his trainer. (Sheikh Mohammed).
Optimum 3-y-o distance: 8f.

175 - KARAMZIN (USA)
Chestnut filly. Nureyev - Kartajana (Shernazar).
February 5. 1st foal.
The dam, a very smart filly, won the Group 1 10.5f Prix Ganay, Group 1 10f Grosser Preis Bayerisches Zuchtrennen, Group 2 10f Nassau Stakes and the Group 2 10f Sun Chariot Stakes. She is a half-sister to the Extel Handicap winner Kazaviyna out of the smart Group 3 12f Princess Royal Stakes winner Karamita (by Shantung) - herself a half-sister to the good winners Kalidar and Karadar, and to the dams of the Group 1 winners Caerlina and Khariyda. **Karamzin** is an attractive filly that has done a fair bit of coughing, but if she stays healthy should be out by July. (Sheikh Mohammed).
Optimum 3-y-o distance: 8-10f.

176 - KERRY RING
Bay filly. Sadlers Wells - Kerrera (Diesis).
February 3. 2nd foal.
Sister to the Irish trained 1994 3-y-o June Moon and half-sister to the 1995 French trained 3-y-o Kerrier (by Nashwan). The dam was a smart filly and winner of 3 races over 6f including the Group 3 Cherry Hinton Stakes and the Sandy Lane Stakes. She was also placed in the 1,000 gns (2nd to Musical Bliss) and in the July Cup (4th to Cadeaux Genereux) and is a half-sister to the very smart, game and genuine colt Rock City and to the very useful 1992 middle distance 3-y-o colt Peto. 2nd dam, Rimosa's Pet (by Petingo), won the Group 3 Musidora Stakes and the Group 3 Princess Elizabeth Stakes. **Kerry Ring** is a small, delicate filly that will take a little time and may be out around September time. (Sheikh Mohammed).
Optimum 3-y-o distance: 8-10f.

177 - L'AMI LOUIS
Chestnut colt. Easy Goer - Jadana (Pharly).
February 7. $225,000.
Half-brother to the smart young sire Jade Hunter (by Mr Prospector), winner of the Grade 1 10f Gulfstream Park Handicap and Grade 1 9f Donn Handicap, to the minor French 3-y-o winner Fraser River (by Forty Niner) and the minor U.S. 3-y-o winner Jade Ridge (by Cox's Ridge). The dam won 3 races in the USA including a minor stakes event, is closely related to the champion 2-y-o and Dewhurst Stakes winner Monteverdi and a half-sister to 2 stakes winners in France. 2nd dam, Janina (by Match II), won as a 3-y-o in France. **L'Ami Louis** was working well in the spring, showing speed, and finished 2nd first time out. (Oakcliff Foals '93).
Optimum 3-y-o distance: 10f.

178 - LAND OF HEROES (USA)
Chestnut colt. Silver Hawk - Made in America (Explodent).
March 18.
Brother to the Grade 1 8.5f Oak Leaf Stakes and Grade 3 7f Sorrento Stakes winner Zoonaqua and half-brother to the U.S. stakes winner Diablo Amigo (by Woodman) and the minor American winners Gatap (by Buckfinder) and Rainy Night (by Caro). The dam won 5 races and was stakes placed in the USA, is a half-sister to the stakes winner and sire Traffic, to the stakes-placed winner Nature (dam of the Grade 3 winner Royal Suite) and to the dam of the Grade 1 winner Gay Style. 2nd dam, Capelet (by Bolero), won the Frizette Stakes and was a half-sister to the top class American filly and broodmare Quill. John Gosden pointed out to me that **Land of Heroes** is "a big, very rangy colt with a big, long stride on him. He looks like he'll stay well and should be out in about September or October." (Sheikh Mohammed).
Optimum 3-y-o distance: 8-10f.

179 - MUKEED
Bay colt. Be My Chief - Rimosa's Pet (Petingo).
May 8.
Half-brother to the high class Coventry, July, Gimcrack, Greenham and Criterion Stakes winner Rock City (by Ballad Rock), the smart Cherry Hinton Stakes winner and 1,000 gns 2nd Kerrera (by Diesis), the 1995 3-y-o Syrian Queen, the fair 1994 3-y-o 8f winner On the Tide (both by Slip Anchor), to the useful 8.3f to 11f winner Peto (by Petoski) and the useful French 10.5f winner Secretariat's Pet (by Secretariat). The dam won the Group 3 8.5f Princess Elizabeth Stakes (at 2 yrs) and the Group 3 10.5f Musidora Stakes. 2nd dam, Rimosa (by Mossborough), won at up to 13f and is closely related to the dam of Track Spare. **Mukeed** goes alright and has grown, though is a little more immature than John thought he'd be. Nevertheless, he should be running around the middle of the season. (Sheikh Ahmed Al-Maktoum).
Optimum 3-y-o distance: 8-10f.

180 - RETICENT
Bay colt. Sadlers Wells - Shy Princess (Irish River).
March 28. 4th foal.
Closely related to the 1994 French 2-y-o 6f listed stakes and 3-y-o Europeaan Free Handicap winner Diffident (by Nureyev). The dam, a smart French 2-y-o 7f winner and 2nd in the Group 1 Prix Morny, won over 6f as a 3-y-o and is a half-sister to the Breeders Cup Mile winner Opening Verse, previously a smart colt in England when 2nd in the Eclipse Stakes. 2nd dam, Shy Dawn (by Grey Dawn II), won no less than 19 races at up to 10f including five Grade 3 stakes and is a half-sister to 3 stakes winners. **Reticent** is a "rather delicate horse that is going to take time to come to hand. Although he is a good mover and I quite like him, he's going to be one for the back-end of the season," his trainer explained. (Sheikh Mohammed).
Optimum 3-y-o distance: 8-10f.

181 - RING OF MUSIC
Bay filly. Sadlers Wells - Glorious Song (Halo).
February 14.
Closely related to the promising 1992 2-y-o 7f winner Singspiel (by In the Wings), to the useful 3-y-o 9f and 10.2f winner Rakeen (by Northern Dancer) - subsequently a Grade 2 winner in South Africa, and the fair 2-y-o 7f winner Haymarket (by Danzig), and half-sister to the very useful colt Rahy - a winner over 6f and 8f here and subsequently winner of the Grade 2 Bel Air Handicap in the USA, to the minor 3-y-o 7.6f winner Morn of Song (both by Blushing Groom) and to a minor winner by Riverman. The dam won 17 races including four Grade 1 events and is a sister to the champion 2-y-o colt Devils Bag and to the Grade 2 Arlington Classic winner Saint Ballado. 2nd dam, Ballade (by Herbager), won over 5f and 6f in the USA. **Ring of Music** goes well and is a strong filly that should be out around June. (Sheikh Mohammed).
Optimum 3-y-o distance: 10f

182 - RUN FOR ME (IRE)
Bay filly. Danehill - Negligence (Roan Rocket).
April 6. 50,000 Ir gns.
Sister to the 1995 3-y-o Dannec and half-sister to the champion 2-y-o filly Negligent, winner of the 7f Rockfel Stakes and 3rd in the 1,000 gns, to the dual 2-y-o 6f winner and 1,000 gns 4th Ala Mahlik (both by Ahonoora), the very useful 22.2f Queen Alexandra Stakes winner Ala Hounak (by Sexton Blake), the useful 1992 3-y-o 8f and 10f winner Zalon (by Flash of Steel) and the quite useful 1993 Irish dual 7f 2-y-o winner Manaafis (by High Estate). The dam, placed once over 10f at 3 yrs, is a half-sister to the dams of the very useful sprinter Governor General and the smart French 10f performer Galunpe. 2nd dam, Malpractice (by Pall Mall), was an unraced half-sister to the dam of the Grade 1 E.P.Taylor Stakes winner Sudden Love. **Run For Me** is a big filly, very heavy and her knees are immature as yet. John also tells me that she'll need give in the ground and should be on the racecourse around September. (Sheikh Ahmed Al-Maktoum).
Optimum 3-y-o distance: 8f.

183 - SACHO (IRE)
Bay colt. Sadlers Wells - Oh So Sharp (Kris).

May 4. 6th foal to live.
Closely related to the very useful 7.3f and 9f English winner and subsequent Grade 2 Long Island Handicap winner Shaima (by Shareef Dancer) and half-brother to the 1994 2-y-o Felitza (by Soviet Star), placed 4th on her only outing, to the smart Group 1 10f Prix Saint Alary winner Rosefinch (by Blushing Groom) and to the minor Irish 3-y-o 8f winner Ben Alisky (by Dunbeath). The dam was a top class filly, and winner of 7 of her 9 races from 5f to 14.6f, notably the fillies Triple Crown (1,000 gns, Oaks and St Leger). She is a sister to the useful 3-y-o 12f and 14f winner Icelandic and a half-sister to 7 winners including the Coronation and Nassau Stakes winner Roussalka (herself dam of the good fillies Ristna and Gayane), the 1,000 gns 2nd Our Home (dam of the useful colt Kristianstad), Jersey Stakes winner Etienne Gerard and the Ribblesdale Stakes 2nd My Fair Niece. 2nd dam, Oh So Fair (by Graustark), won over 10f in Ireland. **Sacho** is a nice horse that goes well and should be out around July time. (Sheikh Mohammed).
Optimum 3-y-o distance: 12f.

184 - SERIF (USA)
Bay colt. Diesis - Ribbon (His Majesty).
April 22.
Brother to the fairly useful 1992 2-y-o 6f winner and 3-y-o 7.3f Fred Darling Stakes 2nd Ribbonwood, and half-brother to the top class colt Risen Star (by Secretariat), winner of the Belmont Stakes and Preakness Stakes and champion 3-y-o colt of 1988, and to the useful 1989 3-y-o 9f York and 12f listed Italian winner Silk Braid (by Danzig). The dam, won 9 races from 6-11f in the USA including the Group 3 Pucker Up Stakes and is a half-sister to the very useful 1988 3-y-o 8-10f winner Polar Gap. 2nd dam, Break Through (by Hail to Reason), was a fairly useful Irish 3-y-o 8f winner. The trainer tells me that **Serif** is a light framed colt that wants to get about his business and will hopefully be running around May. (Sheikh Mohammed).
Optimum 3-y-o distance: 10f.

185 - SHARAF KABEER
Chestnut colt. Machiavellian - Sheroog (Shareef Dancer).
February 27. 1st foal.
The dam, a fair 3-y-o 8f winner, is a sister to the very smart Prix de Pomone winner Colorado Dancer, is closely related to the Grade 1 Gamely Handicap winner Northern Aspen, the Group 1 Grand Prix de Paris winner Fort Wood and the Group 1 July Cup winner Hamas, and a half-sister to the Grade 1 Breeders Cup Juvenile winner Timber Country, the Goodwood Cup winner Mazzacano and the Prix d'Astarte winner Elle Seule - herself dam of the Irish 1,000gns winner Mehthaaf. 2nd dam, Fall Aspen (by Pretense), won 8 races including the Grade 1 7f Matron Stakes. John describes **Sharaf Kabeer** as an extremely tall colt and a good mover. He expects him to be out round about July. (Sheikh Ahmed Al-Maktoum).
Optimum 3-y-o distance: 8f.

186 - SWAN PRINCESS (USA)
Bay filly. Nureyev - Fairy Footsteps (Mill Reef).
January 29. $300,000.
Closely related to the fair 3-y-o 12f winner Haunted Wood (by Nijinsky) and half-sister to the fair 1994 3-y-o 10f winner Fabulous Fairy (by Alydar), the French 2-y-o winner and Group 3 Prix Penelope 3rd Fleet Fairy (by Teenoso) and the fairly useful 3-y-o 11.7f and 12f winner Lovely Fairy (by Beldale Flutter). The dam won the 1,000 gns and is a half-sister to the St Leger winner Light Cavalry. 2nd dam, Glass Slipper (by Relko), was a useful 13.3f winner at 3 yrs, was 2nd in the Musidora Stakes and is a half-sister to Royal Palace. **Swan Princess** is a strong filly with a sharp action, is going well at the moment (mid April) and should be out in May. (Sheikh Mohammed).
Optimum 3-y-o distance: 10-12f.

187 - TRIPLE LEAP
Bay colt. Sadlers Wells - Three Tails (Blakeney).
February 12. 5th foal.
Brother to the 1995 3-y-o 11f winner Tamure and closely related to the fair 1993 12f and 14.8f placed 3-y-o Threemilestone (by Secreto). The dam, a very useful 2-y-o dual 8f winner (including the Group 2 Premio Dormello), improved into a smart, though perhaps not the most genuine

of winners of the Group 2 12f Lancashire Oaks and was 2nd in the Group 1 Prix Vermeille. She is a half-sister to the 1,000 gns and Oaks placed Maysoon, to the Ribblesdale Stakes winner Third Watch and the Prix Foy winner Richard of York. 2nd dam, Triple First (by High Top), won 7 races including the Nassau, Sun Chariot and Musidora Stakes. John tells me that **Triple Leap** is a nice horse and a good mover but that he won't be racing until around September. (Sheikh Mohammed).
Optimum 3-y-o distance: 12f.

188 - WOOD VINE (USA)
Chestnut filly. Woodman - Massaraat (Nureyev).
March 16. 1st foal.
The dam, a French 3-y-o 7f listed stakes winner, is a sister to one of the great racehorses of the Eighties in Miesque, a winner of ten Group/Grade 1 races including the Breeders Cup Mile (twice), the 1,000 gns, Prix Jacques le Marois (twice) and Prix du Moulin - herself dam of the Group 1 winners Kingmambo and East of the Moon. 2nd dam, Pasadoble (by Prove It), won 4 races in France over 8f including two stakes events and is a half-sister to the Grade 1 Brooklyn Handicap winner Silver Supreme. **Wood Vine** has done a bit of coughing but she's a strong filly that should be out by about June time. The 1994 Cheveley Park Stakes winner Gay Gallanta is, like **Wood Vine**, by Woodman and out of a Nureyev mare. (Sheikh Mohammed).
Optimum 3-y-o distance: 8f.

189 - WYBARA
Chestnut filly. Nashwan - Twyla (Habitat).
March 26. 5th foal.
Closely related to the very useful 2-y-o 7f and 8f winner and 3-y-o Group 3 12.3f Dalham Chester Vase winner Twist and Turn (by Groom Dancer) and half-sister to the 1995 3-y-o High Pyrenees (by Shirley Heights). The dam, a useful dual 6f winner, is a sister to the smart 1983 2-y-o sprinter Defecting Dancer. 2nd dam, Running Ballerina (by Nijinsky), won over 6f at 2 yrs and is a half-sister to a number of good winners including Dominion Day, Northern Tavern, Padroug and Sir Penfro, and to the dam of Persian Bold. **Wybara** is a big filly that goes well and should be a staying type. (Sheikh Mohammed).
Optimum 3-y-o distance: 12f.

Michael Grassick

190 - FLAME OF ATHENS (IRE)
Bay colt. Royal Academy - Flame of Tara (Artaius).
March 20. 125,000 Ir gns.
Closely related to the very useful Group 3 10f Prix de Psyche and Irish 1,000 gns Trial winner Danse Royale (by Caerleon), and half-brother to the 1994 3-y-o Song of Tara, to the brilliant filly Salsabil, winner of the 1,000 gns, Oaks, Irish Derby and Prix Vermeille, the very useful 1989 3-y-o 10f and 10.5f winner Nearctic Flame (all three by Sadlers Wells), to the high class Group 1 St James's Palace Stakes winner Marju and the fairly useful 12f and 14.6f winner Rajai (both by Last Tycoon). The dam won 8 races including the Group 2 8f Coronation Stakes and the Group 2 Pretty Polly Stakes and was 2nd in the Champion Stakes. She is a half-sister to the useful dual 2-y-o 7f winner Blaze of Tara and to Fruition - dam of the high class stayer Kneller. 2nd dam, Welsh Flame (by Welsh Pageant), won 4 races at up to 8f and is a half-sister to the Musidora Stakes 2nd Sofala, herself dam of the good stayer Bourbon Boy. 3rd dam, Electric Flash (by Crepello), was a half-sister to the Derby winner Crepello. (Miss P. F. O'Kelly)
Optimum 3-y-o distance: 10f.

John Hammond

191 - BUTTERMERE
Chestnut colt. Polish Precedent - English Spring (Grey Dawn II).

February 5. 5th foal to live.
Half-brother to the useful 1991 3-y-o 10f Lupe Stakes winner Fragrant Hill (by Shirley Heights), the minor 1990 3-y-o 12f winner Spring to Glory (by Teenoso) and the minor 1991 2-y-o 7f winner Brave the Wind (by Dancing Brave). The dam was a very useful winner of 6 races from 8-10f including the Group 2 Prince of Wales's Stakes and is a half-sister to the U.S. Group 1 stakes winner Dance of Life. 2nd dam, Spring is Here (by In Reality), won 6 races and was second in the Grade 2 Molly Pitcher Handicap. (Sheikh Mohammed).
Optimum 3-y-o distance: 8-10f.

192 - CARNIOLA
Bay filly. Rainbow Quest - Carnival Spirit (Kris).
April 23. 2nd live foal.
The dam, a fairly useful 3-y-o 8f winner, is a half-sister to the top class Prix de l'Arc de Triomphe and Grand Prix de Paris winner Saumarez and to the very promising 1994 2-y-o Balliol Boy. 2nd dam, Fiesta Fun (by Welsh Pageant), a sister to the dam of the Gordon Stakes winner John French and a half-sister to the smart 6f and 7f winner Derrylin, was a useful winner of 3 races over 10f at 3yrs and was 3rd in the Group 1 Yorkshire Oaks. (Sheikh Mohammed).
Optimum 3-y-o distance: 8-10f.

193 - IBERIAN (FR)
Bay filly. Belmez - Kiliniski (Niniski).
April 2. 4th foal to live.
Half-sister to the 1991 10f and 12f placed 3-y-o (in two starts) Japonski (by Blushing Groom), to Green Kilt - placed 9 times at 2 and 3 yrs from 8-12f, and the 1993 6f placed 2-y-o (on only start) Kilcoo (both by Green Desert) - all three fair maidens. The dam was a very smart filly, winning the Group 3 12f Lingfield Oaks Trial and running 2nd in the Yorkshire Oaks and 4th in the Epsom Oaks (nearly 12 lengths behind Oh So Sharp). 2nd dam, Kilavea (by Hawaii), won on her only start, at 2 yrs over 5f at Goodwood, and is a half-sister to Nureyev and to the dam of Sadlers Wells. This filly is inbred 3 x 4 to Northern Dancer. (Sheikh Mohammed).
Optimum 3-y-o distance: 12f.

194 - STAGE MANNER
Bay filly. In the Wings - Air Distingue (Sir Ivor),
February 17.
Half-sister to the very promising 1994 2-y-o 8f winner Vettori (by Machiavellian), the quite useful 1991 3-y-o 10f winner Lodestar (by Rainbow Quest), the French 3-y-o 10f winner Decided Air (by Sure Blade) and the minor 1993 3-y-o 9f winner Livonian (by Kris). The dam won the Group 3 8f Prix d'Aumale, was 2nd in the Nassau Stakes and 3rd in the Prix de Diane and is a half-sister to the smart French 2-y-o Eastern Dawn. 2nd dam, Euryanthe (by Nijinsky), is an unraced sister to the Irish St Leger and dual U.S. Group 1 winner Caucasus, is closely related to the champion Canadian turf horse One For All and a half-sister to both the Musidora Stakes winner Last Feather and the dam of Run the Gantlet. (Sheikh Mohammed).
Optimum 3-y-o distance: 10f.

195 - WOODSPELL (USA)
Chestnut filly. Woodman - Beat (Nijinsky).
May 2. 3rd foal.
Half-sister to the 1995 3-y-o Merry Festival (by Private Account). The dam, a Grade 3 stakes-placed winner in the USA, is a half-sister to the smart 1990 3-y-o 7f and 8f winner and Group 1 St James's Palace Stakes 3rd Lord Florey and to the American Grade 1 Maskette Stakes winner Too Chic - herself dam of the Grade 1 stakes winner Chic Shirine. 2nd dam, Remedia (by Dr Fager), won 4 races at 3 and 4 yrs in the USA at up to 8f and is a half-sister to the dam of the dual Ascot Gold Cup winner Sadeem. (Sheikh Mohammed).
Optimum 3-y-o distance: 8-10f.

John Hammond or Jonathan Pease

The following horses were due to be trained by the late Francois Boutin and have now been divided between these two trainers.

196 - MIDNIGHT OASIS (USA)
Bay filly. Java Gold - Northernette (Northern Dancer).
Half-sister to the Grade 1 10f Flower Bowl Handicap winner Scoot, the Group 2 9f Panasonic Beresford Stakes winner Gold Crest (both by Mr Prospector), the fairly useful 2-y-o 8f winner Hilti's Hut and the American 3-y-o winner Groomed to Win (both by Blushing Groom) and to a minor Irish 7f winner by Alydar. The dam, a champion Canadian filly and winner of 13 races including the Grade 1 9f Top Flight Handicap, is a sister to the champion 2-y-o and high class sire Storm Bird and closely related to two stakes winners including Ocean's Answer (winner of the Natalma Stakes and dam of the smart sprinter Al Zawbaah). 2nd dam, South Ocean (by New Providence), won the Canadian Oaks. (Stavros Niarchos).
Optimum 3-y-o distance: 8-10f.

197 - MOON IS UP
Bay filly. Woodman - Miesque (Nureyev).
4th foal.
Closely related to the top class miler Kingmambo, winner of the French 2,000 gns, St James's Palace Stakes and Prix du Moulin and to the French trained 3-y-o Miesque's Son (both by Mr Prospector) and half-brother to the high class French 1,000 gns, Prix de Diane and Prix Jacques le Marois winner East of the Moon (by Private Account). The dam, a great filly and possibly the best miler of the eighties, won ten Group or Grade 1 events including the Breeders Cup Mile (twice), the Prix Jacques le Marois (twice), the 1,000 gns, the French 1,000 gns and the Prix du Moulin. 2nd dam, Pasadoble (by Prove Out), won 4 races in France over 8f including two stakes events, is a sister to the U.S. Grade 1 Brooklyn Handicap winner Silver Supreme and is out of an unraced half-sister to the top class filly Comtesse de Loir. **Moon is Up** is closely related to the John Gosden trained 2-y-o Wood Vine - both of them being by Woodman and out of full-sisters. (Stavros Niarchos). Optimum 3-y-o distance: 8f.

198 - SPINNING WORLD (FR)
Bay colt. Nureyev - Imperfect Circle (Riverman).
1st foal.
The dam was a very useful 2-y-o winner of the listed 6f Firth of Clyde Stakes, was 2nd in the Cheveley Park Stakes and subsequently won over 7f at 3 yrs. She is a half-sister to the very smart filly Chimes of Freedom, winner of the Coronation Stakes, the Moyglare Stud Stakes and the Child Stakes, and to the useful 3-y-o 10.3f winner Binkhaldoun. 2nd dam, Aviance (by Northfields), won the 6f Heinz 57 Phoenix Stakes at 2 yrs and is out of the 7f and 8f winner Minnie Hauk (by Sir Ivor), herself a sister to Malinowski, Gielgud and Monroe (all at least smart) and a half-sister to the dual U.S. Grade 1 winner Blush With Pride and the top class broodmare Sex Appeal (dam of Try My Best and El Gran Senor). (Stavros Niarchos).
Optimum 3-y-o distance: 8f.

199 - VAUTOUR ROUGE (USA)
Bay colt. Sadlers Wells - Coup de Folie (Halo).
6th foal.
Closely related to the very useful Group 2 8f Prix d'Astarte winner and French 1,000gns 2nd Hydro Calido (by Nureyev) and half-brother to the champion European 2-y-o and 2,000 gns 2nd Machiavellian, the smart Group 1 Prix Morny and Group 1 Prix de la Salamandre winner and 1,000gns 3rd Coup de Genie (both by Mr Prospector) and the very smart Group 1 Prix Jacques le Marois winner Exit to Nowhere (by Irish River). The dam won four races from 6f to 10f including the Group 3 8f Prix d'Aumale and was stakes placed in the USA. 2nd dam, Raise the Standard (by Hoist the Flag), is an unraced half-sister to Northern Dancer. (Stavros Niarchos).
Optimum 3-y-o distance: 8-10f.

200 - VINGT ET UNE (FR)
Bay filly. Sadlers Wells - Whakilyric (Miswaki).
January 22. 5th foal.
Sister to the 1995 3-y-o Well's Whisper, to the very useful Group 1 10.5f Prix Lupin and U.S. Grade 2 8f winner Johann Quatz and the 1994 French 3-y-o 13.5f listed stakes winner Walter Willy and half-sister to the top class middle distance colt Hernando (by Ninski), winner of the Group 1 Prix du Jockey Club and Group 1 Prix Lupin and 2nd in the Prix de l'Arc de Triomphe. The dam won over 5.5f and the Group 3 7f Prix du Calvados, was 3rd in the Prix de la Salamandre (all at 2 yrs) and in the Group 1 7f Prix de la Foret. 2nd dam, Lyrism (by Lyphard), was an unraced daughter of the very useful miler and subsequent smart American middle distance performer Pass a Glance. (Stavros Niarchos).
Optimum 3-y-o distance: 10-12f.

201 - WIND OF ROSES (FR)
Bay filly. Lomond - Chimes of Freedom (Private Account).
1st foal.
The dam, a smart filly, won the Group 1 6f Moyglare Stud Stakes and the Group 3 6f Cherry Hinton Stakes at 2 yrs, prior to winning the Group 1 8f Coronation Stakes and the Group 2 8f Child Stakes in her second season. She is a half-sister to the very useful 2-y-o 6f listed Firth of Clyde Stakes winner and Cheveley Park Stakes 2nd Imperfect Circle and to the useful 3-y-o 10.3f winner Binkhaldoun. 2nd dam, Aviance (by Northfields), was a very useful winner of the Group 1 6f Heinz 57 Phoenix Stakes and is out of the 7f and 8f winner Minnie Hauk, herself a sister to the smart winners Gielgud, Malionowski and Monroe and a half-sister to the U.S. Grade 1 Kentucky Oaks winner Blush With Pride and the top class broodmare Sex Appeal - dam of El Gran Senor and Try My Best. (Stavros Niarchos).
Optimum 3-y-o distance: 8f.

202 - YOGYA (USA)
Bay filly. Riverman - Pasadoble (Prove Out).
Half-sister to the great filly Miesque, winner of the Breeders Cup Mile (twice), the 1,000 gns, the French 1,000 gns, the Prix Jacques le Marois (twice), the Prix du Moulin, the Prix d'Ispahan, the Prix de la Salamandre and the Prix Marcel Boussac - all Group or Grade 1 events, to the 1995 3-y-o Ataka and to the French 3-y-o 7f listed stakes winner Massaraat (all by Nureyev). The dam was a very useful winner of 4 races in France over 8f including two stakes events and is a half-sister to the Grade 1 Brooklyn Handicap winner Silver Supreme. 2nd dam, Santa Quilla (by Sanctus II), is an unraced half-sister to the top class middle distance filly Comtesse de Loir. (Stavros Niarchos).
Optimum 3-y-o distance: 8-10f.

Ben Hanbury

203 - CARIBBEAN QUEST
Bay filly. Rainbow Quest - Jammayil (Lomond).
April 3. 1st foal.
The dam, a quite useful filly, ran only at 2 yrs when she won two races over 7f. She is a half-sister to 6 winners including the Nassau Stakes and Musidora Stakes winner Optimistic Lass - herself dam of the high class Coronation Stakes winner Golden Opinion. 2nd dam, Loveliest (by Tibaldo), won at 2 yrs in France, was 2nd in the Prix Penelope and is a half-sister to the U.S. Grade 1 winner Arbees Boy. (Maktoum Al-Maktoum).
Optimum 3-y-o distance: 10f.

204 - JARAH (USA)
Bay colt. Forty Niner - Umniyatee (Green Desert).
February 25. 1st foal.
The dam was a useful 3-y-o winner of two races over 7f and 8f and was 3rd in the Irish 1,000 gns. 2nd dam, Midway Lady (by Alleged), was a high class winner of the 1,000 gns, the Oaks, the Prix Marcel Boussac and the May Hill Stakes and is a sister to the very useful 1994 10f

winner Capias. 2nd dam, Smooth Bore (by His Majesty), was an American stakes winner at around 8f. (Hamdan Al-Maktoum).
Optimum 3-y-o distance: 8-10f.

Richard Hannon

205 - PIGEON HOLE
Bay filly. Green Desert - Cubby Hole (Town and Country).
April 11. 5th foal.
Half-sister to the 1995 3-y-o Juno Purno (by Persian Bold), to the smart filly Niche (by Risk Me), winner of the Lowther Stakes, Nell Gwyn Stakes and Falmouth Stakes and 2nd in the 1,000 gns, the fair 1993 2-y-o 8f winner and 3-y-o 12f winner Alcove (by Faustus) and the fair 1992 2-y-o dual 6f and 3-y-o 7f winner Holetown (by Prince Sabo). The dam, placed twice at 3 yrs over 12.2f and 16f, is a half-sister to the Ascot Gold Cup winner Little Wolf, the very smart stayer Smuggler, the Horris Hill Stakes winner Disguise and the unraced Sanctuary - herself dam of the high class sprinter Sheikh Albadou. 2nd dam, Hiding Place (by Doutelle), won the Nell Gwyn Stakes and is a half-sister to Queen's Hussar. (Highclere Stud Ltd).
Optimum 3-y-o distance: 7-10f.

Guy Harwood

206 - CANDLE SMOKE (USA)
Bay colt. Woodman - Light the Lights (Shirley Heights).
May 12. 2nd foal.
Half-brother to the French trained 3-y-o Light the Heights (by Shirley Heights). The dam was a very smart winner of the Group 2 13.5f Prix de Pomone and is a half-sister to the Group 3 10.5f Prix Fille de l'Air winner Liastra, the Group 3 10f Royal Whip Stakes winner Last Light and the placed Light a Star (by Wollow) - herself dam of the Group 2 Prix Jean de Chaudenay winner Lights Out. The dam won the Group 3 10.5f Prix de Flore, was 2nd in the Group 1 Prix Saint-Alary and is a half-sister to the Group 2 winner King Luthier and to Star in the North - a winner of 2 races and dam of both the U.S. Grade 1 winner Cool and the Yorkshire Cup winner Mountain Kingdom. Guy's assistant, Geoff Lawson, explained to me that **Candle Smoke** is a wonderful specimen of a horse but will be a better 3-y-o. (Mr A. Speelman).
Optimum 3-y-o distance: 10f.

207 - MIDDAY COWBOY (USA)
Bay colt. Houston - Perfect Isn't Easy (Saratoga Six).
April 27. 2nd foal.
Half-brother to a 3-y-o by Polish Navy. The dam is an unplaced half-sister to the smart winners Gielgud, Malinowski and Monroe (herself dam of the Group 3 winners Diese and Masterclass), to the dual U.S. Grade 1 winner Blush With Pride, to the grandam of the Coronation Stakes winner Chimes of Freedom and to the top class broodmare Sex Appeal - dam of El Gran Senor and Try My Best. 2nd dam, Best in Show (by Traffic Judge), was a very useful stakes winner at up to 7f. Again, Geoff Lawson was very pleased with this colt, **Midday Cowboy,** describing him as a "small, sharp, rather plain looking horse that should be a mid-season 2-y-o. There's a lot to like about him - a little tiger!" (Mr Simon Karmel).
Optimum 3-y-o distance: 8f.

Mme Criquette Head

208 - ALL FOR SHOW
Bay colt. Mr Prospector - Aliysa (Darshaan).
April 28. 3rd foal.
Half-brother to the 1994 2-y-o Munaadee (by Green Dancer), last of three over 7f on his only start, and to the 1994 Irish 3-y-o 10f winner Alaiyda (by Shahrastani). The dam won over 9f at

2 yrs and the Group 3 12f Lingfield Oaks Trial at 3, but was disqualified after winning the 1989 Epsom Oaks due to a positive drugs test. She is a half-sister to the good broodmare Aleema - dam of the French Group winners Altayan and Altashar. 2nd dam, Alannya (by Relko), was a smart 8f winner and a half-sister to the dam of Nishapour. (Maktoum Al-Maktoum).
Optimum 3-y-o distance: 10f.

209 - ANSWERED PRAYER
Bay filly. Green Desert - Jet Ski Lady (Vaguely Noble).
March 6. 1st foal. $675,000.
The dam, a winner over 6f and 7f in Ireland as a two-year-old, won a 10f listed event at the Curragh and the Group 1 12f Epsom Oaks the following year. 2nd dam, Bemissed (by Nijinsky), a good American filly, won the Grade 1 Selima Stakes as a two-year-old, was 3rd in the Kentucky Oaks and is a half-sister to the very useful Group 2 12f Princess of Wales's Stakes winner Desert Team. (Maktoum Al-Maktoum).
Optimum 3-y-o distance: 8-10f.

210 - BOLD BOLD
Bay filly. Sadlers Wells - Jasmina (Forli).
March 21. 3rd live foal.
The dam, a winner of 6 races in the USA including a stakes event over an extended 8f, is a half-sister to the top class miler Polish Precedent. 2nd dam, Past Example (by Buckpasser), is an unraced half-sister to the dams of the Group/Grade 1 winners Zilzal, Awe Inspiring and Culture Vulture. 3rd dam, Bold Example (by Bold Lad, USA), won 3 races, was stakes-placed at up to 7f and is a half-sister to In Hot Pursuit (dam of Posse), Discipline (dam of the Grade 1 winner Squander and the Grade 2 winner Duty Dance) and to Uncommitted (dam of the Grade 1 winner Wavering Monarch). (Mr. J. Wertheimer).
Optimum 3-y-o distance: 8-10f.

211 - BRAVALMA (USA)
Bay filly. Danzig - Brave Raj (Rajab).
5th foal.
Closely related to the placed 3-y-o Russian Tango (by Nijinsky) and half-sister to the minor 2-y-o 8.1f winner and 11.5f placed 3-y-o El Rabab (by Roberto). The dam was a champion 2-y-o filly in the USA and winner of 6 races, notably the Grade 1 8f Breeders Cup Juvenile Fillies Stakes and the Grade 2 8f Del Mar Debutante Stakes. She is a half-sister to the minor stakes winner Peal Out. 2nd dam, Bravest Yet (by Bravo), was placed at both 2 and 3 yrs and is a half-sister to two stakes winners including the Grade 3 winner Perfect Poppy. (Mr. J. Wertheimer).
Optimum 3-y-o distance: 8f.

212 - CLASSIC MIX (USA)
Bay colt. Danzig - Bambee T.T. (Better Bee).
April 6.
Brother to the high class middle-distance colts Petit Loup (Gran Premio de Milano, Prix Jean de Chaudeney etc.) and Ascot Knight (placed in the Matchmaker International Stakes, Phoenix Champion Stakes, Mecca-Dante Stakes etc.), closely related to the champion Canadian handicap horse Bounding Away (by Vice Regent) and half-brother to the stakes winner Overreaction (by Nodouble) and to the 1994 7f placed 2-y-o Zahaalie (by Zilzal). The dam won two claiming races at up to 8f. 2nd dam, Golden Beach (by Djeddah), won as a two-year-old. (Maktoum Al-Maktoum).
Optimum 3-y-o distance: 10f.

213 - ECOUTE (USA)
Bay filly. Manila - Soundings (Mr Prospector).
Half-sister to the very smart 1994 French 2,000 gns winner and St James's Palace Stakes and Prix du Moulin placed Green Tune (by Green Dancer), and to the very useful 1992 Group 1 5.5f Prix Robert Papin winner Didyme (by Dixieland Band) - subsequently a winner in the USA. The dam won two races in the USA, is a sister to the very useful 5f and 6f winner Al Zawbaah and a half-sister to 5 other winners. 2nd dam, Ocean's Answer (by Northern Answer), won the

Natalma Stakes and is closely related to Storm Bird. (Mr. J. Wertheimer).
Optimum 3-y-o distance: 8-10f.

214 - EXEMPLAIRE
Bay filly. Polish Precedent - Grecian Beauty (Gorytus).
2nd foal.
Half-sister to the French trained 3-y-o Ploutocrate (by Last Tycoon). The dam won two races in France and is a half-sister to 6 winners out of the very useful Group 3 5f Prix d'Arenburg winner Glancing (by Grundy), herself a half-sister to the high class 2-y-o Middle Park Stakes winner Bassenthwaite. (Mr. J. Wertheimer).
Optimum 3-y-o distance: 6-8f.

215 - NATURAL GOLD (USA)
Bay filly. Mr Prospector - Riviere d'Or (Lyphard).
4th foal.
Half-sister to the smart filly Gold Splash (by Blushing Groom), winner of the Group 1 8f Prix Marcel Boussac and the Group 1 8f Coronation Stakes. The dam, also a smart filly, won the Group 1 10f Prix Saint-Alary, the Group 3 8f Prix d'Aumale and the Group 3 Prix Vanteaux, is closely related to the Group 3 Prix du Lys winner Chercheur d'Or and the French 2,000gns 2nd Goldneyev. 2nd dam, Gold River (by Riverman), won the Prix de l'Arc de Triomphe, the Prix Jean Prat, the Prix du Cadran and the Prix Royal-Oak. **Natural Gold** is, like the high class miler Lycius, by Mr Prospector and out of a Lyphard mare. (Mr. J. Wertheimer).
Optimum 3-y-o distance: 8f.

216 - SEA HILL (USA)
Bay filly. Seattle Slew - Featherhill (Lyphard).
Sister to the very useful French 2-y-o 7f winner Slew the Slewor and half-sister to the top class French colt Groom Dancer (by Blushing Groom), winner of the Prix de Conde as a 2-y-o and the Group 1 10.5f Prix Lupin and Group 3 10f Prix du Prince d'Orange as a 3-y-o, to the French trained 3-y-o Blushing Hector (by Mr Prospector) and the very useful 2-y-o Group 3 9f Prix Saint-Roman winner Tagel (by Cox's Ridge). The dam, a winner over 10f and 12f in France, was placed at 4 yrs in the USA, is closely related to the good class French stayer Le Nain Jeune and a half-sister to the Prix Vermeille winner Indian Rose, the Prix Ganay winner Vert Amande and two other good winners in Woolskin and Mulberry. 2nd dam, Lady Berry (by Violon d'Ingres), won the Group 1 Prix Royal-Oak. (Mr. J. Wertheimer).
Optimum 3-y-o distance: 10-12f.

217 - SENSATION
Bay filly. Soviet Star - Outstandingly (Exclusive Native).
April 3. 6th foal.
Sister to the Irish trained 3-y-o Prominence and half-sister to the quite useful 1992 dual 10f 3-y-o winner Avice Caro (by Caro) and the minor American winner Outlasting (by Seattle Slew). The dam was the champion American 2-y-o filly of 1984 and won the Grade 1 Breeders Cup Juvenile Fillies Stakes and the Grade 1 8.5f Hollywood Starlet Stakes. She is closely related to the Grade 3 9f Miss Grillo Stakes winner Loveliest (by Affirmed) and a half-sister to the fair 3-y-o 11f winner Wace. 2nd dam, La Mesa (by Round Table), a minor winner at 4 yrs in the USA, is out of a half-sister to the Horse of the Year Buckpasser. (Sheikh Mohammed).
Optimum 3-y-o distance: 8-10f.

218 - SET IN MOTION (USA)
Chestnut filly. Mr Prospector - Cadeaux d'Amie (Lyphard).
May 13. 5th foal.
Half-sister to the 1995 3-y-o Tawakal (by Slew O'Gold), the 1993 3-y-o dual 10f listed stakes winner Insijaam (by Secretariat) and the 1994 3-y-o 12f listed stakes winner Fasateen (by Alysheba) - all trained in France. The dam, a winner over 8f at 2 yrs and 10f at 3 yrs in France, was 3rd in the Group 3 8f Prix d'Aumale and is a half-sister to the champion 2-y-o filly and Prix Vermeille and Prix de Diane winner Mrs Penny. 2nd dam, Tananarive (by Le Fabuleux), won 3 times at up to 14f in France and is a half-sister to the stakes winners Tahitian King and Tuxpan.

(Maktoum Al-Maktoum).
Optimum 3-y-o distance: 10f.

219 - SILWANA
Bay filly. Nashwan - Riviere d'Argent (Nijinsky).
5th foal.
Half-sister to the 1995 3-y-o Louisinsky (by Saumarez) and to the minor 1992 French 3-y-o 10f winner Little Wassl (by Wassl). The dam, a French 3-y-o 12f winner, is closely related to the Group 1 Prix Saint-Alary winner Riviere d'Or and to the Group 3 Prix du Lys winner Chercheur d'Or. 2nd dam, Gold River (by Riverman), won the Prix de l'Arc de Triomphe, Prix Jean Prat, Prix du Cadran and Prix Royal-Oak - all Group 1 events, and is a half-sister to the dam of the smart French 1980 2-y-o Greenway. (Mr. J. Wertheimer).
Optimum 3-y-o distance: 10-12f.

220 - SILVERSTORM
Bay colt. Saumarez - Silvermine (Bellypha).
Half-brother to the 1995 3-y-o Silvering (by Polish Precedent), to the very smart 1991 3-y-o Group 1 9.2f Prix Jean Prat and 4-y-o Group 2 9.7f Prix Dollar winner Sillery (by Blushing Groom) and the French 2-y-o 8f and 3-y-o 10f winner Signorelli (by Cox's Ridge). The dam, a high class filly, won the French 1,000 gns, was 2nd in the 9.2f Prix de l'Opera and is a half-sister to the champion 2-y-o Saint Cyrien. 2nd dam, Sevres (by Riverman), was a very useful winner from 7.5f to 9f.
(Mrs Alec Head).
Optimum 3-y-o distance: 10f.

221 - UNDERSTOOD
Bay colt. Green Desert - Untold (Final Straw).
April 26. 5th live foal.
Half-brother to the 1995 3-y-o Muffle (by Sadlers Wells). The dam was a high class winner of 4 races from 7-12f including the Group 1 Yorkshire Oaks and the Group 3 Hoover Fillies Mile, was 2nd in the Epsom Oaks and 3rd in the Yorkshire Oaks. She is a half-sister to the Group 3 Waterford Candelabra Stakes winner Shoot Clear and to the very smart Yorkshire Oaks and Ribblesdale Stakes winner Sally Brown. 2nd dam, Unsuspected (by Above Suspicion), won 8 races from 8-14f. (Sheikh Mohammed).
Optimum 3-y-o distance: 8-10f.

222 - XAYMARA
Bay filly. Sanglamore - Nimble Folly (Cyane).
Half-sister to the 2-y-o 5f winners Nimble Feet (herself dam of the very smart 1994 2-y-o Eltish) and Old Alliance, to the Grade 1 7f Arlington-Washington Lassie Stakes winner Contredance (all by Danzig) and to the 3-y-o 10f winner Shotiche (by Northern Dancer). The dam is an unraced half-sister to the U.S. Grade 1 placed Misgivings - herself dam of the Rockfel Stakes winner At Risk. 2nd dam, Instant Sin, won in the States at 3 yrs. (Khaled Abdulla).
Optimum 3-y-o distance: 10f.

Major Dick Hern

223 - MAMDOOH (USA)
Brown colt. Dayjur - Life's Magic (Cox's Ridge).
March 30. 6th foal.
Closely related to the moderate 1992 6f and 8f placed 3-y-o Alfaari (by Danzig) and half-brother to the minor American winner Magic Prospect (by Mr Prospector) and the quite useful 1991 12f placed 3-y-o Alrayed (by Alydar). The dam was a champion 3-y-o filly and champion older mare in the USA. She won five Grade 1 races from 8.5f to 10f, namely the Breeders Cup Distaff, Beldame Stakes, Oak Leaf Stakes, Mother Goose Stakes and Alabama Stakes, and is a half-sister to Herb Water, a very useful American colt of 1980. 2nd dam, Fire Water (by Tom Rolfe), won

7 races including a stakes event in the USA. (Hamdan Al-Maktoum).
Optimum 3-y-o distance: 6-8f.

224 - MIN ELREEH (USA)
Bay filly. Danzig - Roseate Tern (Blakeney).
January 20. 1st foal.
The dam, a very smart filly, won the Group 1 12f Yorkshire Oaks, Group 2 12f Jockey Club Stakes and Group 3 12f Lancashire Oaks. She is a half-sister to 4 winners including the high class middle distance colt Ibn Bey, winner of the Irish St Leger, Gran Premio d'Italia and Geoffrey Freer Stakes and 2nd in the Breeders Cup Classic. 2nd dam, Rosia Bay (by High Top), a useful 7.5f and 8f winner, is a half-sister to the top class Queen Elizabeth II Stakes and Budweiser Arlington Million winner Teleprompter. (Hamdan Al-Maktoum).
Optimum 3-y-o distance: 10f.

225 - NO-AMAN
Bay colt. Nashwan - Ghanimah (Caerleon).
February 2. 4th foal.
Brother to the 1995 3-y-o Afifah, placed 3rd over 7f on her only outing at 2 yrs, and half-brother to the fair 1992 2-y-o 7f winner Faez (by Mtoto). The dam, a useful 2-y-o dual 6f winner, is a half-sister to the champion 2-y-o and 3-y-o filly Marwell - herself dam of the high class filly Marling and the smart colt Caerwent. 2nd dam, Lady Seymour (by Tudor Melody), won the 5f Phoenix Stakes (from only two starts). (Hamdan Al-Maktoum).
Optimum 3-y-o distance: 8-10f.

226 - SHAWKEY (IRE)
Chestnut colt. Nashwan - Rosia Bay (High Top).
April 21.
Brother to the fair 1994 10.5f to 12f placed 3-y-o Taqreem and half-brother to the 1995 3-y-o Al Helal (by In the Wings), unplaced on his only start at 2 yrs, the high class middle distance colt Ibn Bey (by Mill Reef), winner of 10 races including the Irish St Leger, Gran Premio d'Italia, Geoffrey Freer Stakes etc., and 2nd in the Breeders Cup Classic, to the smart filly Roseate Tern (by Blakeney), winner of the Yorkshire Oaks, Lancashire Oaks and Jockey Club Stakes etc., the fairly useful 3-y-o 14f and 14.6f winner Barakat (by Bustino), the fair 1993 3-y-o 14f winner Barraak (by El Gran Senor) and a minor 2-y-o 5f winner by Mummy's Pet. The dam, a useful 7.5f and 8f winner, is a half-sister to the top class Queen Elizabeth II Stakes and Budweiser Arlington Million winner Teleprompter. 2nd dam, Ouija (by Silly Season), was a useful dual 8f winner at 3 yrs. (Hamdan Al-Maktoum).
Optimum 3-y-o distance: 10-12f.

Lady Herries

227 - CELTIC WING
Chestnut filly. Midyan - Celtic Ring (Welsh Pageant).
March 24. 3rd foal.
Half-sister to the outstanding 1994 champion European 2-y-o Celtic Swing (by Damister), winner of all three of his 2-y-o starts including the Group 1 8f Racing Post Trophy, and to the quite useful 1992 2-y-o 7f winner Cissbury Ring (by Jalmood). The dam was a fairly useful winner of two races, over 10f and 12f, out of the twice raced Pencuik Jewel (by Petingo), herself a half-sister to the Ascot Gold Cup winner Ragstone and to the top class broodmare Castle Moon - dam of the Group 1 winners Moon Madness and Sheriff's Star. (Lavinia, Duchess of Norfolk).
Optimum 3-y-o distance: 10-12f.

228 - GRETNA GREEN
Bay filly. Hansel - Greenland Park (Red God).
May 17.
Half-sister to the 1994 2-y-o Golden Tune (by Nureyev), placed 2nd over 6f on her only outing, to the high class filly Fitnah (by Kris), winner of the Prix Saint-Alary, Prix Vanteaux, Prix de la

Nonette and Prix du Prince d'Orange, and to the minor French winner Falcon Eye (by Touching Wood). The dam was a high class filly herself, winning the Queen Mary, Molecomb and Cornwallis Stakes', is a sister to the Coventry Stakes winner Red Sunset and a half-sister to the unraced Mary Martin, herself dam of the very useful filly Marina Park. 2nd dam, Centre Piece (by Tompion), was placed once over 6f. (Maktoum Al-Maktoum).
Optimum 3-y-o distance: 8f.

229 - MOON MISCHIEF
Bay colt. Be My Chief - Castle Moon (Kalamoun).
March 18.
Half-brother to the 1995 3-y-o Moon Magic (by Polish Precedent), to the St Leger and Grand Prix de Saint-Cloud winner Moon Madness, the useful 10f winner Wood Chanter (both by Vitiges), the Coronation Cup and Grand Prix de Saint-Cloud winner Sheriff's Star (by Posse), the Goodwood Cup winner Lucky Moon (by Touching Wood) and to minor winners by Comedy Star and Welsh Pageant. The dam won from 8-13f, is a sister to the very smart middle distance stayer Castle Keep and a half-sister to the Gold Cup winner Ragstone. 2nd dam, Fotheringay (by Right Royal V), won over 8f. (Lavinia, Duchess of Norfolk).
Optimum 3-y-o distance: 10f.

Barry Hills

230 - AMBASSADOR (USA)
Bay colt. Hansel - Taba (Table Play).
February 4.
Half-brother to 6 winners including the Grade 1 10f Marlboro Cup Handicap, Grade 1 10f Widener Handicap and $2 million winner Turkoman (by Alydar), the U.S. stakes winner Slow Fuse (by Fluorescent Light) and to the unraced dam of the minor U.S. stakes winner Now Dance. The dam, champion 2-y-o filly in Argentina in 1975, won the Argentinian 1,000 gns, is a sister to two other Argentinian Grade 1 winners in Telescopico (champion 3-y-o) and Telefonico and a half-sister to the dam of yet another - Cerbatana. Although rather big and backward in the spring, **Ambassador** has good limbs and a good attitude, according to Barry Hills. 2nd dam, Filipina (by Fomento), won twice at 3 yrs in Argentina. (Maktoum Al-Maktoum).
Optimum 3-y-o distance: 10f.

231 - FILLY MI GNONNE (IRE)
Chestnut filly. Nashwan - Christabelle (Northern Dancer).
June 2. 5th foal. 120,000 Ir gns.
Sister to the 3-y-o Alisidora and half-sister to the fairly useful 1994 3-y-o 10f winner - stayed 14.8f - Caladesi (by Slip Anchor), the 2-y-o 6f winner Na-Ayim (by Shirley Heights) and to the minor Belgian winner Christalaw (by Law Society). The dam was placed once at 2 yrs in Ireland and is a half-sister to the Group 3 Prix de Minerve winner I Will Follow (dam of Rainbow Quest), to the Group 3 Fred Darling Stakes winner Slightly Dangerous (dam of Commander in Chief, Warning and Deploy) and to the unraced Idyllic (dam of Scenic). 2nd dam, Where You Lead (by Raise a Native), won the Group 3 Musidora Stakes and was 2nd in the Epsom Oaks. (Wafic Said).
Optimum 3-y-o distance: 10-12f.

232 - LIGHT REFLECTIONS
Bay colt. Rainbow Quest - Tajfah (Shadeed).
March 26. 2nd foal.
Half-brother to the 1995 3-y-o Tabbasamm (by Dancing Brave). The dam is an unraced half-sister to the very smart 6f and 7f winners Great Commotion and Lead on Time and to the very useful miler Keyala. 2nd dam, Alathea (by Lorenzaccio), showed no form but is a half-sister to the very smart 2-y-o R.B.Chesne out of a sister to Vaguely Noble. (Maktoum Al-Maktoum). Another horse that will not be seen out until mid-summer at the earliest, Barry says that **Light Reflections** has done plenty of cantering but not much else at this stage. Nevertheless, he is a horse with good limbs that should go nicely at around 7 furlongs this year. (Maktoum Al-

Maktoum).
Optimum 3-y-o distance: 10f.

233 - MADAME STEINLEN
Bay or brown filly. Steinlen - Equadif (Abdos).
April 10. 60,000 gns.
Half-sister to the 1995 3-y-o Wanderlake (by Woodman), to the 4 time Spanish winner La Potita (by Dom Pasquini) and the top class Group 1 12f Grand Prix de Saint-Cloud, Group 1 10.5f Prix Lupin, Group 2 10.5f Prix Greffulhe and Group 3 12f Prix Niel winner Epervier Bleu (by Saint Cyrien). The dam won 2 minor races in France over 9f and 12f. 2nd dam, Gracilla (by Prince Bio), was 2nd in the 10.5f Prix Cleopatre. Bought at Deauville, Barry would like to run **Madame Steinlen** in the money-spinning 2-y-o race there if she proves good enough. She won't be out until late June, early July. (Sir Eric Parker).
Optimum 3-y-o distance: 10f.

234 - POLINESSO
Bay colt. Polish Precedent - Lypharita (Lightning).
February 4. 4th foal to live.
Half-brother to the French trained 3-y-o Rasak and to the quite useful 1991 3-y-o 7.6f and 8f winner Swordstick (by Sure Blade). The dam was a high class winner of the Group 1 10.5f Prix de Diane and was placed in the Prix Vermeille and Prix Cleopatre. 2nd dam, Gracefully (by Lyphard), was a minor 10f winner in France and is a sister to the Prix Fille de l'Air 3rd Model Girl (herself dam of the very useful 8f winners Arousal and In Focus) and a half-sister to the Group 3 Lingfield Oaks Trial 2nd Grace Note (dam of the top class middle distance colt Belmez). A colt that Barry feels will benefit by 6 furlongs or more this year, **Polinesso** is likely to be running by mid-season. (Sheikh Mohammed).
Optimum 3-y-o distance: 8-10f.

235 - RUZNAMA (USA)
Chestnut filly. Forty Niner - Last Feather (Vaguely Noble).
April 20.
Half-sister to the fairly useful 1990 3-y-o 8f winner Contessa, the 1993 middle distance placed 3-y-o Bawaeth (both by Blushing Groom), the Irish 10f winner Limber Dancer (by Nijinsky), the French 9f winner Phar Feather (by Lyphard) and the fair 1994 7-10f placed 3-y-o Eqtesaad (by Danzig). The dam, a smart 2-y-o 7.3f and 3-y-o Group 3 10.5f Musidora Stakes winner, was 3rd in the Oaks behind Time Charter and Slightly Dangerous and is a half-sister to the Irish St Leger winner Caucasus, to the champion Canadian grass horse One For All and to the dam of Run the Gantlet. 2nd dam, Quill (by Princequillo), was a top class American winner of 14 races including the Acorn Stakes, the Matron Stakes, the Mother Goose Stakes and the Delaware Handicap. **Ruzama** is another one of Barry's 2-y-o's that will be running later on in the year, though he feels that she's a nice filly. (Hamdan Al-Maktoum).
Optimum 3-y-o distance: 10f.

236 - SHAWANNI
Grey filly. Shareef Dancer - Negligent (Ahonoora).
April 5. 1st foal.
The dam, a very useful filly, won the 7f Rockfel Stakes at 2 yrs when she was champion filly and was subsequently 3rd in the 1,000 gns behind Salsabil on the first of her three outings at 3 yrs. She is a sister to the dual 2-y-o 6f winner and 1,000 gns 4th Ala Mahlik and a half-sister to the very useful 22.2f Queen Alexandra Stakes winner Ala Hounak and the useful 3-y-o 8f and 10f winner Zalon. 2nd dam, Negligence (by Roan Rocket), was placed once over 10f at 3 yrs and is a half-sister to the dams of the very useful sprinter Governor General and the smart French 10f performer Galunpe. "I like this filly, **Shawanni**, very much but she's going to take a bit of time," commented Barry. (Sheikh Mohammed).
Optimum 3-y-o distance: 8-10f.

237 - THREE HILLS
Bay colt. Danehill - Three Stars (Star Appeal).
January 28. 6th foal.

Half-brother to the very smart Group 1 12f Irish Oaks and Group 2 12f Ribblesdale Stakes winner Bolas (by Unfuwain) and to the French 12f winner Star of Dance (by Sadlers Wells). The dam, a fairly useful 3-y-o dual 12f winner, is a half-sister to the Ascot Gold Cup, Goodwood Cup and Doncaster Cup winner Longboat and to the useful middle distance colt Sailor's Dance. 2nd dam, Pirogue (by Reliance II), a useful 3-y-o 8f winner, is a half-sister to the good stayers Sloop, Tepukei and Torpid and to Cutle - dam of the St Leger winner Cut Above and the Irish 2,000 gns winner Sharp Edge. A good-limbed horse, according to the trainer, Barry hopes that **Three Hills** will have have some speed injected into what is essentially a stout pedigree by the sire Danehill. (Khaled Abdulla).
Optimum 3-y-o distance: 10-12f.

238 - WILAWANDER
Chestnut colt. Nashwan - Wilayif (Danzig).
April 4. 1st foal.
The dam, a fair 7f winner (in a 2 runner race) and 8-10f placed 3-y-o, is a half-sister to the Grade 1 Ashland Stakes and Grade 1 Holllywood Oaks winner Gorgeous, to the Grade 1 Kentucky Oaks winner Seaside Attraction - herself dam of the Cherry Hinton Stakes winner Red Carnival, to the Canadian dual Grade 3 winner Key to the Moon and the Group 3 Princess Margaret Stakes winner Hiamm. 2nd dam, Kamar (by Key to the Mint), was a champion Canadian 3-y-o filly and is a sister to the Grade 1 winner Love Smitten and a half-sister to the U.S. stakes winners Dancing on a Cloud and Stellarette - dam of the Grade 1 winner Cuddles. (Maktoum Al-Maktoum). Optimum 3-y-o distance: 8-10f.

John Hills

239 - DANCING SHOES (IRE)
Bay filly. Sadlers Wells - Producer (Nashua).
February 22.
Sister to the useful 1994 3-y-o 10f winner, Lingfield Oaks Trial 2nd and Italian Oaks 3rd Las Flores, closely related to the useful Irish fillies, Dancing Goddess (by Nijinsky) a winner over 6f and 10f, and Music And Dance (by Northern Dancer) a winner over 5f and 6f, and half-sister to the fair 3-y-o 12f winner Certain Creator (by Alleged). The dam, a top class winner of the Group 1 7f Prix de la Foret and Group 2 Prix de l'Opera, was 2nd in the Irish Oaks and is a half-sister to the Grade 3 stakes winners Deb Marion and D.O. Lady and to the dam of the triple Grade 1 winner Yankee Affair. 2nd dam, Marion (by Tantieme), won 3 minor events over 5f, 7f and 8f in France and is closely related to Manush, herself dam of the good French winners Mourtazam, Croque Monsieur, Mannshour and Masmouda. (Abbot Racing Partners).
Optimum 3-y-o distance: 10-12f.

240 - SCARPETTA (USA)
Chestnut filly. Seattle Dancer - Pump (Forli).
February 13. 6th foal.
Closely related to the 1989 3-y-o Classic Sport, winner of two poorly contested listed events in Ireland over 10f and 11f, to the 1990 3-y-o 8f and 9f Leopardstown winner Classic Legend and to Spike Heel (all by Nijinsky), a minor American winner of two races at 3 yrs, and half-sister to Filao Beach (by Alysheba), a winner of 3 races in France and Switzerland including the 12f Swiss Derby. The dam is an unraced daughter of Espadrille (by Hoist the Flag), winner of 3 races including the 8.3f Busanda Stakes and half-sister to Thatch (Group1 Sussex Stakes and a good sire), King Pellinore (Grade 1 Oak Tree Invitational Handicap) and Special (dam of Nureyev and grandam of Sadlers Wells). The dam of this filly then, is a three-parts sister to Thatch and Special. (Mr J. Barber).
Optimum 3-y-o distance: 10f.

Lord Huntingdon

241 - DOCTOR GREEN (FR)
Bay colt. Green Desert - Highbrow (Shirley Heights).
March 5. 3rd foal.
Half-brother to the 1995 3-y-o Beyond Doubt (by Belmez), 2nd over 7f on her only start at 2 yrs. The dam, a very useful 2-y-o 8f winner and Group 2 12f Ribblesdale Stakes 2nd, is closely related to the good middle distance colt Milford and a half-sister to the Princess of Wales's Stakes winner Height of Fashion - herself dam of Nashwan and Unfuwain, and to the dam of the Epsom Oaks 2nd Wind in Her Hair. 2nd dam, Highclere (by Queens Hussar), won the 1,000 gns and French Oaks in 1973. (The Queen).
Optimum 3-y-o distance: 10f.

242 - STATE CIRCUS
Bay filly. Soviet Star - Wily Trick (Clever Trick).
February 19. 1st foal.
The dam, a quite useful maiden, was placed four times at 3 yrs from 7-8f. She is a half-sister to the Group 2 12f Princess of Wales's Stakes winner Height of Fashion - herself dam of the 2,000 gns and Derby winner Nashwan, to the good middle-distance colt Milford and to Burghclere - dam of the Oaks 2nd Wind in Her Hair. 2nd dam, Highclere (by Queens Hussar), won the 1,000 gns and Prix de Diane. (The Queen).
Optimum 3-y-o distance: 8f.

Michael Jarvis

243 - ET FREM (IRE)
Bay colt. Posen - New Light (Reform).
March 26. 32,000 Ir gns.
Half-brother to the high class miler Then Again (by Jaazeiro), winner of the Waterford Crystal Mile, Queen Anne Stakes and Lockinge Stakes (all Group 2 events), the listed Brazilian winner Babil (by Young Emperor), herself dam of two Brazilian stakes winners, to the minor Irish 2-y-o winner Kamplight (by Kampala) and the minor 3-y-o winners Martie's Light (by Martinmas) Tordo (by Bob Back) and Warm December (by He Loves Me). The dam won over 10f at 3 yrs and is a half-sister to the top class broodmare Sunny Valley, dam of Sun Princess and Saddlers Hall. 2nd dam, Sunland (by Charlottesville), won at 3 yrs and was 3rd in the Park Hill Stakes. (Mrs Anita Green).
Optimum 3-y-o distance: 8-10f.

William Jarvis

244 - LA PAPAYA (USA)
Bay filly. Alleged - La Papagena (Habitat).
April 17. 5th foal.
Half-sister to the champion 1993 2-y-o Grand Lodge (by Chief's Crown), winner of the Group 1 7f Dewhurst stakes and, at 3 yrs, the Group 1 8f St James's Palace Stakes, to the 1995 3-y-o Zygo (by Diesis), unplaced on his only outing at 2 yrs and to the minor 1993 3-y-o 11.5f winner Rose Noble (by Vaguely Noble). The dam is an unraced half-sister to the very useful 3-y-o 7f and 8f winner Pamina, the very useful 3-y-o 11f and 12.5f winner Lost Chord and the useful 11f Scottish Derby winner Eagling. 2nd dam, Magic Flute (by Tudor Melody), won the Cheveley Park Stakes and the Coronation Stakes and was very smart at up to 8f. (Lord Howard de Walden). **La Papaya** is bred on the same Alleged - Habitat cross as the smart colt Nomrood and Alleging.
Optimum 3-y-o distance: 10-12f.

245 - SCHERMA
Bay filly. Green Desert - Escrime (Sharpen Up).

April 2. 2nd foal.
Full sister to the 1995 3-y-o Feinte, unplaced on her only outing at 2 yrs. The dam, a fairly useful 3-y-o 8f and 10f winner, is a sister to the top class miler and sire Kris and the champion 2-y-o and high class sire Diesis, and a half-sister to the Group 2 Forte Mile winner Rudimentary and to Pris - herself dam of the useful colts Prismatic and Perpendicular. 2nd dam, Doubly Sure (by Reliance II), was placed over 12f. (Lord Howard de Walden).
Optimum 3-y-o distance: 8-10f.

246 - SULAWESI (IRE)
Bay filly. In the Wings - Royal Loft (Homing).
March 23. 6th foal.
Closely related to the quite useful 1994 2-y-o 7f winner Wigberto (by Old Vic) and half-sister to the fairly useful 6-8f winner Olette (by Rousillon), the Irish 3-y-o 7f and 9f winner Sir Slaves (by Salse) and the minor 3-y-o 6f winner Desert Ditty (by Green Desert). The dam, a useful filly, won 2 races including the listed 7f Oak Tree Stakes, was 4th in the Group 3 7f Hungerford Stakes and is a half-sister to the Belgian Group 1 winner Sharpset (by Sharpen Up). 2nd dam, Well Off (by Welsh Pageant), is an unplaced half-sister to the useful 6-7f performer Doc Marten. (Mr James H. Slade).
Optimum 3-y-o distance: 7-8f.

Mark Johnston

247 - BEACONTREE
Chestnut colt. Lycius - Beaconaire (Vaguely Noble).
April 1.
Half-brother to the dual U.S. Grade 1 winning filly Sabin (by Lyphard), to the smart 10.5f Musidora Stakes winner Fatah Flare (by Alydar), the very useful 1985 2-y-o 6f winner Soughaan (by Riverman), the fairly useful 1994 3-y-o 10.5f winner Fire Worshipper (by Sadlers Wells) and the fair 1990 3-y-o 10f winner Nadma (by Northern Dancer). The dam, a stakes winner of 3 races at up to 10f in France, is a half-sister to the high class filly Kittiwake (herself dam of the excellent American filly Miss Oceana and grandam of the Coronation stakes winner Magic of Life) and to the stakes winner Oilfield. 2nd dam, Ole Liz (by Double Jay), won 6 races including a stakes event. (Sheikh Mohammed).
Optimum 3-y-o distance: 8-10f.

248 - GREEN BARRIES
Bay colt. Green Desert - Barari (Blushing Groom).
February 23. 3rd foal to live.
Half-brother to the Belgian winner Zahabi (by Jareer). The dam is an unraced half-sister to the Canadian Grade 1 winner Rainbows For Life and to the Group 2 Prix de l'Opera winner Colour Chart. 2nd dam, Rainbow Connection (by Halo), a champion 2-y-o and 3-y-o filly in Canada, is a half-sister to 3 stakes winners including the Canadian Grade 1 winners Archdeacon and Hangin' on a Star. **Green Barries** is an exceptionally nice, strong, sprinting type and will be relatively early. (Maktoum Al-Maktoum).
Optimum 3-y-o distance: 7-9f.

249 - HALEAKALA (IRE)
Chestnut filly. Kris - Haiati (Alydar).
March 24. 3rd foal.
Half-sister to the 1995 3-y-o Nashotah (by Nashwan). The dam was a very useful 2-y-o 6f and 7f winner, was 2nd in the Group 1 Hoover Fillies Mile and 2nd over 10f as a three year old before ending her racing career in fifth place in the Ribblesdale Stakes over 12f. 2nd dam, Northern Fable (by Northern Dancer), a smart stakes winner at around 8f, is a half-sister to the dam of the 2-y-o 8f May Hill Stakes winner Majmu. (Sheikh Mohammed).
Optimum 3-y-o distance: 10-12f.

250 - MARCOMIR (USA)
Bay colt. Dayjur - Mariella (Roberto).
April 9. 6th foal.
Closely related to the quite useful 1994 3-y-o 11.9f winner Duke of Warsaw (by Danzig) and half-brother to the Group 1 placed Mariemma (by Nureyev), the minor U.S. winner Queluz (by Saratoga Six) and the minor middle-distance placed 3-y-o's Ballet Russe and Marionetta (both by Nijinsky). The dam was a useful winner of 3 minor events over 12f (twice) and 13.8f and was 2nd in the Princess Royal Stakes. She is a half-sister to the very useful Sun Chariot Stakes 3rd Elect (herself dam of 5 winners), to the very smart U.S. stakes winner Pressing Date and to the dams of Lord Florey (St James's Palace Stakes 3rd), Too Chic (Grade 1 Maskette Stakes winner), Sadeem (Ascot Gold Cup winner) and Prima Voce (Champion Stakes 3rd). 2nd dam, Monade (by Klairon), won the Oaks and Prix Vermeille in 1962. (Sheikh Mohammed).
Optimum 3-y-o distance: 10f.

251 - MASK FLOWER (USA)
Bay filly. Dayjur - Nom de Plume (Nodouble).
April 26. 4th foal.
Closely related to the 1995 3-y-o Stylo (by Danzig), unplaced on both his outings at 2 yrs over 8f, and half-sister to the useful 1994 3-y-o 7f winner and Group 3 7.3f Fred Darling Stakes 2nd Pen Point (by Diesis). The dam, a very useful filly, won 4 races at 3 yrs from 8f to 10.5f including the Group 2 Nassau Stakes and is a half-sister to the high class 1982 2-y-o Total Departure. 2nd dam, Life Style (by Manifesto), is an unraced half-sister to the U.S. Grade 1 winner Life Cycle. (Sheikh Mohammed).
Optimum 3-y-o distance: 6-8f.

252 - METAL BADGE (IRE)
Bay colt. Doyoun - Sharaya (Youth).
May 18. 12,500 Ir gns.
Half-brother to the 3-y-o winners Shanasara (by The Minstrel) and Sharadiya (by Akarad) and to the 1995 3-y-o Sheriyza (by Caerleon). The dam, a high class filly, won the Group 1 12f Prix Vermeille and the Group 3 10f Prix de la Nonette, and is a half-sister to the very useful Group 3 12f Prix de Minerve and Group 3 12.5f Prix de Royallieu winner Sharaniya. 2nd dam, Shanizadeh (by Baldric II), was a useful French 6f and 8f winner. Not yet in training in March and a late foal, I'll take my hat off to Mark if he gets Metal Badge to win this year. A exceptionally cheap yearling considering his pedigree, it will be interesting to watch him develop next season. (Mr. C. Bryan).
Optimum 3-y-o distance: 10-12f.

253 - MIGHTY KEEN
Chestnut colt. Keen - Mary Martin (Be My Guest).
May 9.
Half-brother to the very useful 1992 2-y-o Group 3 6f Princess Margaret Stakes and 3-y-o 5f listed stakes winner Marina Park (by Local Suitor), to the fair 1994 3-y-o 8f winner Robbies Rainbow (by Rainbow Quest), the quite useful 2-y-o 6f winner Pacific Gem (by Valiyar), the fair sprint winners Boy Martin and Maria Cappuccini (both by Siberian Express) and the 1994 5f-7f placed 2-y-o Boldina Bay (by Never So Bold). The dam is an unraced half-sister to the Coventry Stakes winner Red Sunset and to the Molecomb, Queen Mary and Cornwallis Stakes winner Greenland Park - herself dam of the high class French filly Fitnah. 2nd dam, Centre Piece (by Tompion), ran four times at 2 yrs and was placed 4th once. (Greenland Park Ltd).
Optimum 3-y-o distance: 6-8f.

Gaye Kelleway

254 - SCENIC SPIRIT (IRE)
Bay filly. Scenic - Quality of Life (Auction Ring).
February 18. 3rd foal.
Half-sister to the modest 1994 6-10f placed 3-y-o Life's Too Short (by Astronef) and to the high

class colt Bob's Return (by Bob Back), winner of the 10f listed Zetland Stakes at 2 yrs, the Group 1 14.6f Coalite St Leger, Group 2 11.9f Great Voltigeur Stakes and Group 3 11.5f Lingfield Derby Trial at 3 yrs, and placed in the Group 1 Prix Ganay, Eclipse Stakes and Irish St Leger at 4 yrs. The dam was a minor Irish 2-y-o 6f winner. 2nd dam, Flirting Countess (by Ridan), was placed once at 2yrs over 6f and is out of the Chesham Stakes winner Narrow Escape. (Mr A. Al-Radi).
Optimum 3-y-o distance: 8f.

David Loder

255 - BLUE DUSTER (USA)
Bay filly. Danzig - Blue Note (Habitat).
March 3. 4th foal.
Sister to the smart Group 1 6f Middle Park Stakes, Group 2 7f Challenge Stakes, Group 3 5f Prix d'Arenburg and Group 3 8f Prix de Fontainebleau winner Zieten and to the 1995 3-y-o Koheilan, and closely related to the French 1993 2-y-o 6f and 6.7f and 3-y-o listed 8f winner Slow Jazz (by Chief's Crown). The dam won 5 races from 5-7f in France including the Group 2 Prix Maurice de Gheest and the Group 3 Prix de le Porte Maillot. 2nd dam, Balsamique (by Tourangeau), won 7 races at up to 11.5f and 2 jumping events in France. David Loder was quite specific about this filly's ability - "**Blue Duster** is a strong type that's going to be ready to run in about May. She's going to be a very nice filly indeed." (Sheikh Mohammed).
Optimum 3-y-o distance: 5-7f.

256 - DIMAKYA (USA)
Bay filly. Dayjur - Reloy (Liloy).
May 6. 4th foal.
Half-sister to the useful 1994 2-y-o 5f and listed 6f Firth of Clyde Stakes winner Loyalize (by Nureyev) and to the minor American winner Periscopic (by Secreto). The dam was a smart winner of the Group 3 10.5f Prix de Royaumont, was 2nd in the Group 1 12f Prix Vermeille and went on to win two Grade 1 events in the USA. She is a half-sister to the very useful French performers En Calcat and Roi Guillaume and the smart French 8f winner Reine Imperiale. 2nd dam, Rescousse (by Emerson), a top class filly, won the Prix de Diane and was 2nd in the Prix de l'Arc de Triomphe behind San San. Another nice filly, **Dimakya** may not be ready until June, but David does seem to like her quite a bit. (Sheikh Mohammed).
Optimum 3-y-o distance: 6-9f.

257 - INCARVILLEA (USA)
Bay filly. Mr Prospector - In the Groove (Night Shift).
April 20. 1st foal.
The dam was a top class middle distance filly and won seven races, notably the Irish 1,000 gns, Juddmonte International, Dubai Champion Stakes and Coronation Cup - all Group 1 events - and in so doing belied her relatively low profile pedigree. In the Groove is a half-sister to 4 winners, including the fairly useful miler Spanish Pine, out of the quite useful dual 12f winner Pine Ridge (by High Top) - herself out of the minor 12f and 14f winner Wounded Knee (by Busted). When I spoke to David in the spring, **Incarvillea** was ready to run and he expressed his opinion that she would be suited by 6f or 7f later on this season. (Sheikh Mohammed).
Optimum 3-y-o distance: 10f.

258 - LAVANDA
Bay filly. Soviet Star - One Life (L'Emigrant).
February 23. 4th foal.
Half-sister to the quite useful 1994 2-y-o 7.5f winner Tenoria (by Law Society), to the French 3-y-o winner of 3 races from 7-9f Lithuania (by Ti King) and the minor French winner No Rehearsal (by Baillamont). The unraced dam is closely related to the outstanding filly Miesque - herself dam of the Group 1 winners Kingmambo and East of the Moon. 2nd dam, Pasadoble (by Prove It), won four races in France including two stakes events over 8f and is a half-sister to the U.S. Grade 1 winner Silver Supreme. "**Lavanda** has been held up because of one or two

niggling problems, but she should be ready to run in May or June even though I haven't been able to do a lot with her," David commented.
Optimum 3-y-o distance: 8f.

259 - MOONFIRE
Bay filly. Sadlers Wells - Moon Cactus (Kris).
March 9. 2nd foal.
Sister to the highly promising 1995 3-y-o Moonshell, winner of her only outing, over 8f, at 2 yrs. The dam was a smart winner of the 7f Sweet Solera Stakes at 2 yrs and the 10f Lupe Stakes at 3 yrs, was placed in the Group 1 Prix de Diane and Group 2 Nassau Stakes and is a sister to the very smart Diomed Stakes winner Shining Steel. 2nd dam, Lady Moon (by Mill Reef), won 3 races from 11f to 12.3f and is out of the Oaks 3rd Moonlight Night. David told me that, although **Moonfire** is reputedly a very nice filly, she had to be operated on for a bad colic attack and was not yet in his yard. (Sheikh Mohammed).
Optimum 3-y-o distance: 10-12f.

260 - MOUNTAIN HOLLY
Bay filly. Shirley Heights - Ela Romara (Ela Mana Mou).
April 7. 3rd foal.
Half-sister to the 1995 3-y-o Vicenza (by Old Vic) and to the smart 1994 3-y-o Group 2 12f King Edward VII Stakes winner Foyer (by Sadlers Wells). The dam was a high class winner of the Group 3 6f Lowther Stakes (at 2 yrs) and the Group 2 10f Nassau Stakes and is a half-sister to 7 winners including the very useful 10f colt Roman Gunner. 2nd dam, Romara (by Bold Lad, Ire), was a useful winner over 7f and 8f at 3 yrs and was 4th in the Irish 1,000 gns. Very backward, **Mountain Holly** had immature knees and was not in the yard in spring. (Sheikh Mohammed).
Optimum 3-y-o distance: 10-12f.

261 - NANDA
Chestnut filly. Nashwan - Pushy (Sharpen Up).
February 19.
Sister to the smart 1994 2-y-o 6f and 3-y-o Nell Gwyn Stakes winner Myself and half-sister to the smart 2-y-o 6f Princess Margaret Stakes and 3-y-o 6f Prix de Seine et Oise winner Bluebook (by Secretariat), the useful 3-y-o 8f winner and 4-y-o Trusthouse Forte Mile 4th Phountzi (by Raise a Cup), the fairly useful 2-y-o 6f winner Eye Drop (by Irish River), the fair 3-y-o 5f winner Pushoff (by Sauce Boat) and the minor 4-y-o Macau winner Performance (by Shadeed). The dam was a very useful 2-y-o winner of 4 races including the Group 2 Queen Mary Stakes and is a half-sister to the high class 2-y-o Precocious, the Group 1 Japan Cup winner Jupiter Island, the good 2-y-o Krayyan and 6 other winners including the 2-y-o 5f winner Putupon (dam of the smart French sprinter Pole Position). 2nd dam, Mrs Moss (by Reform), won over 5f at 2 yrs (her only season to race). **Nanda** is quite backward at this stage (mid-April) and has been turned out for the moment. (Sheikh Mohammed).
Optimum 3-y-o distance: 7f.

262 - PINK CASHMERE
Bay or brown filly. Polar Falcon - Old Domesday Book (High Top).
March 8. 5th foal.
Half-sister to the 1995 3-y-o Great Inquest (by Shernazar), to the high class Group 1 6f July Cup, Group 2 6f Moet and Chandon Rennen at Baden-Baden, Group 3 6f Cork and Orrery Stakes and Group 3 6f Duke of York Stakes winner Owington (by Green Desert) and to the fair 2-y-o 8f (all-weather) winner Common Council (by Siberian Express). The dam was a fairly useful 3-y-o 10.4f winner and was 3rd in the listed 10f Sir Charles Clore Memorial Stakes. 2nd dam, Broken Record (by Busted), was a useful winner of four races from 12-15f, was 3rd in the Jockey Club Gold Cup and 4th in the Tote Ebor Handicap. "A chunky filly and very much a 2-y-o type, **Pink Cashmere** should be ready to run in May and is certainly above average," the trainer tells me. (A. Steigenberger)
Optimum 3-y-o distance: 8f.

263 - PRANCING
Bay filly. Prince Sabo - Valika (Valiyar).
February 11. 4th foal.
Sister to the 1995 3-y-o Keyhinge Boy, last of 4 over 6f on the 2nd of his two outings at 2 yrs, and half-sister to the very smart 1993 2-y-o First Trump, winner of 5 races over 6f including the Group 1 Middle Park Stakes, the Group 3 July Stakes and the Group 3 Richmond Stakes and to the quite useful 1993 3-y-o 7f winner First Veil (both by Primo Dominie). The dam was placed three times from 8-12f at 3 yrs and is a half-sister to the high class sprinter Mr Brooks and to the smart 3-y-o dual 7f winner Larionov. 2nd dam, Double Finesse (by Double Jump), was a fairly useful winner over 6f (at 2 yrs), 7f and 8f (at 4 yrs). **Prancing** is a filly to take note of, as David specifically told me that he is very pleased with her, that she's a very nice filly with scope and that she should be ready by June. (Cheveley Park Stud)
Optimum 3-y-o distance: 6-8f.

Willie Muir

264 - WOODBURY (USA)
Chestnut colt. Woodman - Habibti (Habitat).
March 24. 55,000 gns. 6th live foal.
Half-brother to the fair Irish 1994 2-y-o 5f winner Desert Lily (by Green Desert) and to the fair 1990 dual 6f placed 2-y-o Reem Albaraari (by Sadlers Wells). The dam, a brilliant sprinter, won the July Cup, William Hill Sprint Championship, Prix de l'Abbaye and Kings Stand Kakes (all Group 1 events) and the Group 2 Vernons Sprint Cup. She also finished 4th, promoted to 3rd, in the 1,000 gns and is closely related to the fairly useful 2-y-o sprinter Khedive and a half-sister to the useful Irish sprinter Knesset and to Eight Carat, dam of two Grade 1 winners in Australia and New Zealand. 2nd dam, Klairessa (by Klairon), won once at just under 6f, is a sister to the good sprinter D'Urberville and is closely related to Lora, herself dam of the 1,000 gns winner On the House. (Linkslade Partnership).
Optimum 3-y-o distance: 6f.

Aidan O'Brien

265 - GRAND CONCERTO (IRE)
Bay colt. Sadlers Wells - Passamaquoddy (Drone).
March 11. 120,000 gns.
Brother to the 1995 3-y-o Rosy Sweetheart and to the 1993 French 8f 2-y-o winner and very useful middle distance placed 3-y-o Papago, closely related to the useful 1992 2-y-o 6f Chesham Stakes winner Humam (by Nijinsky) and half-brother to the useful 2-y-o 5f and 6f winner Tamim (by Topsider) and the U.S. winner of 3 races and stakes placed Tammany (by Mr Prospector). The dam won 7 races including 2 stakes events and is a sister to Navajo Princess (the Grade 2 winning dam of Dancing Brave) and a half-sister to a Grade 3 stakes winner. 2nd dam, Olmec (by Pago Pago), won 5 races at 3 yrs including a minor stakes event.
Optimum 3-y-o distance: 10-12f.

Charles O'Brien

266 - EPIGRAM (IRE)
Bay colt. Royal Academy - Perlita (Baldric II).
March 11.
Half-brother to the high class French colt Persepolis (by Kalamoun), winner of the Group 1 10.5f Prix Lupin, Group 2 11f Prix Noailles etc., to the useful 2-y-o 6f and 4-y-o 7f winner Chaddleworth (by Ahonoora), to minor winners by Lyphard, Nonoalco and Rheingold, and to the maiden Seattle Rockette (by Seattle Slew) - herself dam of the very useful 6-8f colt Redoubtable. The dam was placed four times at up to 8f in France and is a half-sister to the top class broodmare Val Divine - dam of Vayrann, Yashgan (both Group 1 winners) and Valiyar,

2YO 1995

and grandam of the French Derby 4th Natroun. 2nd dam, Pola Bella (by Darius), was a champion French 2-y-o filly and winner of the French 1,000 gns and Prix du Moulin.
Optimum 3-y-o distance: 8f.

267 - HAPPY MEDIUM (IRE)
Bay colt. Fairy King - Belle Origine (Exclusive Native).
April 26. 200,000 Ir gns.
Half-brother to the very smart sprinter Lavinia Fontana (by Sharpo), winner of the Group 1 6f Haydock Sprint Cup, Group 2 6f Premio Umbria, Group 3 5f Prix du Petit-Covert and Group 3 7f Premio Chiusura and to the moderate 1994 Irish 5f placed 2-y-o Ceide Dancer (by Alzao). The dam, a minor winner over 9.5f at 3 yrs in France, is a half-sister to the French listed stakes winners Bel Sorel and My Volga Boatman. 2nd dam, Bella Sorella (by Ribot), won 3 races at 3 yrs and is a sister to the champion 2-y-o Ribofilio.
Optimum 3-y-o distance: 6-8f.

John Oxx

268 - CHARLOCK (IRE)
Chestnut filly. Nureyev - Charmante (Alydar).
May 17. 3rd foal.
Closely related to the 1995 3-y-o Dragontina (by Danzig), and half-sister to the fairly useful 1994 dual 14f 3-y-o winner Alinova (by Alleged). The dam, a winner over 7f at 2 yrs in Ireland and a minor 8f stakes in the USA, is a half-sister to the top class miler Zilzal. 2nd dam, French Charmer (by Le Fabuleux), won 5 races at 3 yrs including a Grade 2 stakes event in the USA, and is a half-sister to the dams of the Group 1 winners Polish Precedent, Awe Inspiring and Culture Vulture. John said that "**Charlock** has been at home on the farm and has missed a good deal of the early training. She is a nice filly and moves well but has a lot of ground to make up on the others." (Sheikh Mohammed).
Optimum 3-y-o distance: 8f.

269 - KASORA (IRE)
Brown filly. Darshaan - Kozana (Kris).
Half-sister to the 1995 3-y-o Khozabad, to the useful Irish 1991 7.8f 2-y-o winner and 3-y-o 8f listed stakes winner Khanata (both by Riverman), the 1992 2-y-o 7f winner, Group 1 National Stakes 3rd and 3-y-o Group 1 8f Premio Parioli 2nd Khoraz (by The Minstrel), the quite useful Irish 14f and 2 mile winner Kausar (by Vaguely Noble), the useful 1994 Irish 1,000 gns Trial winner Kotama and the 1991 Irish 3-y-o 10f winner (his only race) Khazari (both by Shahrastani). The dam, a top class filly, won four races at 3 yrs over 8f (3 times) and 10f including the Prix de Malleret and Prix de Sandringham, and was 3rd in the Prix de l'Arc de Triomphe. 2nd dam, the French 1,000 gns winner Koblenza (by Hugh Lupus), has also bred the Prix du Cadran winner Karkour and the useful 10f winners Reine de Lenza and Korinetta (herself dam of the Cumberland Lodge Stakes winner Kazaroun). "**Kasora** is a nice looking filly with good conformation. She will take time but will hopefully have a race or two in the Autumn," commented her trainer. (H.H. Aga Khan).
Optimum 3-y-o distance: 10-12f.

270 - MASAFIYA (IRE)
Bay filly. Shernazar - Masarika (Thatch).
April 11.
Half-sister to the very useful 1993 3-y-o 7f Irish 2,000 gns Trial and 10f Gallinule Stakes winner Massyar (by Kahyasi), to the U.S. Grade 3 8f Arcadia Handicap winner Madjaristan (by Irish River) - previously a winner 5 times in France, to the quite useful 1994 Irish 3-y-o 8f winner Masawa (by Alzao) and to the minor French 10f winner Masskana (by Darshaan). The dam, a smart filly, won the French 1,000 gns and Prix Robert Papin and is a half-sister to the very useful middle-distance performer Maiymad. 2nd dam, Miss Melody (by Tudor Melody), was a smart 5f 2-y-o and a half-sister to the Champion Stakes 3rd Lord David. (H.H. Aga Khan).
Optimum 3-y-o distance: 10f.

271 - MAZAMET (USA)
Bay colt. Elmaamul - Miss Mazepah (Nijinsky).
May 4.
Half-brother to the smart stayer and dual Ascot Gold Cup winner Sadeem (by Forli), to the quite useful 1994 3-y-o 8.2f winner Apache Plume (by Gone West) and to four minor winners by Blushing Groom. The dam won 3 minor races at 3 yrs in the USA and is a half-sister to the U.S. stakes winner and Group 1 placed Pressing Date and to the dams of Too Chic (Grade 1 Maskette Stakes) and Prima Voce (Group 1 Grand Prix Prince Rose). 2nd dam, Monade (by Klairon), won both the Epsom Oaks and the Prix Vermeille and was 2nd in the Prix de l'Arc de Triomphe. "**Mazamet** is the biggest 2 year old in the yard and will be lucky to have a race towards the end of the year. He's a nice colt, despite his size, moves well and has a very good temperament." John told me. (Sheikh Mohammed).
Optimum 3-y-o distance: 10-12f.

272 - ORIANE
Chestnut filly. Nashwan - Rappa Tap Tap (Tap on Wood).
April 20. 6th live foal.
Half-sister to the fair 1994 Irish 7f placed 2-y-o Winger (by In the Wings), to the very useful 1988 2-y-o 7f winner and Group 1 Hoover Fillies Mile 2nd Pick of the Pops (by High Top) and the fairly useful 1993 3-y-o dual 10f winner Tap on Air (by Caerleon). The dam was a useful winner of 3 races from 6f to 8f including the Blue Seal Stakes and is a half-sister to the Irish Oaks winner Colorspin (herself dam of the top class colt Opera House) and to the Group 2 Prix de l'Opera winner Bella Colora (dam of the high class colt Stagecraft). 2nd dam, Reprocolor (by Jimmy Reppin), won the 12f Lingfield Oaks Trial and the Lancashire Oaks in 1979. (Lady Clague).
Optimum 3-y-o distance: 8-10f.

273 - POWER PLAY
Bay colt. Nashwan - Game Plan (Darshaan).
April 22. 2nd foal.
Half-brother to the 1995 3-y-o Chaturanga (by Night Shift). The dam was a smart winner of the Group 2 10f Pretty Polly Stakes at the Curragh, was 2nd in the Epsom Oaks to Salsabil and is a half-sister to four minor winners. 2nd dam, Formulate (by Reform), was a very smart 2-y-o winner of the Hoover Fillies Mile and the Waterford Candelabra Stakes and was 2nd in the 10f Lupe Stakes at 3 yrs. "**Power Play** is a nice colt and a good mover. He has had an uninterrupted training routine so far and I am hoping he will race by July." says John. (Sheikh Mohammed).
Optimum 3-y-o distance: 10-12f.

274 - SHERAKA (IRE)
Bay filly. Doyoun - Sherzana (Great Nephew).
April 22. 3rd foal.
Half-sister to the 1995 3-y-o Shemaran (by Kahyasi), 2nd over 8f on his only outing at 2 yrs. The dam is an unraced sister to the top class Derby, King George and Irish Derby winner Shergar and a half-sister to the high class September Stakes and Geoffrey Freer Stakes winner Shernazar (by Busted). 2nd dam, Sharmeen (by Val de Loir), won over 10.5f in France and is a half-sister to the very smart Prix Hocquart winner Naasiri. John says "**Sheraka** is a nice filly but will take time. None of this family reach their full potential until 3 years old." (H.H. Aga Khan).
Optimum 3-y-o distance: 10-12f.

275 - SOCIALITE (IRE)
Bay filly. Alzao - Merriment (Go Marching).
March 29.
Sister to the high class miler Second Set, winner of the Sussex Stakes and placed in the St James's Palace Stakes, Queen Elizabeth II Stakes and Queen Anne Stakes and half-sister to the Belgian listed stakes winner Lonely Reef (by Pas de Seul) and to minor winners by Trepan (in France) and Taufan (in Malaysia). The dam was placed three times in France and is a sister to the high class French miler Brinkmanship. 2nd dam, Tiddlywinks (by Court Martial), was an unraced half-sister to the Hollywood Oaks winner Paris Pike. "**Socialite** is small but with good conformation. She has not yet been in full training so it remains to be seen if she will reach the

racetrack before the end of the season." (J.P. Mangan).
Optimum 3-y-o distance: 8f.

276 - ZAYNAL (IRE)
Bay colt. Shernazar - Zariya (Blushing Groom).
May 26.
Half-brother to the 3-y-o Zaridiya (by Doyoun), to the smart 7f Greenham Stakes winner and Group 2 12f King Edward VII Stakes 2nd Zayyani and half-sister to the fairly useful 1988 3-y-o Zerzaya (by Beldale Flutter), a winner of four 10f handicaps. The dam, a quite useful winner of two races over 7f at 2 yrs, is out of the placed Zahra (by Habitat), herself a daughter of Petite Etoile. According to his trainer "**Zaynal** has good enough conformation but is excitable like a lot of his family. He had a setback recently and will have to rest for a couple of months. I don't know if he will be able to race this year." (H. H. Aga Khan).
Optimum 3-y-o distance: 10-12f.

Henri A. Pantall

277 - VIVONNE
Bay filly. Unfuwain - Viole d'Amour (Luthier).
March 26.
Closely related to the top class filly Luth Enchantee (by Be My Guest), winner of 4 races over 8f including the Group 1 Prix Jacques le Marois and Group 1 Prix du Moulin, and to the stakes-placed colt Sheikh Dancer (by Shareef Dancer) and half-sister to the useful French middle-distance winners Luth Celtique (by Thatch) and Luth d'Or (by Noir Et Or) and the minor Irish 3-y-o winner Romantic Age (by Mill Reef). The dam, a very useful filly, won 2 races in France over middle-distances including the listed Prix des Tuileries and was 2nd in the Group 3 10.5f Prix Fille de l'Air. 2nd dam, Mandolinette (by Yorik), was also a very useful middle-distance winner. (Sheikh Mohammed).
Optimum 3-y-o distance: 12f.

Kevin Prendergast

278 - ASHBAL (USA)
Chestnut colt. Elmaamul - Hooriah (Northern Dancer).
April 19. 3rd foal.
Half-brother to the 1995 3-y-o Jahaz (by Reference Point) and to the 1993 Irish 8f placed 2-y-o Arkub (by Mtoto). The dam, placed twice at 3 yrs, is a half-sister to the Fred Darling Stakes winner and Oaks 2nd Slightly Dangerous (dam of Commander in Chief, Deploy and Warning), to the smart middle distance winner I Will Follow (dam of Rainbow Quest) and to the unraced dam of the Dewhurst Stakes winner (in a dead-heat) Scenic. 2nd dam, Where You Lead (by Raise a Native), won the 1973 Musidora Stakes and was 2nd in the Oaks. (Hamdan Al-Maktoum).
Optimum 3-y-o distance: 10f.

Sir Mark Prescott

279 - ASPEN SNOW
Bay filly. Lyphard - Looks Sensational (Majestic Light).
May 15. 30,000 Ir gns.
Closely related to the quite useful 2-y-o 5f winner and 5-6f placed 3-y-o Yakin (by Nureyev). The dam ran twice in the USA without success but is a half-sister to the dual Grade 1 stakes winner Awe Inspiring. 2nd dam, Highest Regard (by Gallant Romeo), won 7 races including 3 stakes events and is a half-sister to the top class broodmares French Charmer (dam of Zilzal), Past Example (dam of Polish Precedent) and Perfect Example (dam of Culture Vulture). Sir Mark informed me that this filly had been turned out early in the year and would not be seen on

a racecourse until late in the season. (Prince Faisal Salman).
Optimum 3-y-o distance: 8f.

Gary Rimmer

280 - EXTREMELY FRIENDLY
Chestnut colt. Generous - Water Woo (Tom Rolfe).
January 19.
Half-brother to the 1995 3-y-o Action Jackson (by Hadeer), unplaced three times at 2 yrs, to the high class Group 1 10f Eclipse Stakes and Group 2 10.5f Wm Hill Dante Stakes winner Environment Friend (by Cozzene), the U.S. winner and Group 2 placed Prince Everett (by Sensitive Prince) and to minor winners by Coastal (in Italy) and Buckfinder (in the USA). The dam won once, a listed race over 6f in France at 3 yrs, and is a half-sister to 5 winners including the smart 2-y-o 6f and 7f winner and Queen Anne Stakes, Royal Lodge Stakes and Wm Hill Futurity Stakes placed Water Cay. 2nd dam, Waterloo (by Bold Lad, Ire), won the 1,000 gns and the Cheveley Park Stakes. (W. J. Gredley).
Optimum 3-y-o distance: 8-10f.

Jean-Claude Rouget

281 - HOOK LINE
Bay or brown filly. Shaadi - Hooked Bid (Spectacular Bid).
March 20. 4th foal.
Half-sister to the quite useful 1994 6f and 7f 2-y-o winner Caerphilly (by Caerleon) and to the fair 1993 14f 3-y-o winner Hoosie (by Niniski). The dam, a minor 3-y-o 10f winner, is a half-sister to the useful 1988 2-y-o 6f and 7f winner Thorn Dance. 2nd dam, Barb's Bold (by Bold Forbes), was a very useful French filly at around 10f and a half-sister to Lyphard, Nobiliary and Tertiary (dam of the smart colt Kefaah). (Sheikh Mohammed).
Optimum 3-y-o distance: 8-10f.

Alain de Royer-Dupre

282 - BEHARIYA (IRE)
Bay filly. Sadlers Wells - Behera (Mill Reef).
April 20. 3rd foal.
Half-sister to the useful 1994 Group 3 15.5f Prix Berteux winner Bayrika (by Kahyasi) and to the 1995 3-y-o Behariya (by Rainbow Quest). The dam was a top class winner of the Group 1 10f Prix Saint-Alary and the Group 3 10.5f Prix Penelope, and was placed in the Prix de l'Arc de Triomphe (2nd to Carroll House), the Breeders Cup Turf and the Prix de la Nonette. 2nd dam, Borushka (by Bustino), won 4 races from 12-14f including the Group 2 Park Hill Stakes and the Galtres Stakes and is out of a winning half-sister to the Prix de Diane winner Crepellana. **Behariya** is bred on the same lines as the very useful middle distance filly Spring. (H.H. Aga Khan).
Optimum 3-y-o distance: 10-12f.

283 - BERRY ROSE (FR)
Chestnut filly. Dancing Spree - Lady Berry (Violon d'Ingres).
April 21.
Half-sister to the Group 1 Grand Prix de Paris winner Le Nain Jeune, the Group 1 Prix Vermeille winner Indian Rose, the Group 1 Prix Ganay winner Vert Amande, to two other good winners in Woolskin and Mulberry, and to Featherhill, dam of the high class French colt Groom Dancer. The dam, a smart filly, won six of her eight races including the the Group 1 Prix Royal-Oak (French St Leger) and the Prix de Pomone. 2nd dam, Moss Rose (by Mossborough), was a minor French 3-y-o 10f winner. (Baron Guy de Rothschild).
Optimum 3-y-o distance: 10-12f.

284 - DARAZARI (IRE)
Bay colt. Sadlers Wells - Darara (Top Ville).
May 27. 5th foal.
Closely related to the 1992 French 2-y-o 8f winner Dardjini (by Nijinsky) and half-brother to the 1995 3-y-o Dariyani (by Doyoun) and the very useful Group 1 14f Gran Premio de Madrid winner and Group 1 20f Prix du Cadran 3rd Dariyoun (by Shahrastani). The dam, a top class filly, won the Group 1 12f Prix Vermeille and the Group 3 10f Prix de Psyche and is a half-sister to the Prix du Jockey Club winner Darshaan and the Group 2 Prix de Royallieu winner. 2nd dam, Delsy (by Abdos), won over 12f and was 3rd in the Prix de Pomone. (H.H. Aga Khan).
Optimum 3-y-o distance. 12f.

285 - DUNAYSIR (FR)
Bay colt. Kahyasi - Dumayla (Shernazar).
May 30. 2nd foal.
Half-brother to the French trained 3-y-o Dumayra (by Lashkari). The dam was placed on both her outings, over 8f and 10f at 3 yrs, and is a half-sister to the high class 2,000 gns winner Doyoun, the sprinter Dafayna and the miler Dalsaan - both very smart. 2nd dam, Dumka (by Kashmir II), won the French 1,000 gns in 1974. (H.H. Aga Khan).
Optimum 3-y-o distance: 10-12f.

286 - KARANPOUR (IRE)
Bay colt. Darshaan - Karamita (Shantung).
June 8.
Half-brother to the very smart filly Kartajana (by Shernazar), winner of the Group 2 10f Nassau Stakes at 3 yrs, the Group 1 10.5f Prix Ganay and Group 1 10f Grosser Preis Bayerisches Zuchtrennen at 4 yrs and subsequently successful in America as a 5-y-o, and to the fairly useful 10f Extel Handicap winner Kazaviyna (by Blakeney). The dam was a smart winner of the Group 3 12f Princess Royal Stakes at 3 yrs and is a half-sister to the very useful Jockey Club Cup winner Karadar, the smart middle distance winner Kalidar and to the dams of the Group 1 winners Caerlina and Khariyda. 2nd dam, Shahinaaz (by Venture VII), was a useful winner at up to 13f in France. (H.H. Aga Khan).
Optimum 3-y-o distance: 10-12f.

287 - SEVRES ROSE (IRE)
Bay colt. Caerleon - Indian Rose (General Holme).
April 4. 2nd foal.
The dam was a high class winner of three middle-distance races at 3 yrs, notably the Group 1 Prix Vermeille and the Group 3 Prix Cleopatre. She is a half-sister to the Group 1 Prix Ganay winner Vert Amande, the Group 1 Grand Prix de Paris winner Le Nain Jeune, to two other good winners in Mulberry and Woolskin, and to the French middle-distance winner Featherhill - dam of the top class Group 1 Prix Lupin winner Groom Dancer. 2nd dam, Lady Berry (by Violon d'Ingres), won the Prix Royal-Oak. (Baron Guy de Rothschild).
Optimum 3-y-o distance: 12f.

David Smaga

288 - ROYAL HOSTESS (IRE)
Bay filly. Be My Guest - Edinburgh (Charlottown).
March 8.
Half-sister to the smart Group 1 20f Prix du Cadran and Group 2 15f Prix Kergorlay winner Sought Out (by Rainbow Quest), the very useful 7f (at 2 yrs) and 14.6f winner Queen Helen (by Troy), the French 10f and 12f winner Greektown (by Ela Mana Mou), the fairly useful 3-y-o 12f winner Castle Peak (by Darshaan), the fair 3-y-o 12f winner Scots Lass (by Shirley Heights) - herself dam of the Great Voltigeur Stakes winner Bonny Scot, and to a minor winner in France by Lightning. The dam was a very useful winner of the Group 3 8f Prix des Reservoirs at 2 yrs and was 2nd in both the Group 3 Prix de la Nonette and the Group 3 Prix Vanteaux. 2nd dam, Queen's Castle (by Sovereign Path), was a fairly useful 3-y-o 8f winner and a half-sister to

Reform. (Lord Weinstock).
Optimum 3-y-o distance: 10-12f.

Alec Stewart

289 - NASEEM EL FAJR (IRE)
Bay filly. Green Desert - Flying Bid (Auction Ring).
March 31. 52,000 Ir gns.
Half-sister to the 1989 Group 1 2-y-o Moyglare Stud Stakes winner Flutter Away, to the fair Irish 1994 listed 9.5f 3-y-o winner Copper Mountain (both by Lomond), the fair 3-y-o 7f winner Vision of India (by Vision), the Irish 1993 3-y-o 7-9f winner Rienroe (by Caerleon), the moderate 3-y-o 7.2f winner Flying Biddy (by Affirmed), the plating class 3-y-o 12f winner Rahwah (by Northern Baby) and the winning hurdler Soneeto (by Teenoso). The dam, a fair 4-y-o 10f winner in Ireland, is a sister to the Group 1 2-y-o Prix Robert Papin winner Maelstrom Lake and a half-sister to 6 winners. 2nd dam, Skyway (by Skymaster), won as a 3-y-o.
Optimum 3-y-o distance: 7-8f.

290 - SABAAH ELFULL
Chestnut filly. Kris - Putupon (Mummy's Pet).
January 30. 5th foal to live.
Sister to the 1995 3-y-o Placement, closely related to the smart 1989 2-y-o Group 3 Prix Eclipse and 3-y-o Group 3 Prix de Meautry winner Pole Position (by Sharpo), and half-sister to the fair 1993 3-y-o 5f winner Putout (by Dowsing). The dam, a fairly useful 2-y-o 5f winner, is a half-sister to 9 winners including the Japan Cup winner Jupiter Island, the high class 2-y-o Precocious and two other good 2-y-o's in Krayyan and Pushy (herself dam of the smart filly Bluebook). 2nd dam, Mrs Moss (by Reform), also won over 5f at 2 yrs. (Sheikh Ahmed Al-Maktoum).
Optimum 3-y-o distance: 7f.

291 - SHAHRUR (USA)
Bay or brown colt. Riverman - Give Thanks (Relko).
February 17. 6th foal.
Brother to the 1995 3-y-o Bilad and half-brother to the quite useful 1990 10.4f placed 3-y-o Ghzaalh (by Northern Dancer), the quite useful 1989 3-y-o 12.2f winner (awarded race) Saffaanh (by Shareef Dancer) and to the fair 1993 7-10.4f placed 3-y-o Makin (by Danzig). The dam, a game and genuine filly, won 6 races at 3 yrs from 9-12f including the Irish Oaks, Musidora Stakes, Lancashire Oaks and Lingfield Oaks Trial. 2nd dam, Parthica (by Parthia), was a useful 8f winner and a half-sister to the dams of Amaranda, Ashayer, Braiswick, Favoridge, Old Country, Teenoso and Topsy. (Hamdan Al-Maktoum).
Optimum 3-y-o distance: 10-12f.

Michael Stoute

292 - BEREG (USA)
Bay or brown colt. Danzig - Balidaress (Balidar).
March 13.
Half-brother to the Irish Oaks and Ribblesdale Stakes winner Alydaress (by Alydar), to the Cheveley Park Stakes winner and 1,000 gns 3rd Desirable (by Lord Gayle) - herself dam of the high class filly Shadayid, to the Cheveley Park winner Park Appeal (by Ahonoora), the Group 3, 9f Hennesey Ballymacoy Stakes winner Nashamaa (by Ahonoora), the fairly useful 1994 Irish 3-y-o 7f and 10f winner Kilconnell (by Mr Prospector) and to 2 minor winners by Sallust including the dam of the very useful Peking Opera. The dam won 3 races from 7-10f in Ireland. 2nd dam, Innocence (by Sea Hawk II), won twice over 9f. The trainer, Michael Stoute, told me that **Bereg** would not be out until towards the end of the season, as he is big and immature at this stage. (Sheikh Mohammed).
Optimum 3-y-o distance: 8-9f.

293 - BUSH ROSE
Bay filly. Rainbow Quest - Bustara (Busted).
March 6. 5th foal.
Half-sister to the 1995 3-y-o Discorsi (by Machiavellian), to the smart 1991 Group 3 11f September Stakes winner Young Buster (by Teenoso), the minor 1992 3-y-o 10f and 12f placed El Taranda (by Ela Mana Mou) and the 1994 all-weather 10f placed 4-y-o Rising Wolf (by Shirley Heights). The dam, a fairly useful 6f 2-y-o winner, stayed 10f at 3 yrs and is a half-sister to the high-class Group 2 Nassau Stakes winner Ela Romara (herself dam of the smart Group 2 12f King Edward VII Stakes winner Foyer). 2nd dam, Romara (by Bold Lad, Ire), was a useful 3-y-o 7f and 8f winner and was 4th in the Irish 1,000 gns. Michael tells me that **Bush Rose** is a very attractive, staying type of filly. He added that Rainbow Quest isn't known for his 2-y-o winners and that this filly too, will take a bit of time. (Sheikh Mohammed).
Optimum 3-y-o distance: 10-12f.

294 - CASTING FOR GOLD (IRE)
Chestnut filly. Hansel - Mesmerize (Mill Reef).
May 2. 6th foal.
Closely related to the champion 1990 2-y-o colt Mujtahid, winner of the Group 2 6f Gimcrack Stakes, Group 3 6f Anglia TV July Stakes etc., and to the fairly useful 1994 2-y-o 6f winner Nuriva (both by Woodman), and half-sister to the very useful 1994 3-y-o Group 2 10f Guillaune d'Ornano and 8f Thirsk Classic Trial winner Just Happy, the fair 3-y-o 6f winner Jaazim (both by Night Shift) and the minor U.S. 4-y-o winner Paenula (by State Dinner). The dam is an unraced half-sister to the champion Italian 2-y-o filly Marina Duff and to the three times winner Cornish Gem (also third in the 2,000 gns Trial). 2nd dam, Jeanie Duff (by Majestic Prince), won twice at 3 yrs. "An athletic filly, **Casting For Gold** should be a good 2-y-o," said Michael. (Maktoum Al-Maktoum).
Optimum 3-y-o distance: 8-10f.

295 - CLASH OF SWORDS
Bay colt. Shaadi - Swept Away (Kris).
February 2. 5th foal.
Half-brother to the 1995 3-y-o Foehn (by Dancing Brave). The dam, a useful filly, won two of her six races including the Group 3 9f Prix Chloe and is a half-sister to the Group 3 7f Gladness Stakes winner Great Lakes, the 8f Easter Stakes winner Severn Bore and the Irish 3-y-o 7f listed stakes winner Inishdalla - all useful. 2nd dam, Costly Wave (by Caro), won 5 races including the Group 2 Premio Ribot. (Sheikh Mohammed).
Optimum 3-y-o distance: 8-10f.

296 - CLERKENWELL (USA)
Bay colt. Sadlers Wells - Forlene (Forli).
May 3.
Brother to the useful 3-y-o 10f and 4-y-o 14f winner Jungle Dancer, closely related to the fair Irish 2-y-o 7f winner Palais Glide, the dual French listed stakes winner Gloria's Dancer (both by Northern Dancer) and the minor American winner Battistello (by Storm Bird) and half-brother to the quite useful 4-y-o 10.8f winner Mesleh (by Alleged). The dam won the Group 3, 8f Silken Glider Stakes and is a half-sister to 5 winners including Dark Lomond (Irish St Leger) and South Atlantic (Blandford Stakes). 2nd dam, Arkadina (by Ribot), a smart 3-y-o filly of 1972, won the 7f Athasi Stakes, was placed in the Epsom Oaks, the Irish Oaks and the Irish 1,000 gns, and is a sister to the high class stayer Blood Royal - unbeaten in four races including the Jockey Club Cup and the Queens Vase. **Clerkenwell** is a "good-actioned, attractive horse. Rather big, he will need a bit of time," according to his trainer. (Sheikh Mohammed).
Optimum 3-y-o distance: 10-12f.

297 - COLOR PRECEDENT
Bay filly. Polish Precedent - Colorspin (High Top).
March 25. 5th foal.
Sister to the quite useful 1994 8f and 10f placed 3-y-o Polanski and half-sister to the 1995 3-y-o Stencil (by Nashwan), the top class Opera House (by Sadlers Wells), winner of the King George VI and Queen Elizabeth Diamond Stakes, Coral-Eclipse Stakes, Coronation Cup,

Tattersalls Rogers Gold Cup, Cumberland Lodge Stakes and Brigadier Gerard Stakes, and the very useful 10f and 11.7f winner and Brigadier Gerard Stakes and Hardwicke Stakes placed Highland Dress (by Lomond). The dam won 3 races, notably the Irish Oaks, and is a half-sister to the Group 2 Prix de l'Opera winner Bella Colora, herself dam of the high class colt Stagecraft. 2nd dam, Reprocolor (by Jimmy Reppin), won 3 races including the Group 3 Lingfield Oaks Trial and the Group3 Lancashire Oaks. A very immature filly around the knees, Michael explained that **Color Precedent** has gone back to the stud and may not be trained this year.
Optimum 3-y-o distance: 10f.

298 - DANCE SEQUENCE (USA)
Chestnut filly. Mr Prospector - Dancing Tribute (Nureyev).
March 14. 1st foal.
The dam, a very useful 2-y-o 6f and 3-y-o 8f winner, was 2nd in the Group 2 7f Bisquit Cognac Challenge Stakes and later won in the USA. She is closely related to the French 3-y-o 10f winner Belle et Deluree out of the very smart American 2-y-o winner and Grade 1 Oak Leaf Stakes 2nd Sophisticated Girl (by Stop the Music). **Dance Sequence** is " a mature filly, quite precocious and she could be out before Royal Ascot." The best example of this Mr Prospector - Nureyev cross is the top class miler Kingmambo.
Optimum 3-y-o distance: 8f.

299 - DEVIL'S DANCE (FR)
Bay colt. Mujtahid - Dance of Leaves (Sadlers Wells).
March 25.
Half-brother to the very promising 1995 3-y-o winner Charnwood Forest (by Warning). The unraced dam is a sister to the Group 1 Grand Prix de Paris winner Fort Wood, is closely related to the Group 1 July Cup winner Hamas, the Group 2 Prix de Pomone winner Colorado Dancer and the Group 1 Gamely Handicap winner Northern Aspen, and a half-sister to the Group 3 Prix d'Astarte winner Elle Seule (herself dam of the Irish 1,000 gns winner Mehthaaf), the Group 3 Goodwood Cup winner Mazzacano and the champion American 2-y-o of 1994, Timber Country, winner of the Grade 1 Breeders Cup Juvenile. 2nd dam, the outstanding broodmare Fall Aspen (by Pretense), won 8 races including the Grade 1 8f Matron Stakes. Incidentally, Timber Country, being by Woodman (the sire of Mujtahid) and out of Fall Aspen, is bred on the same lines as this colt. "A big, tall horse, **Devil's Dance** may have one or two runs later in the year." (Sheikh Mohammed).
Optimum 3-y-o distance: 8f.

300 - EARTH SHAKER (USA)
Chestnut colt. Zilzal - Snow Bride (Blushing Groom).
February 3. 3rd foal.
Half-brother to the very promising 1994 2-y-o 7f Washington Singer Stakes winner Lammtarra (by Nijinsky). The dam was awarded the 1989 Oaks on the disqualification of Aliysa and won the Musidora Stakes and the Princess Royal Stakes. She had also won both her 2-y-o starts over 7f and 8f and is a half-sister to the useful middle distance filly Habaayib and the Grade 3 U.S. winner Jarraar. 2nd dam, Awaasif (by Snow Knight), won the Group 1 Yorkshire Oaks and the Group 1 Gran Premio del Jockey Club and is a half-sister to the good American colt Akureyri and to the dams of the Group winners Proskona, Majuscule and Royal Cielo. Michael was quick to point out that "None of the Zilzal's are particularly precocious - he wasn't himself - but **Earth Shaker** is a stronger model than Zilzal and looks like being a mid-sason 2-y-o." (Saaed Maktoum Al-Maktoum).
Optimum 3-y-o distance: 10f.

301 - EBEN NAAS (USA)
Bay colt. Dayjur - Regal State (Affirmed).
February 6. 4th foal.
The dam was a high class 2-y-o winner of the Group 1 6f Prix Morny and was 2nd in both the Group 1 7f Prix de la Salamandre and the Group 1 8f Prix Jacques le Marois. She is a half-sister to another Prix Morny winner in Seven Springs - herself dam of the high class miler Distant View. 2nd dam, La Trinite (by Lyphard), was a very useful winner of two races at around 6f and was placed in the French 1,000 gns. Michael tells me that **Eben Naas** is a a big colt and as such

will not be rushed. Probably a back-end type. (Sheikh Ahmed Al-Maktoum).
Optimum 3-y-o distance: 6-8f.

302 - EXPENSIVE TASTE
Bay filly. Cadeaux Genereux - Um Lardaff (Kris).
May 21. 3rd foal.
Half-sister to the Irish trained 3-y-o Hatalee (by Kris). The dam, a winner at 3 yrs in France, is a sister to the Derby winner and high class sire Shirley Heights and a half-sister to the good mare Bempton - dam of the Group 3 winners Mr Pintips and Banket and of the Group 2 winner Gull Nook (herself dam of the very useful filly Spring). 2nd dam, Hardiemma (by Hardicanute), was a quite useful 3-y-o 11f winner, after winning over 7f at 2 yrs. Quite a mature filly, according to her trainer, **Expensive Taste** ought to have a 2-y-o season. (Maktoum Al-Maktoum).
Optimum 3-y-o distance: 7-9f.

303 - GET AWAY WITH IT (IRE)
Bay colt. Last Tycoon - Royal Sister II (Claude).
May 2.
Brother to the high class, if enigmatic, Ezzoud, winner of the Group 1 10f Eclipse Stakes, Group 1 10.4f Juddmonte International Stakes (twice) and Group 3 9f Earl of Sefton Stakes, and half-brother to the top class miler Distant Relative (by Habitat), winner of the Sussex Stakes, Prix du Moulin, Hungerford Stakes, Beefeater Gin Celebration Mile and Bisquit Cognac Challenge Stakes, to the minor 3-y-o 10f winner Lightning Thunder (by Dara Monarch) and the minor 1994 3-y-o 14f winner Jundi (by Sadlers Wells). The dam, a winner over 10f at 4 yrs in Ireland, also won 7 races in Italy from 3-5 yrs and is a half-sister to 4 winners. 2nd dam, Ribasha (by Ribot), is a half-sister to Natashka (dam of Gregorian), Arkadina (dam of Irish St Leger winner Dark Lomond) and to the high class stayer Blood Royal. Michael told me that **Get Away With It** is a bigger horse than his brother, Ezzoud, and would need more time to come to hand. (Maktoum Al-Maktoum).
Optimum 3-y-o distance: 8-10f.

304 - HAMMERSTEIN
Bay colt. Kris - Musical Bliss (The Minstrel).
April 6. 2nd foal to live.
Half-brother to the 1995 3-y-o Maquina (by Machiavellian). The dam, a very useful filly, won the 7f Rockfel Stakes at 2 yrs and the 1,000 gns at 3 yrs. She is a half-sister to the Grade 1 La Canada Stakes winner Safe Play (herself dam of the Grade 1 Man O'War Stakes winner Defensive Play). 2nd dam, Bori (by Quadrangle), is a placed half-sister to the Grade 3 winner Bob's Majesty and to the Dewhurst Stakes 2nd Draw the Line. "A medium-sized horse and not too backward, **Hammerstein** is a colt I would expect to be quite an early a 2-y-o," said Michael. (Sheikh Mohammed).
Optimum 3-y-o distance: 10f.

305 - HIDDEN OASIS
Bay colt. Green Desert - Secret Seeker (Mr Prospector).
February 3. 1st foal to live.
The dam, a winner of 2 races at 3 yrs in the USA, is a sister to the Grade 1 Dwyer Stakes winner Gone West (sire of Zafonic) and to the smart Greenham Stakes and Horris Hill Stakes winner Lion Cavern. 2nd dam, Secrettame (by Secretariat), won 6 races including a stakes event, was 2nd in the Grade 2 Gazelle Handicap and is a half-sister to the champion miler, 2,000 gns, Middle Park Stakes and Queen Elizabeth II Stakes winner Known Fact, to the triple Grade 1 winner Tentam, the U.S. Grade 2 winner Terete and to the dam of the triple Grade 1 winner Tappiano. Michael reports that **Hidden Oasis** is a little bit on the leg at the moment but expects to get some racing into him this season. (Sheikh Mohammed).
Optimum 3-y-o distance: 8f.

306 - KEBILI (IRE)
Bay filly. Green Desert - Pebbles (Sharpen Up).
March 11. 6th foal.
Closely related to the 1995 3-y-o Lapillus (by Polish Precedent). The dam, Pebbles, was one of

the most outstanding fillies of the 80's and won 8 races from 6-12f, notably the Breeders Cup Turf, 1,000 gns, Champion Stakes and Eclipse Stakes. 2nd dam, La Dolce (by Connaught), was a useful winner of 2 races over 8f (at Beverley and Ascot) at 3 yrs, was 5th in the Oaks and is a half-sister to Princess Zena (dam of the smart colt Supreme Leader) and Port Ahoy (dam of the useful winners Pretty Pol, Top Hope and Wylfa). Sadly, Pebbles has been extremely disappointing as a broodmare, as her first five foals have yet to see a racecourse. "**Kebili** is a good actioned filly and I can't complain about her at the moment. It's just a worry that the dam has been disappointing up to now," Michael mused. (Sheikh Mohammed).
Optimum 3-y-o distance: 8f.

307 - KING'S FLAME * (See page 85)
Bay colt. Kris - Nearctic Flame (Sadlers Wells).
February 14. 2nd foal.
Half-brother to the fairly useful 1994 3-y-o 10f and 12f winner Blushing Flame (by Blushing Groom). The dam was a very useful winner of two of her five races, over 10f and 10.5f at 3 yrs, and was 3rd in the Group 2 12f Ribblesdale Stakes. She is a sister to the top class Irish Derby, Prix Vermeille and 1,000 gns winner Salsabil, closely related to the Prix de Psyche winner Danse Royale and a half-sister to the high class St James's Palace Stakes winner Marju. 2nd dam, Flame of Tara (by Artaius), won eight races including the Group 2 Coronation Stakes and the Group 2 Pretty Polly Stakes at the Curragh, was 2nd in the Champion Stakes and is a half-sister to the Lupe Stakes 2nd Fruition - herself dam of the Tote Ebor, Doncaster Cup and Jockey Club Cup winner Kneller and of the smart 1994 French middle-distance stayer Northern Spur. "Only just medium-sized and light framed, **King's Flame** needs to grow a fair bit and start to mature."
Optimum 3-y-o distance: 10-12f.

308 - MOHAWK RIVER (IRE)
Bay colt. Polish Precedent - High Hawk (Shirley Heights).
March 26.
Half-brother to the top class middle distance colt In the Wings, winner of the Breeders Cup Turf, Coronation Cup, Grand Prix de Saint-Cloud and Prix du Prince d'Orange, to the smart 1993 3-y-o Group 2 10.5f Prix Greffulhe winner Hunting Hawk and the very useful 1994 3-y-o 10f and 11.5f winner Hawker's News (all by Sadlers Wells). The dam won 6 races from 10f to 14.5f including the Group 1 Premio Roma, Group 2 Ribblesdale Stakes, Group 2 Park Hill Stakes and Group 3 Prix de Royallieu, and is a half-sister to the useful miler Heron's Hollow and to the dam of Infamy (Rothman's International, Sun Chariot Stakes, etc). 2nd dam, Sunbittern (by Sea Hawk II), a very useful 2-y-o 6f and 7f winner, was 4th in the Cheveley Park Stakes. A backward colt, **Mohawk River,** won't be seen out until the end of the season. (Sheikh Mohammed).
Optimum 3-y-o distance: 10f.

309 - NATIONAL TREASURE
Bay filly. Shirley Heights - Brocade (Habitat).
March 15.
Sister to the very useful 1989 2-y-o 7f Somerville Tattersall Stakes winner and 1,000 gns 4th, Free at Last - subsequently winner of an 8.5f stakes event in the USA, and half-sister to the high class Breeders Cup Mile, Irish 2,000 gns and Queen Anne Stakes winner Barathea, the unraced 1994 2-y-o Bracco (both by Sadlers Wells) and the smart colt Zabar (by Dancing Brave), winner of the Prix du Chemin de Fer du Nord, the Prix du Muguet and the Prix Perth - all Group 3 8f races. The dam was a high class filly at up to 8f, winning five races including the Group 1 7f Prix de la Foret and the Group 3 7f Bisquit Cognac Challenge Stakes. She is a sister to the very useful 2-y-o Cause Celebre and a half-sister to 5 winners. 2nd dam, Canton Silk (by Runnymede), was a useful winner of 4 races over 5f. Not a very big filly from a family that needs time to come to hand, **National Treasure** will not be seen out until later this season. Arizelos, Acclimatise and Free at Last are three good examples of this Shirley Heights - Habitat cross. (Cheveley Park Stud).
Optimum 3-y-o distance: 8-10f.

310 - OPAL JEWEL
Bay filly. Sadlers Wells - Optimistic Lass (Mr Prospector).

February 9.
Half-sister to the 1995 3-y-o Joyful (by Green Desert), to the top class 1989 3-y-o filly Golden Opinion (by Slew O'Gold), winner of the Group 1 8f Coronation Stakes, Group 3 8f Prix du Rond-Point etc, and placed in the French 1,000 gns and July Cup, and to the minor 7f to 8.3f placed 3-y-o Webspinner (by Shadeed). The dam, a winner over 6f at 2 yrs, was a smart 3-y-o winner of the Group 2 10f Nassau Stakes and the Group 3 10.5f Musidora Stakes. 2nd dam, Loveliest (by Tibaldo), was a very useful winner at up to 10.5f in France and 9f in the USA and is a half-sister to the US Grade 1 winner Arbees Boy. (Sheikh Mohammed).
Optimum 3-y-o distance: 10f.

311 - PATRIA (USA)
Bay filly. Mr Prospector - Lypatia (Lyphard).
March 14. $275,000.
Sister to the Group 1 6f Middle Park Stakes winner and 2,000 gns, Irish 2,000 gns, July Cup, Prix Jacques le Marois and Prix du Moulin placed Lycius and to the useful 1994 2-y-o Group 3 Prix de Cabourg winner and Group 1 7f Moyglare Stud Stakes 2nd Tereshkova. Half-sister to the dual U.S. Grade 2 winner (over 9.5f and 12f), Akabir (by Riverman), the U.S. stakes winner Book Collector (by Irish River) and to minor winners by Irish River, Valdez and Temperance Hill. The dam, a minor 6.5f 3-y-o French and 8f 4-y-o American winner, is a half-sister to the Park Hill Stakes 3rd Lynwood Sovereign. 2nd dam, Hypatia (by High Hat), won over 8f at Warwick at 2 yrs. "A barely medium-sized filly out of a nice mare, **Patria** should make a useful 2-y-o," Michael tells me. (Hesmonds Stud).
Optimum 3-y-o distance: 8f.

312 - POSSESSIVE ARTISTE
Bay filly. Shareef Dancer - Possessive (Posse).
March 22. 5th foal.
Sister to the very smart 1991 Irish Oaks and Italian Oaks winner Possessive Dancer and half-sister to the promising 1994 2-y-o 6f winner (on only start), Desert Courier (by Green Desert) and the moderate 3-y-o dual 8f winner Possessive Lady (by Dara Monarch). The dam is an unraced half-sister to 10 winners including the smart miler Long Row and the Norfolk Stakes winner Colmore Row. 2nd dam, Front Row (by Epaulette), won the Irish 1,000 gns, as did her half-sister Black Satin. Michael tells me that **Possessive Artiste** is a smaller, more mature type than her half-brother Desert Courier and that she should be on the racecourse by mid-season. (Mrs D. Swinburn).
Optimum 3-y-o distance: 10-12f.

313 - RAHEEN (USA)
Bay colt. Danzig - Belle de Jour (Speak John).
March 18.
Brother to the fair 1991 2-y-o 6f winner and subsequent 3-y-o American winner Jode and to the minor American 3-y-o winner Bill Mooney, closely related to the U.S. stakes-placed winner Prancing Ballerina (by Nijinsky) and to the minor U.S. winner of 8 races Joined (by One For All), and half-brother to the American Kentucky Derby winner Spend a Buck (by Buckaroo), to five minor winners by Buckaroo (2), Far Out East, Giacometti and Raise a Cup and to the 1994 2-y-o Crown of Sheba (by Alysheba). The dam won 2 races over 6f at 3 yrs in the USA and is a half-sister to the U.S. stakes winner Savage Love. 2nd dam, Battle Dress (by Jaipur), won at 4 and 5 yrs in America and is a half-sister to the dam of the Graded stakes winners Groshawk and Sea Songster. Michael expressed slight doubts about **Raheen's** dam, as she hasn't bred anything much in the last few years and is rather old, but nevertheless he feels that this colt should be a decent 2-y-o and will be out around mid-season. (Mana Al-Maktoum).
Optimum 3-y-o distance: 7-8f.

314 - ROCKY OASIS (USA)
Bay colt. Gulch - Knoosh (Storm Bird).
April 17. 3rd foal.
Half-brother to the 1995 3-y-o Ranosh (by Rahy). The dam, a winner over 7f on her only start as a 2-y-o, was a very useful winner of three listed races at 3 yrs including the 12f Glorious Stakes at Goodwood and the 12f Galtres Stakes at York. 2nd dam, Fabulous Salt (by Le

Fabuleux), a fairly useful winner of the 8f Masaka Stakes and 3rd in the 10f Playboy Pretty Polly Stakes at 3 yrs, won in the USA at 4 yrs and is a half-sister to the 8f Senorita Stakes winner Ballare - herself dam of the U.S. stakes winner Balladry and the Group 3 Kiveton Park Stakes winner Gold Seam. **Rocky Oasis** isn't an early type, according to the trainer, but he looks like being a decent 2-y-o. (Maktoum Al-Maktoum).
Optimum 3-y-o distance: 8-10f.

315 - ROSSEL (USA)
Bay colt. Blushing John - Northern Aspen (Northern Dancer).
May 6.
The dam, winner of the Grade 1 9f Gamely Handicap in the USA and the Group 2 8f Prix d'Astarte in France, is closely related to the Group 1 Grand Prix de Paris winner Fort Wood, the Group 1 July Cup winner Hamas, the very smart Prix de Pomone winner Colorado Dancer and the fair 3-y-o 8f winner Sheroog and a half-sister to the 1994 Grade 1 Breeders Cup Juvenile winner Timber Country, the Goodwood Cup winner Mazzacano and the Prix d'Astarte winner Elle Seule - herself dam of the Irish 1,000gns winner Mehthaaf. 2nd dam, Fall Aspen (by Pretense), won 8 races including the Grade 1 7f Matron Stakes. **Rossel** is "a medium-sized colt, quite well-developed at this stage, but being a late foal will take until the middle of the season before ready to race." (Sheikh Mohammed).
Optimum 3-y-o distance: 10f.

316 - TIME ALLOWED
Bay filly. Sadlers Wells - Time Charter (Saritamer).
April 2. 5th live foal.
Half-sister to the very useful Group 3 12f Jockey Club Stakes winner and Group 3 St Simon Stakes 3rd Zinaad and to the useful 1988 2-y-o 7f winner and 3-y-o Cheshire Oaks 2nd By Charter (both by Shirley Heights). The dam was an exceptionally talented filly and winner of the Oaks, King George VI and Queen Elizabeth Diamond Stakes, Champion Stakes, Coronation Cup, Prix Foy and Sun Chariot Stakes. 2nd dam, Centrocon (by High Line), won 4 races including the Lancashire Oaks and is a sister to the high class horses Nicholas Bill and Centroline. Michael explained that this is not a family of big horses and that **Time Allowed** is in the same mould, as indeed is her half-brother Zinaad, both of them being quite light-framed individuals. Michael seemed pleased with **Time Allowed**, describing her as a nice, athletic filly. (Mr R. Barnett).
Optimum 3-y-o distance: 12f.

317 - TREASON
Bay filly. Polish Precedent - Talon d'Aiguille (Big Spruce).
March 19. 4th foal.
Half-sister to the promising 1994 2-y-o 6f winner Deceive (by Machiavellian) and the 3-y-o 8f winner Decant (by Rousillon). The dam, a winner at 3 yrs in France and 3rd in the Group 3 10.5f Prix de Flore, is a half-sister to the high class French filly Proskona and to the smart Prix Chloe winner Korveya - herself dam of the French 2,000 gns winners Hector Protector and Shanghai. 2nd dam, Konafa (by Damascus), a winner over 7f at 2 yrs and 2nd in the 1,000 gns, is a half-sister to the Yorkshire Oaks winner Awaasif - dam of the Oaks winner Snow Bride, to the high class American colt Akureyri and to the unraced Royal Stance - dam of the Group 3 winners Majuscule and Royal Cielo. (Cheveley Park Stud).
Optimum 3-y-o distance: 8f.

318 - TRUE JOY (IRE)
Chestnut filly. Zilzal - Foreign Courier (Sir Ivor).
June 2.
Closely related to the fairly useful 1992 2-y-o 5f winner Moumayaz (by Nureyev), and half-sister to the high class colt and sire Green Desert, a winner of 5 races from 5f to 7f including the Group 1 Norcros July Cup, the Vernons Sprint Cup, the European Free Handicap and the Flying Childers Stakes, to the useful 2-y-o 6f winner Kissogram Girl, the quite useful 2-y-o 6f winner Yousefia, the 1994 2-y-o 6f winner Blue Ocean (all four by Danzig) and the 5f winner Lillah Darak (by Shadeed). The dam is an unraced half-sister to 13 winners, notably the Grade 1 winners Althea (herself dam of the U.S. Grade 3 winner Destiny Dance), Ali Oop and Ketoh,

and the Grade 2 winners Aishah, Aquilegia and Twining. 2nd dam, Courtly Dee (Never Bend), won 4 races at up to 6f. (Maktoum Al-Maktoum).
Optimum 3-y-o distance: 6-7f.

319 - UNITUS (IRE)
Bay colt. Soviet Star - Unite (Kris).
May 12. 5th foal.
Closely related to the smart 1994 Group 2 10f Sun Chariot Stakes winner La Confederation (by Nureyev) and half-brother to the 1995 3-y-o Uniondale (by Sadlers Wells) and the fairly useful 1992 3-y-o 8f and 10f winner United Kingdom (by Danzig). The dam, a top class 3-y-o filly, won both the Epsom and Irish Oaks and was retired after breaking a blood vessel in the King George VI and Queen Elizabeth Diamond Stakes. Her career was woefully short, consisting as it did of just five races including a win in the 8f Insulpak Graduation Stakes at 3 yrs and a 2nd in the Blue Seal Stakes at 2 yrs. 2nd dam, Pro Patria (by Petingo), won over 5f and 6f at 2 yrs, is a half-sister to the smart miler Patris and is out of a half-sister to Lady Seymour (the dam of Marwell). Michael told me that **Unitus** is an attractive sort of horse that should be a useful 2-y-o. (Sheikh Mohammed).
Optimum 3-y-o distance: 10f.

320 - VAGUELY REGAL (USA)
Bay filly. Sadlers Wells - Reine Mathilde (Vaguely Noble).
March 24. 5th foal.
Sister to the 1995 3-y-o Empress Matilda and to the minor 1993 14f and 16.4f placed 3-y-o Menhaad, closely related to the French 3-y-o 8.5f winner Reine des Iles (by Nureyev) and half-sister to the minor 1994 dual 5-y-o winner Swordking (by Kris). The dam, a very smart filly, won 7 races in France and the USA including the 10f Prix de Malleret, the 9.2f Prix de l'Opera and the 10f E.P.Taylor Stakes - all Group/Grade 2 events, and is a half-sister to the U.S. stakes winner Shelter Half. 2nd dam, the high class Gay Matelda (by Sir Gaylord), won 9 races in the USA at up to 10f including five stakes events. (Cheveley Park Stud).
Optimum 3-y-o distance: 12f.

321 - WEE HOPE (USA)
Bay colt. Housebuster - Tell Me Sumthing (Summing).
May 20. 4th foal.
Half-brother to the promising 1994 2-y-o 7f winner Star of Zilzal (by Zilzal), to the minor American 4-y-o winner Sum Secret (by Devil's Bag) and to the 1994 German 8f listed placed 3-y-o Star Carnival (by Nashwan). The dam, a winner of 4 races at 3 and 4 yrs in the USA at up to 7f, is a half-sister to the champion 2-y-o and 3-y-o miler Green Forest, to the very smart French miler Green Paradise and to the very smart American filly Honest and True - herself dam of the Grade 1 Breeders Cup Juvenile Fillies winner Epitome. 2nd dam, Tell Meno Lies (by The Axe II), won 2 small races in the USA at 5f and 8f. Michael seems to like **Wee Hope**, calling him "a quite mature, fairly well-developed and tough little colt." (Maktoum Al-Maktoum).
Optimum 3-y-o distance: 8f.

Saeed Bin Suroor

322 - CORONATION GOLD (USA)
Bay colt. Mr Prospector - Lyphka (Lyphard).
April 20. 4th foal.
Brother to the French trained 3-y-o Copperbelt. The dam, winner of the 8f listed Prix des Lilas, is closely related to the top class miler Soviet Star and a half-sister to the Grade 1 10f Santa Barbara Handicap winner The Very One. 2nd dam, Veruschka (by Venture VII), won at around 8f in France at 3 yrs, was 2nd in the 8f Prix de la Calonne and won in the USA at 4 yrs. Like the high class miler Lycius, **Coronation Gold** is by Mr Prospector and out of a Lyphard mare. (Godolphin).
Optimum 3-y-o distance: 7-9f.

323 - FOREST HILLS
Bay filly. Woodman - Line Call (The Minstrel).
March 1. 4th foal.
Closely related to the 1992 Irish 2-y-o 10f winner Missaukee (by Miswaki) and half-sister to the 1995 3-y-o Wentworth (by Diesis) and the quite useful 1994 3-y-o 10.3f winner Line Out (by Private Account). The dam won over 8f in France at 3 yrs and is closely related to the useful York 3-y-o 10.4f winner King Athelstan. 2nd dam, Wimbledon Star (by Hoist the Flag), won 3 races in the USA including a minor stakes event and is a half-sister to Six Crowns (dam of the two Grade 1 winners Chief's Crown and Classic Crown) and to the unraced Nijinsky Star (dam of the stakes winner and Grade 1 2nd Hometown Queen). 3rd dam, Chris Evert (by Swoon's Son), a champion 3-y-o filly in the USA, is a half-sister to the dams of the Group/Graded stakes winners Beyton, Missed the Storm, Two Timing and Winning Colors. (Godolphin).
Optimum 3-y-o distance: 8-10f.

324 - MUDALLEL
Bay colt. Machiavellian - Sonic Lady (Nureyev).
May 26. 5th foal.
Half-brother to the 1995 3-y-o Soyuz (by Nashwan), to the very useful 1992 3-y-o colt Hazaam, winner of four races from 7-8f at 3 yrs including the Group 3 Supreme Stakes and to the very useful 1993 3-y-o Group 3 8f Prix de la Jonchere winner Sharman (both by Blushing Groom). The dam was a top class miler and won 8 races, notably the Irish 1,000 gns, Coronation Stakes, Sussex Stakes and Prix du Moulin - all Group 1 events. She was rated 4th in the International Classifications in front of the likes of Highest Honor, Sure Blade, Baiser Vole, Flash of Steel and Then Again. 2nd dam, Stumped (by Owen Anthony), was a smart winner of 4 races from 6-8f including the Child Stakes. (Godolphin).
Optimum 3-y-o distance: 8f.

325 - PHANTOM CREEK
Bay filly. Mr Prospector - Danseur Fabuleux (Northern Dancer).
February 1. 5th foal.
Sister to the fairly useful 1993 2-y-o Evry 8f winner Columbus Day, closely related to the French 2-y-o 7.5f winner Fortrose (by Forty Niner), and half-sister to the French 2-y-o 6f winner River Sunset (by Irish River) and the great 1991 2-y-o Arazi (by Blushing Groom), winner of the Breeders Cup Juvenile, Prix Robert Papin, Prix Morny, Prix de la Salamandre and Ciga Grand Criterium - all Group 1 events between 5f and 8.5f, and subsequently winner of the 8f Prix Omnium and 8f Prix du Rond-Point at 3 yrs. The dam was placed in the Group 3 12f Prix de Minerve and is closely related to the very useful 12f winner Fabulous Dancer. 2nd dam, Fabuleux Jane (by Le Fabuleux), won 4 races including the Group 3 Prix de Pomone and is a half-sister to Formidable and Ajdal. Ravinella and Rhythm are just two of the good horses bred on this Mr Prospector - Northern Dancer cross. (Godolphin).
Optimum 3-y-o distance: 8f.

326 - WALL STREET (USA)
Chestnut colt. Mr Prospector - Wajd (Northern Dancer).
February 20. 1st foal.
The dam, a very smart filly, won the Group 2 12f Grand Prix d'Evry and the Group 3 12f Prix de Minerve, is closely related to the Group 1 Prix Lupin, Grade 1 Century Handicap, Grade 1 San Juan Capistrano Invitational Handicap and San Luis Rey Stakes winner Dahar and to the Grade 2 Jersey Derby winner Llandaff (both by Lyphard), and a half-sister to the triple U.S. Grade 1 winner Rivlia (by Riverman), the Grade 1 winner Delegant (by Grey Dawn II) and the 1994 5-y-o Grade 1 Flower Bowl Handicap winner Dahlia's Dreamer (by Theatrical). 2nd dam, Dahlia (by Vaguely Noble), was a brilliant and tough mare. She won 15 races, notably the King George VI and Queen Elizabeth Stakes (twice), the Benson and Hedges Gold Cup (twice), the Irish Oaks, Grand Prix de Saint-Cloud, Prix Saint-Alary, Man O'War Stakes, Washington D.C. International, Hollywood Invitational Handicap and the Canadian International Championship. (Godolphin).
Optimum 3-y-o distance: 10f.

Harry Thomson-Jones

327 - ALFAHAAL (IRE)
Bay colt. Green Desert - Fair of the Furze (Ela Mana Mou).
February 10. 5th foal. 280,000 Ir gns.
Brother to the useful 1991 3-y-o Elfaslah, winner of 3 races from 10f to 10.4f including a listed race in Ireland, and half-brother to the top class Group 1 12f Italian Derby winner and King George VI and Queen Elizabeth Diamond Stakes 2nd White Muzzle (by Dancing Brave) and to the fair 1994 Irish 10f placed 3-y-o Penza (by Soviet Star). The dam, a very useful winner of the Group 2 10f Tattersalls Rogers Gold Cup, is a half-sister to the listed stakes winners Majestic Role (in Ireland), Norman Style (in Germany) and Proconsular (in France). 2nd dam, Autocratic (by Tyrant), won over 5f at 2 yrs in Ireland. (Hamdan Al-Maktoum).
Optimum 3-y-o distance: 10f.

328 - ASHJAR (USA).
Bay colt. Kris - Jathibiyah (Nureyev).
April 24. 2nd foal.
The dam was a fairly useful 2-y-o 7f winner, was placed from 7-10f at 3 yrs and is closely related to the Irish 1,000 gns and Nell Gwyn Stakes winner Ensconse. 2nd dam, Carefully Hidden (by Caro), won two minor 7f events at 3 yrs in the USA, and is a half-sister to Crown Treasure (dam of Glint of Gold and Diamond Shoal), Diomedia (dam of Media Starguest), Frontonian (dam of I Want to Be and grandam of Armiger) and the very useful Group 3 Princess Elizabeth Stakes winner Kanz. (Hamdan Al-Maktoum).
Optimum 3-y-o distance: 10f.

329 - BALSAM (IRE)
Chestnut filly. Kris - Zumurrudah (Spectacular Bid).
April 30. 5th foal.
Sister to the 1995 3-y-o Musrif, and closely related to the fair 1989 2-y-o 7f and 4-y-o 8f winner Mustahil, subsequently a winner over hurdles, and to the fair 1993 3-y-o 7f winner Qamoos (both by Sure Blade). The dam, a winner over 8f at 3 yrs, is a half-sister to the Group 1 12f Yorkshire Oaks and Group 1 12f Gran Premio del Jockey Club winner Awaasif (dam of the Oaks winner Snow Bride), to the high class American colt Akureyri, the 1,000 gns 2nd Konafa (dam of the smart French fillies Proskona and Korveya - the latter herself dam of the French 2,000 gns winners Hector Protector and Shanghai) and to the unraced dam of the Group 3 winners Majuscule and Royal Cielo. 2nd dam, Royal Statute (by Northern Dancer), a 2-y-o 5f winner, is a half-sister to the Canadian champion handicap horse Dance Act. (Hamdan Al-Maktoum). Optimum 3-y-o distance: 8-10f.

330 - MITHALI
Bay colt. Unfuwain - Al Bahathri (Blushing Groom).
May 1. 6th foal.
Closely related to the 1995 3-y-o Goalwah and the fair 1993 3-y-o 8f winner and 10f placed Alyakkh (both by Sadlers Wells) and half-brother to the very useful 1991 Irish 3-y-o 8f listed stakes winner and Group 1 Coronation Stakes 2nd Hasbah (by Kris). The dam was a high class winner of 6 races from 6-8f, notably the Irish 1,000 gns, Coronation Stakes, Child Stakes and Lowther Stakes. She is a half-sister to Geraldine's Store, an American stakes-winning filly at up to 10f, and to the Cheshire Oaks winner Peplum. 2nd dam, Chain Store (by Nodouble), won 8 races including a 9f stakes event. (Hamdan Al-Maktoum).
Optimum 3-y-o distance: 8-10f.

Peter Walwyn

331 - AZWAH (USA)
Bay or brown filly. Danzig - Magic Slipper (Habitat).
Aprol 19. 6th foal.
Closely related to the useful 1994 2-y-o 6f and 7f winner Muhab (by Lyphard), to the fair winner

of 4 races at around 7f, Wali (by Lomond) and to the quite useful 1992 3-y-o 7f winner Ahbab (by Ajdal). The dam, a useful 10f and 11.5f winner, is a half-sister to the 1,000 gns winner Fairy Footsteps and to the St Leger winner Light Cavalry. 2nd dam, Glass Slipper (by Relko), a useful 13.3f winner at 3 yrs and 2nd in the Musidora Stakes, is a half-sister to Royal Palace. **Azwah** is bred on similar lines to the Middle Park and Challenge Stakes winner Zieten - being by Danzig and out of a Habitat mare. (Hamdan Al-Maktoum).
Optimum 3-y-o distance: 7-8f.

Bill Watts

332 - AMUSING ASIDE (IRE)
Chestnut filly. In the Wings - Most Amusing (Blushing Groom).
March 14. 2nd foal.
Closely related to the 1995 3-y-o Lorelei Lee (by Old Vic). The dam is an unraced half-sister to the top class American 2-y-o colt and useful sire Saratoga Six, winner of the Grade 1 8f Del Mar Futurity Stakes, and to the high class 2-y-o colt Dunbeath, winner of the Group 1 William Hill Futurity Stakes and the Group 2 Royal Lodge Stakes. 2nd dam, Priceless Fame (by Irish Castle), won twice over sprint distances and is a sister to the Kentucky Derby and Belmont Stakes winner Bold Forbes. (Sheikh Mohammed).
Optimum 3-y-o distance: 10-12f.

Dermot Weld

333 - CAER MELYN
Bay filly. Caerleon - Marwell (Habitat).
April 30.
Sister to the good 5-8f colt Caerwent, winner of 4 races and placed in the Prix de l'Abbaye, Irish 2,000 gns, St James's Palace Stakes and Vernons Sprint Cup, closely related to the 1994 6f placed 2-y-o Otterbourne (by Royal Academy) and half-sister to the high class filly, Marling (by Lomond), winner of 7 races from 5-8f notably the Cheveley Park Stakes, Irish 1,000 gns, Coronation Stakes and Sussex Stakes - all Group 1 events, and to the useful 1990 3-y-o 8f winner Selaah (by Rainbow Quest). The dam, like her daughter Marling, was a champion filly, and an even better one, winning 10 races, notably the July Cup, Prix de l'Abbaye, Kings Stand Stakes and Cheveley Park Stakes. 2nd dam, Lady Seymour (by Tudor Melody), won the 5f Phoenix Stakes and has bred numerous other winners including Lord Seymour (Mill Reef Stakes). (Mr. E. Loder).
Optimum 3-y-o distance: 6-8f.

334 - DANCE DESIGN
Bay filly. Sadlers Wells - Elegance in Design (Habitat).
February 18. 2nd foal.
The dam was a useful Irish winner over 6f at 2 yrs and a listed 6f event at 3 yrs and is a sister to the high class Coronation Stakes winner Chalon - dam of the Prix Ganay and Prix d'Ispahan winner Creator - and a half-sister to the good Irish 8-10f winner Executive Perk and the useful 12f winner Costly Lesson. 2nd dam, Areola (Kythnos), won the 5f Phoenix Stakes, was a very useful 2-y-o and was inbred 3x3 to Nasrullah. **Dance Design,** being by Sadlers Wells and out of a Habitat mare, is bred on the same lines as Barathea, Batshoof and Alnasr Alwasheek. (Moyglare Stud Farm).
Optimum 3-y-o distance: 8-10f.

335 - DIALI (USA)
Bay filly. Dayjur - Past Example (Buckpasser).
June 3. $200,000.
Closely related to the top class miler Polish Precedent (by Danzig), winner of the Group 1 8f Prix Jacques le Marois and the Group 1 8f Prix Moulin and half-sister to the U.S. stakes winner, over an extended 8f, Jasmina (by Forli). The dam is an unraced half-sister to the dams of the

Group/Grade 1 winners Zilzal, Awe Inspiring and Culture Vulture. 2nd dam, Bold Example (by Bold Lad, USA), won 3 races and was stakes-placed at up to 7f and is a half-sister to In Hot Pursuit (dam of Posse), Discipline (dam of the Grade 1 winner Squander and the Grade 2 winner Duty Dance) and to Uncommitted (dam of the Grade 1 winner Wavering Monarch). (Hamdan Al-Maktoum).
Optimum 3-y-o distance: 7-8f.

336 - EASY DEFINITION
Brown colt. Alzao - Easy to Copy (Affirmed).
February 4. 5th foal.
Half-brother to the 1992 Irish 3-y-o 8f winner Clear Procedure (by The Minstrel). The dam was a useful winner of 5 races from 8-12f in Ireland and Italy including the Group 2 Premio Legnano and subsequently performed well in Graded stakes company in America. She is a sister to the Irish 1,000 gns winner Trusted Partner, the useful Irish listed 2-y-o 6f winner Low Key Affair and the useful 7f and 9f winner Epicure's Garden. 2nd dam, Talking Picture (by Speak John), the champion American filly of 1973, won at up to 7f. (Moyglare Stud Farm).
Optimum 3-y-o distance: 10f.

337 - FLAMING FEATHER
Bay colt. Shirley Heights - Forest Flower (Green Forest).
March 31. 4th foal.
Brother to the quite useful gelding Hill of Dreams, a winner of 4 races from 11.8f to 14f, and closely related to the 1995 3-y-o Eastwood Hall (by Reference Point). The dam was a high class winner of the Irish 1,000 gns, Mill Reef Stakes, Queen Mary Stakes and Cherry Hinton Stakes. 2nd dam, Leap Lively (by Nijinsky), was a smart filly herself and won 3 races including the Hoover Fillies Mile and the Lingfield Oaks Trial and was 3rd in the Oaks behind Blue Wind. (Mrs B. Maxwell Moran).
Optimum 3-y-o distance: 12f.

338 - HAMAD
Bay colt. Sadlers Wells - Dead Certain (Absalom).
March 1. 2nd foal.
Half-brother to the unplaced 1994 2-y-o Full Cover (by Thatching). The dam was a very smart filly and winner of the Group 1 6f Cheveley Park Stakes, the Queen Mary Stakes and the Lowther Stakes at 2 yrs, and the Group 2 6.5f Prix Maurice de Gheest as a three-year-old when she was was also 2nd in the Cork and Orrery Stakes but was very disappointing for the rest of the season. Dead Certain is a half-sister to 6 winners, including the fairly useful 10f handicapper Fire Top, out of the French 8-10f winner Sirnelta (by Sir Tor) - herself a daughter of a half-sister to the French Derby winner Sanctus II. (Saleh Y Al Homaizi).
Optimum 3-y-o distance: 6-9f.

339 - IN GENEROSITY
Bay filly. Generous - Aptostar (Fappiano).
March 24. 3rd foal.
Half-sister to the fairly useful 1994 Irish 3-y-o 12f and 14f winner In Anticipation (by Sadlers Wells). The dam won 6 races, notably the Grade 1 8f Acorn Stakes and the Grade 2 8f Bed O'Roses Handicap, is a sister to 2 winners including the fair 3-y-o 8.5f winner Mutakallam and a half-sister to the Grade 3 winner Man Alright. 2nd dam, Stark Drama (by Graustark), won 3 races at up to 10f, was 2nd in the Grade 3 Comely Stakes and is a half-sister to the Grade 1 2nd Damascus Drama. (Moyglare Stud Farm).
Optimum 3-y-o distance: 8-10f.

340 - MOVIE LEGEND
Bay filly. Affirmed - Talking Picture (Speak John).
Sister to the very useful Irish 1,000 gns winner Trusted Partner, to the useful Irish 8f and 12f winner Easy to Copy, the useful Irish 7f and 9f winner Epicure's Garden and the 2-y-o 6f winner and Group 1 Moyglare Stud Stakes 3rd Low Key Affair - all three at least useful - and half-sister to the 1988 Irish 2-y-o winner Seperate Issue (by Saratoga Six) and to three minor winners in the USA by Hoist the Flag (2) and Sir Ivor. The dam, champion American 2-y-o filly of 1973,

won at up to 7f. 2nd dam, Poster Girl (by Nasrullah), was unraced but also bred the Native Dancer Handicap winner Illustrious. (Moyglare Stud Farm).
Optimum 3-y-o distance: 10f.

341 - NIGHT SPELL (IRE)
Bay filly. Fairy King - Moonsilk (Solinus).
March 23. 130,000 Ir gns.
Closely related to the minor 8f (at 2 yrs) and 10f winner Ilkomo (by Glenstal) and to the 1995 3-y-o Nordic Spree (by Nordico) and half-sister to the very smart 1994 Group 1 14.6f St Leger and Group 1 15.5f Prix Royal-Oak winner Moonax (by Caerleon) and to the dual Italian 3-y-o winner Wassilk (by Wassl). The dam was placed over 9f in France and is a half-sister to the 1,000 gns winner Nocturnal Spree and the Prix Saint-Alary winner Tootens (herself grandam of the useful 1994 2-y-o filly Jural). 2nd dam, Night Attire (by Shantung), was an unplaced sister to the smart middle distance filly Setsu - herself dam of the Group 2 Premio Melton winner Tres Gate. (Mr Michael Tabor).
Optimum 3-y-o distance: 8-10f.

342 - TOUCH JUDGE (USA)
Bay colt. Nijinsky - Hush Dear (Silent Screen).
January 18. $300,000.
Closely related to the minor American 2-y-o winner of 2 races Dear Birdie (by Storm Bird) and to the minor Australian winner Danzig Corridor (by Danzig), and half-brother to the American 2-y-o stakes winner Noactor (by Theatrical) and the Japanese 3-y-o winner Triple Cast (by Private Account). The dam won 11 races including the 12f Long Island Handicap, the 11f Tidal Handicap and the 9f Diana Handicap (twice) - all Grade 2 events on the turf. She is a half-sister to a stakes winner and to the dam of the Middle Park Stakes 2nd Silvino. 2nd dam, You All (by Nashua), won 4 races including a stakes event. (Michael Watt).
Optimum 3-y-o distance: 10-12f.

343 - TRUST IN LUCK
Chestnut filly. Nashwan - Trusted Partner (Affirmed).
May 8. 4th foal.
Half-sister to the 1995 3-y-o Archive Footage (by Sadlers Wells) and to the 1993 Irish 3-y-o 9f winner Brave Raider (by Dixieland Band). The dam, a very useful filly, won both her 2-y-o races including the Group 3 7f C.L.Weld Park Stakes and next season won the Irish 1,000 gns and was 2nd in the Mount Coote Matron Stakes at the Curragh. She is a sister to the useful middle distance performers Easy to Copy and Epicure's Garden and to the useful 1993 2-y-o Low Key Affair. 2nd dam, Talking Picture (by Speak John), was the top American 2-y-o filly of 1973 and won at up to 7f. (Moyglare Stud Farm).
Optimum 3-y-o distance: 8-10f.

Ernie Weymes

344 - WEDGEWOOD (USA)
Chestnut filly. Woodman - Woodstream (Northern Dancer).
April 29.
Half-sister to the 1995 3-y-o Royal Canal, the 1993 Irish 2-y-o 7f winner Crystal Lake (both by Shirley Heights), the Irish 2-y-o 6f winners Seattle Centre and Tributary (both by Seattle Slew) and the minor Irish 4-y-o and dual hurdles winner Head of Chambers (by Alleged). The dam, a very useful filly, won the Group 1 6f Cheveley Park Stakes and the Group 1 6f Moyglare Stud Stakes, was 2nd in the Irish 2,000 gns and is a half-sister to the Irish 2,000gns and Sussex Stakes winner Jaazeiro. 2nd dam, Rule Formi (Forli), though unraced, bred 4 other useful winners. (Mr. G. Middlebrook).
Optimum 3-y-o distance: 8f.

John Wharton

345 - KOTA
Bay colt. Kris - Lady Be Mine (Sir Ivor).
April 25.
Half-brother to the champion 2-y-o of 1989, Be My Chief, winner of the Group 1 8f Racing Post Trophy, the Imry Solario Stakes and the Lanson Champagne Stakes etc., to the fair 2-y-o 5f winner Run Little Lady (by J.O.Tobin) and the fair 3-y-o 8f winner Albemine (by Al Nasr). The dam, a minor 3-y-o 8f winner at Yarmouth, is a half-sister to Mixed Applause, herself dam of the high class miler Shavian and the Gold Cup winner Paean. 2nd dam, My Advantage (by Princely Gift), won over 5f at 2 yrs and is a half-sister to the dam of Marwell. (Mr. P. W. Lambert).
Optimum 3-y-o distance: 8-10f.

Stuart Williams

346 - CLASSIC COLOURS (USA)
Chestnut colt. Blushing John - All Agleam (Gleaming).
April 12.
Half-brother to the French 3-y-o Sweet Gleam (by Easy Goer), to the very smart Group 2 8f Child Stakes winner and Coronation Stakes 2nd Magic Gleam (by Danzig), to the South African Group 1 winner Flying Snowdrop (by Soy Numero Uno) and to 2 minor winners by Full Out. The dam is an unraced half-sister to the top class American filly Davona Dale - winner of five Grade 1 events and herself dam of the Belmont Stakes 3rd Le Voyageur. 2nd dam, Regal Entrance (by Tim Tam), won 7 minor races in the USA and is a half-sister to the dam of the Preakness Stakes winner Gate Dancer. (Classic Bloodstock Plc).
Optimum 3-y-o distance: 10f.

347 - CLASSIC JENNY (IRE)
Bay filly. Green Desert - Eileen Jenny (Kris).
February 20. 1st foal.
The dam was a very useful winner at 3 yrs of a 12f listed event in Milan and a 12f Curragh maiden and was 3rd in the Irish Oaks. She is a half-sister to the 3-y-o 12f listed stakes winner Kasmayo, the Lingfield Oaks Trial winner Bahamian (dam of the high class filly Wemyss Bight), the Irish miler Captivator, the Irish 7f winner Klarifi and the middle-distance stayer West China - all at least useful. 2nd dam, Sorbus (by Busted), was disqualified after winning the Irish Oaks and was 2nd in the Irish 1,000 gns, Irish St Leger and Yorkshire Oaks. (Classic Bloodstock Plc).
Optimum 3-y-o distance: 10f.

348 - CLASSIC VINTAGE (USA)
Bay colt. Lear Fan - Reve de Reine (Lyphard).
May 17.
Brother to the fairly useful French 8f winner and Group 3 placed Rose de Thai and half-brother to the French 2-y-o dual 8f winner and 3-y-o Group 3 9.2f Prix de Guiche winner Roi de Rome (by Time For a Change), the minor French and American winner Venetian Red (by Blushing Groom) and the 1995 3-y-o Cas Royaux (by Woodman). The dam won 3 races from 8.5f to 9.2f in France including the listed Grand Prix du Nord and is a half-sister to the very useful Riviere Doree. 2nd dam, Riverqueen (by Luthier), won the 1976 French 1,000 gns and the Grand Prix de Saint-Cloud and is a half-sister to the good French winners River King and River River, and to the dams of the French Group winners Malakim and Rachmaninov. (Classic Bloodstock Plc).
Optimum 3-y-o distance: 8-10f.

Geoff Wragg

349 - CHARLOTTE CORDAY
Bay filly. Kris - Dancing Rocks (Green Dancer).
March 9.
Sister to the very useful Gai Bulga, winner of three races over 10f at 3 yrs, and half-sister to the very useful 1993 2-y-o Group 3 7f Prestige Stakes winner Glatisant (by Rainbow Quest), the fairly useful 3-y-o 8f winner Gale Yaka (by Habitat) and the fair Lingfield (all-weather) 3-y-o 12f winner Pippa's Song (by Reference Point). The dam was a good filly, winning over 5f and 6f at 2 yrs and the Group 2 10f Nassau Stakes at 3 yrs, and is a half-sister to the very useful 7f winner Cragador. 2nd dam, Croda Rossa (by Grey Sovereign), won 3 races including the 10f Premio Lydia Tesio and is a half-sister to the Italian Derby winner Cerreto. The very smart filly Divine Danse is, like this filly, by Kris and out of a Green Dancer mare. (Sir Philip Oppenheimer). Optimum 3-y-o distance: 10f.

350 - QUESTING STAR
Chestnut filly. Rainbow Quest - Guest Artiste (Be My Guest).
April 20. 3rd foal.
Half-sister to the 1995 3-y-o St Rhadegund (by Shirley Heights). The dam, a very useful 3-y-o 8f winner, was placed in the Coronation, Child and Nell Gwyn Stakes and is a half-sister to the Child Stakes winner Inchmurrin, herself dam of the smart 7f colt Inchinor, and to the Mill Reef Stakes winner Welney. 2nd dam, On Show (by Welsh Pageant), was a fairly useful 3-y-o 10f winner and was 2nd in the 12f November Handicap. (Sir Philip Oppenheimer).
Optimum 3-y-o distance: 8-10f.

351 - SASURA
Bay colt. Most Welcome - Sassalya (Sassafras).
May 4.
Brother to the quite useful 1993 2-y-o 6f winner Tzu'mu and half-brother to the fairly useful 1994 2-y-o dual 7f winner Baltic Raider (by Polish Precedent), the high class 7f Jersey Stakes and Challenge Stakes winner Sally Rous (by Rousillon), the Welsh Derby winner Assemblyman (by General Assembly), the 7f and 7.5f winner Bold Indian (by Bold Lad, Ire), the 12f winner Chauve Souris (by Beldale Flutter) - all very useful, the useful Schweppes Golden Mile Handicap winner Little Bean (by Ajdal), the 3-y-o dual 7f winner Etosha (by Green Desert) and the 3-y-o 10.4f winner Krisalya (by Kris) - both fairly useful. The dam won over 10f in Ireland and is a half-sister to the smart colts Beau Sham and Lafontaine. 2nd dam, Valya (by Vandale), won 3 races including the 13.5f Prix de Pomone. (Sir Philip Oppenheimer).
Optimum 3-y-o distance: 10f.

352 - STAR AND GARTER
Chestnut filly. Soviet Star - On Show (Welsh Pageant).
April 24.
Half-sister to the 1995 3-y-o Wild Rice (by Green Desert), to the very useful filly Inchmurrin, winner of 6 races including the Group 2 6f Child Stakes and herself dam of the very smart colt Inchinor, to the fair 1993 3-y-o 8f winner Balnaha (both by Lomond), the very useful 1989 3-y-o dual 8f winner Guest Artiste, the quite useful 1991 dual 2-y-o 8f winner Waterfowl Crest (both by Be My Guest), the very useful Group 2 6f Mill Reef Stakes winner Welney (by Habitat), and the fair 1991 3-y-o 7f winner Sohrab (by Shernazar). The dam, a fairly useful 3-y-o 10f winner, is out of the Park Hill Stakes winner African Dancer (by Nijinsky). (Sir Philip Oppenheimer).
Optimum 3-y-o distance: 8f.

353 - TASSILI (IRE)
Bay colt. Old Vic - Topsy (Habitat).
February 17.
Half-brother to the top class middle distance colt Most Welcome, winner of the Lockinge Stakes and the Select Stakes and placed in the Champion Stakes, Epsom Derby, Sussex Stakes, Turf Classic and Breeders Cup Mile, the useful 3-y-o 10-12f winner Top Guest (both by Be My Guest), the useful 3-y-o 11.5-16f winner and Lancashire Oaks 3rd Bourbon Topsy (by Ile de

Bourbon) the fair 1993 2-y-o 6f winner and 3-y-o 10f placed Tansy (by Shareef Dancer)and to 2 minor winners by Ile de Bourbon and Troy. The dam was a very smart winner of the Sun Chariot Stakes, Prix d'Astarte and Fred Darling Stakes, and is a half-sister to the Derby winner Teenoso. 2nd dam, Furioso (by Ballymoss), won over 10f and was 2nd in the Oaks and is a half-sister to the dams of Amaranda, Ashayer, Braiswick, Favoridge, Give Thanks, Old Country and Percy's Girl. (Sheikh Mohammed).
Optimum 3-y-o distance: 12f.

Note: A last minute addition:
*   **307 - KING'S FLAME - has died**

100 TO FOLLOW THIS SEASON

An exciting addition to the book this year is this section on two-year-olds housed with those trainers noted for producing fast, early sorts. The horses have been chosen, in the main, because of their relatively early foaling dates, for the noted ability of their sires in producing juvenile winners - the exceptions being promising first season sires - and, most important of all, because of suggestions from the trainers themselves.

I say "in the main" with regard to early foaling dates because, where a trainer was particularly bullish about a late foal's ability, I have still included him in what is primarily a section devoted to fast two-year-olds. Incidentally, the percentage of winners to runners given with each trainer refers only to runners in Britain.

ROBERT ARMSTRONG

Although the filly below isn't as well bred as Robert's two representatives in the book's premier section, he urged me to mention her. **Mujtahida** is a very attractive filly with presence and a great action. We can expect her to be ready for mid-May and she should be his earliest 2-y-o filly. 13% of Robert's 2-y-o runners won last year - disappointing considering his excellent previous year's total of 23%.

MUJTAHIDA
Bay filly. Mujtahid - Domino's Nurse (Dom Racine).
April 29. 5th foal. 45,000 gns.
Half-sister to Archi Moore, a winner of 5 races in Italy, to the quite useful 1994 2-y-o 5f and 7f winner Romios (both by Common Grounds) and to the Irish 3-y-o 10f winner Domino's Ring (by Auction Ring). The dam won 3 races including a listed event in Ireland and was placed in the Nassau Stakes and the Meld Stakes. She is a half-sister to 8 winners out of the minor 3-y-o winner Pall Nan (by Pall Mall), herself a half-sister to the dam of the smart miler Last Fandango.

ALAN BAILEY

Tarporley based Alan Bailey will be hoping to improve upon his 1994 statistics of 10% 2-y-o winners to runners and punters should take note that he hasn't had a first time out 2-y-o winner in the last two seasons. However, Alan feels he has at least two 2-y-o's with good prospects of winning this term. **Braes 'o' Shieldhill** is a filly that he was keen for me to mention, as she is working very well and is expected to win races. Alan feels she'll be ready to race in May, possibly at the Chester meeting. The gelding **Crabbies Pride**, a full brother to 5 winners, is also a nice sort. Owned by a syndicate from the Turks Head public house in St Helens (apparently he is named after a recently deceased local character), Alan says they can certainly expect the gelding to win races for them.

BRAES 'O' SHIELDHILL
Chestnut filly. Music Maestro - Dalchroy (Hotfoot).
March 7. 5,000 gns. (Doncaster St Leger).
Sister to the minor 1989 3-y-o 7f, 7.5f and 8f winner Asithappens and half-sister to 3 minor winners, namely the 1989 2-y-o 5f winner Ermo Express (by Bay Express) - subsequently a winner of 11 races in Italy, the 1993 3-y-o dual 7f winner Fuchu and the hurdles winner Curtain Factory (both by Jupiter Island). The dam only ran at 2 yrs and was never placed. She is a half-

sister to 4 winners including the Lincoln Handicap winner Quizair. 2nd dam, Amber Breeze (by Arctic Storm), won as a 2-y-o and is a half-sister to 7 winners.

CRABBIES PRIDE (IRE)
Chestnut gelding. Red Sunset - Free Rein (Sagaro).
April 10. 11,500 gns (Doncaster 2-y-o's in Training Sales).
Brother to six winners (the dams first six foals), namely the quite useful 1994 2-y-o 7f winner Chance Bid, the fair 3-y-o 10f winner Ice Magic, the fair 3-y-o 8f and 8.2f winner Sunset Reins Free, the moderate 1993 2-y-o 5f winner Hiltons Travel, the modest 3-y-o 7f and 4-y-o 8f winner Perdition and the modest La Reine Rouge - a winner of three 12f events on the all-weather. The dam is an unraced half sister to one winner on the flat and another over hurdles. 2nd dam, Silk Rein (by Shantung), won at 3 yrs and is a half-sister to the outstanding colt Troy, winner of the Derby, the King George, the Irish Derby etc., and to the Prince of Wales's Stakes winner Admetus. (Turks Head Racing Club).

MICHAEL BELL

The Fitzroy House 2-y-o's did exceptionally well last year with no less than 19% winners to runners. This year Michael has helped me single out eight very promising young horses with two more back end 2-y-o's in the premier section of this book, devoted to the very best bred horses in training. His early colts will include **Dankeston** - "as sharp as a dart, has plenty of speed on his dam's side and looks a nice colt," **Hoh Returns** - "a strong, ready made 2-y-o with good quarters and a good engine. Has everything you could want in a 2-y-o," **Princely Sound** - "a very nice, sharp 2-y-o" and **Snow Falcon** - "a nice type and a very good mover." Among his fillies, **Flash in the Pan** "has plenty of speed and will require 5f on good ground," **Paloma Bay** is "a nice, scopey filly that will need 7f" and **Rose of Siberia** "has got speed, will make a 2-y-o and is a nice, long-striding filly. She will make her debut at 6f." Finally, mid-summer should see the emergence of a useful colt in **Hamlet**. Michael describes him as "a giraffe to look at, but is very well balanced and seems sure to make up into a very nice 2-y-o indeed."

DANKESTON (USA)
Bay colt. Elmaamul - Last Request (Dancer's Image).
February 25. 37,000 Ir gns (Goffs).
Half-brother to the fairly useful dual 7f winner Mawsuff - subsequently a winner of 5 races in America and Grade 2 placed, to the fair 2-y-o 8f winner Arz (both by Known Fact), the fairly useful 9-10f winner Wishiah (by Persian Bold), the minor 2-y-o 6f winner Al Mawoud (by Doulab) and the Scandinavian 5-time winner Alrazzi (by Shirley Heights) - previously placed over 2 miles here. The dam a fairly useful 10f winner at 2 yrs, is a half-sister to the dam of the French Group winners Lou Piquet and Chamisene. 2nd dam, Torrefranca (by Sicambre), won twice in France and was a half-sister to the Sussex Stakes winner Carlemont and the good broodmares Cambrienne (dam of Critique) and Princesse Tora (dam of the Group 3 winner Boreale and grandam of the Prix de la Salamandre winner Princesse Lida). (Mr L. Gaucci).

FLASH IN THE PAN (IRE)
Chestnut filly. Bluebird - Tomona (Linacre).
March 12. 22,000 Ir gns (Goffs).
Half-sister to the useful 2-y-o 7f winner Full of Pluck (by Try My Best) and the Irish 3-y-o 10f winner Hegemonic (by Godswalk). The dam won from 11-12f and over hurdles in Ireland. 2nd dam, Strokestown Girl (by Henry Higgins), won as a 2-y-o in Ireland, was placed in the listed Marble Hill Stakes and is a half-sister to the Group 2 placed Beggar's Bridge. (Mr P. A. Phillips).

HAMLET (IRE)
Bay colt. Danehill - Blasted Heath (Thatching).
April 3. 3rd foal. 28,000 gns - failed to reach reserve - (Newmarket Highflyer).
Half-brother to the 1993 Irish 2-y-o 5f winner Wave the Wand (by Fairy King). The dam was a useful Irish winner of a 5f listed event at 2 yrs and an 8f listed race at 3 yrs. She is a half-sister

to the 2-y-o Group 1 6f Middle Park Stakes winner Balla Cove, to the minor U.S. stakes winner Burning Issue and the Irish listed Silver Flash Stakes winner Tribal Rite. 2nd dam, Coven (by Sassafras), won 4 races at 3 yrs in Ireland from 6-10f and is a half-sister to 4 winners including the French listed stakes winner Interdit and the dam of the Dee Stakes winner Cicerao. (Mrs M. B. Hawtin).

HOH RETURNS (IRE)
Bay colt. Fairy King - Cipriani (Habitat).
March 14. 3rd foal. 72,000 gns (Newmarket Houghton).
Half-sister to the 1995 3-y-o Cyphell (by Sadlers Wells). The dam won at 2 yrs and the listed 7f Ballycorus Stakes at 4 yrs in Ireland and is a half-sister to 5 minor winners. 2nd dam, La Mer (by Copenhagen), was a champion 2-y-o filly and 3-y-o filly in New Zealand and won a total of 24 races in Australia and New Zealand including 3 Grade 1 events. (Mr. D. F. Allport).

PALOMA BAY (IRE)
Bay filly. Alzao - Adventurine (Thatching).
April 6. 4th foal. 36,000 gns (Newmarket Highflyer).
Half-sister to the minor 1994 6f and 9.4f placed 2-y-o Sandra Dee (By Be My Guest) and to Cliff Edge (by Diesis), placed in 2 minor races in Ireland at 2 and 3 yrs. The dam won 3 races over sprint distances at 2 and 3 yrs in Ireland, is a sister to the Group 3 6f Greenlands Stakes winner Rustic Amber and a half-sister to Mushref, a winner of 4 races here and in the USA. 2nd dam, Forever Amber (by Bold Lad, Ire), won once as a 3-y-o and is a half-sister to the Lancashire Oaks winner Istiea out of the Irish Oaks winner Ambergris. (Mr. T. Harris).

PRINCELY SOUND
Bay colt. Prince Sabo - Sound of the Sea (Windjammer).
April 12. 5th foal. 32,000 gns (Newmarket October).
Half-brother to the fair 1994 2-y-o dual 5f winner Endless Wave (by Indian Ridge) and to the Irish 2-y-o 5f and 6f winner and listed placed Cu Na Mara (by Never So Bold). The dam was a fairly useful winner of 6 races at up to 7f from 2 to 5 yrs and is a half-sister to 7 minor winners. 2nd dam, Running Cedar (by Bryan G), won twice in the USA and is a half-sister to the dams of the U.S. Grade 3 winners Slip Screen and Bemis Heights - herself dam of Grade 1 winner Bemissed and thus grandam of the Oaks winner Jet Ski Lady. (Mr. G. Byrne).

ROSE OF SIBERIA (USA)
Grey filly. Siberian Express - Exuberine (Be My Guest).
April 3. 42,000 gns (Newmarket Highflyer).
Sister to the useful filly Ancestral Dancer, a winner from 5f to 7.5f at 2 yrs and of the Italian 1,000 gns at 3 yrs and half-sister to the fairly useful Italian listed 2-y-o 7.5f winner Michelle Hicks (by Ballad Rock) and the minor 12f+ winners Classy Trick (by Head For Heights) and Pharoah's Guest (by Pharly). The dam was quite useful and won over 8f at 3 yrs. She is a half-sister to 4 winners out of the minor French 2 mile winner Exuberance (by Val de Loir). (Mrs J. M. Corbett).

SNOW FALCON
Bay colt. Polar Falcon - Cameroun (African Sky).
February 14. 6th foal to live. 19,000 gns (Newmarket Highflyer).
Half-brother to the fair Black Mischief (by Salse), placed on both her outings - over 7f at 2 yrs and 8f at 3 yrs - and to the minor 7f to 8.5f winner Eternal Flame (by Primo Dominie). The dam, a useful filly, won 3 races at 2 yrs including the listed 5f Goffs Silver Flash Stakes and was placed in the Cheveley Park Stakes and the Queen Mary Stakes. She is a half-sister to 4 winners out of the unplaced Texly (by Lyphard). (Mrs. G. Rowland - Clark).

JACK BERRY

Choosing 2-y-o winners from Jack Berry's Moss Side Stables can't be too difficult, one might imagine, as his acumen for training juvenile winners is legendary - (an excellent average of 14%

winners to runners in the past two years). With Jack's invaluable assistance however, I have narrowed the list down somewhat and all the 2-y-o's mentioned here should visit the winners enclosure this season. First of all, the colts Jack was particularly concerned to point out to me are **Playmaker** (quite possibly a Royal Ascot type), the Godolphin owned colts **Larghetto, Lilburne** and **West Austria** (all working very well) and **Kuwam** (a lovely horse in the making). The best of his fillies may well be **My Melody Parkes** (Jack hopes she'll make the Queen Mary Stakes at Royal Ascot and the injection of stamina via her sire Teenoso may be for the better as her half-sister, the useful Lucky Parkes, barely gets 5f). Other good ones to note are **Il Doria** (a good sort from a family Jack knows well and owned by the England footballer David Platt), **Gwespyr** (benefitted from his run in the Brocklesby and won next time out) and **Limerick Princess** (a nice filly by Polish Patriot and a half-sister to a listed winner trained by Jack last year, Limerick Belle). Some colts not to miss are **Jack's Treat** (a lovely horse with plenty of scope for further improvement as the season goes on), **Miletrian City** (really nice, goes well and is an early sort), **Pekay** (a lovely, sharp type) and **Albert the Bear** (a lovely, placid colt that will win races). Finally, three others that aren't quite as good but will win their share of races are **Laurel Crown** (owned by the same syndicate that own the prolific winner Laurel Queen who has just produced a foal by Selkirk for them), **Distinctly Red** and **Noble Colours.** Jack is particularly keen to see the latter two in the winner's enclosure as they are both by the sire Distinctly North, a good horse he trained to win the Flying Childers Stakes in 1990. Jack explained that all the foals of Distinctly North he'd seen appeared to have lovely temperaments and he is very keen for the sire to do well.

ALBERT THE BEAR
Bay colt. Puissance - Florentynna Bay (Aragon).
March 7. 4th foal. 21,000 gns (Doncaster St Leger).
Half-brother to the minor 1994 7f and 8.5f (all-weather) placed 3-y-o Supercool (by Superlative) and to the 1994 2-y-o Charnwood Queen (by Cadeaux Genereux) - unplaced on both her outings. The dam, a fair 2-y-o 5f winner, is a half-sister to 3 winners including the very useful 1988 2-y-o Superpower - winner of 7 races at 2 yrs from 5-6f including the Group 1 Heinz 57 Phoenix Stakes. 2nd dam, Champ d'Avril (by Northfields), was a fairly useful sprinter and won 2 races at 2 and 3 yrs. (Mr. C. Deuters).

DISTINCTLY RED
Bay colt. Distinctly North - Persian Mistress (Persian Bold).
April 11. 2nd foal. 13,500 gns (Doncaster St Leger).
Half-brother to the unplaced 1994 2-y-o Ballywillian (by Prince Rupert). The dam is an unraced half-sister to 5 winners including the high class sprinter Hallgate, winner of the Cornwallis Stakes, Diadem Stakes and Palace House Stakes and to the unplaced dam of the very useful sprinter Mistertopogigo. 2nd dam, Beloved Mistress (by Rarity), was a minor 2-y-o 5f winner. (Antonia Deuters).

GWESPYR
Chestnut colt. Sharpo - Boozy (Absalom).
April 7. 1st foal. 46,000 gns (Newmarket Highflyer).
The dam, a very useful sprinter, won three 5f events at 2 and 3 yrs including the Group 3 Phoenix Flying Five and was placed in the Palace House Stakes and the Molecomb Stakes. She is a half-sister to 2 minor winners out the unplaced High Dancer (by High Line), herself a half-sister to 3 minor winners. (Lord Mostyn).

IL DORIA (IRE)
Chestnut filly. Mac's Imp - Pasadena Lady (Captain James).
April 28. 5th foal. 30,000 gns.
Half-sister to the useful sprinter Palacegate Episode, a winner of 7 races here and abroad including listed events in Germany, to the fair sprinter Another Episode (both by Drumalis), a winner of 11 races from 2-5 yrs, to the useful sprinter Palacegate Jack (by Neshad), a winner of 5 races at 2 and 3 yrs and to the fair sprinter Sports Post Lady (by M Double M), winner of four 5f events at 2 and 3 yrs. The dam is an unraced half-sister to 4 minor winners out of the 3-y-o winner Gliding Gay (by Hill Gail) - herself a half-sister to the Prix Gladiateur winner Alciglide.

JACK'S TREAT (IRE)
Bay colt. Thatching - Just a Treat (Glenstal).
March 12. 1st foal. 37,000 gns (Newmarket Highflyer).
The dam, a moderate 2-y-o 5f winner, is a half-sister to 3 winners and to the unplaced Rare Mint - herself dam of the Group winners Mystery Rays and Robin des Pins. 2nd dam, Another Treat (by Cornish Prince), was an unplaced half-sister to the dams of Golden Fleece and Be My Guest. (Trevor Hemmings).

KUWAM
Bay colt. Last Tycoon - Inshad (Indian King).
May 23.
Half-brother to the useful 1994 3-y-o Mareha (by Cadeaux Genereux), a winner over 7f (twice) and 8f. The dam, a quite useful winner over 6f at 2 yrs and twice over 7f at 3, is a sister to one winner and a half-sister to 5 others. 2nd dam, Glancing (by Grundy), was a very useful winner of the Group 3 5f Prix d'Arenburg and is a half-sister to the Middle Park Stakes winner Bassenthwaite. Optimum 3-y-o distance: 7-8f. (Sheikh Ahmed Yousef Al-Sabah).

LARGHETTO
Chestnut colt. Lycius - Spoilt Again (Mummy's Pet).
April 17. 4th foal.
Half-brother to the minor 1994 4-y-o 10f winner Teen Jay (by Teenoso) and the 1995 3-y-o Florismart (by Never So Bold) - unplaced on his only outing at 2 yrs. The dam was a fairly useful 9f and 10f winner and a half-sister to the useful 2-y-o 8f winner War Whoop and the fairly useful middle-distance winners Feltwell and Kenninghall. 2nd dam, Reload (by Relko), a smart filly, won the Group 2 Park Hill Stakes and was a half-sister to the 1,000 gns winner Full Dress II. (Godolphin).

LILBURNE
Bay colt. Lycius - Hayat (Sadlers Wells).
February 13. 2nd foal.
Half-brother to the 3-y-o Haya Ya Kefaah (by Kefaah). The dam is an unraced half-sister to the smart French colt Lichine out of the U.S. stakes winner, at up to 9f, Stylish Genie (by Bagdad), herself a half-sister to the top class Sussex Stakes and Eclipse Stakes winner Artaius and the Ascot 1,000 gns Trial winner Embroidery. (Godolphin).

LIMERICK PRINCESS
Chestnut filly. Polish Patriot - Princess of Nashua (Crowned Prince).
May 14.
Closely related to the useful 1994 2-y-o Limerick Belle (by Roi Danzig), a winner of 3 races from 5-6f including a listed event, to the fairly useful 2-y-o triple 5f winner It's All Academic (by Mazaad), the fairly useful 2-y-o 5f winner Sky Royale (by Skyliner), to a winner of numerous races in Italy by Kampala and to the moderate winner of four 6f races, Elton Ledger (by Cyrano de Bergerac). The dam is an unraced granddaughter of the very smart Victoria Cross. (Mr T. Docherty).

LAUREL CROWN (IRE)
Bay colt. Thatching - Laureon (Caerleon).
March 13. 2nd foal. 12,000 gns (Newmarket October).
Half-brother to the minor 1994 2-y-o dual 5f winner (including one win on the all-weather) Poly Laureon (by Fairy King). The dam ran once, unplaced, at 2 yrs and is a half-sister to 4 winners including the Group 3 Cheshire Oaks winner Helenetta. 2nd dam, Lauretta (by Relko), won the listed Pretty Polly Stakes at Newmarket, was placed in the Musidora Stakes and the Lancashire Oaks and was a half-sister to the Dante Stakes winner Hobnob. (Laurel Leisure).

MILETRIAN CITY
Grey colt. Petong - Blueit (Bold Lad, Ire).
April 19. 21,000 gns (Newmarket October).
Half-brother to Blues Indigo (by Music Boy), a useful winner of 3 races at 2 yrs over 5f and one race over 6f at 3 yrs, to the fairly useful 2-y-o dual 5f winner Tino Tere (by Clantime), the quite

useful 5f (at 2 yrs) and 6f winner King of Spades (by King of Spain) and the fair 2-y-o dual 5f winner Indigo (by Primo Dominie). The dam, a useful 2-y-o 5f winner, is a half-sister to 3 winners out of the equally useful 2-y-o 5f winner Blue Butterfly (by Majority Blue). (Miletrian plc).

MY MELODY PARKES
Bay filly. Teenoso - Summerhill Spruce (Windjammer).
February 12.
Half-sister to the useful mare Lucky Parkes (by Full Extent), winner of 13 races over 5f from 2-5 yrs and to a winner in Holland by Jupiter Island. The dam, a fair winner of a 6f seller at 3 yrs, is out of the unraced Sharper Still (by Sharpen Up). (Mr.J. Heler).

NOBLE COLOURS
Bay colt. Distinctly North - Kentucky Tears (Cougar, CHI).
March 3. 4th foal. 22,000 gns (Newmarket October).
Half-brother to the plating-class Kentucky Dreams (by Dreams to Reality) and En-Cee-Tee (by Risk Me) - winners of 2-y-o sellers over 7f and 5f respectively. The dam, an unraced half-sister to 5 winners including the French listed stakes winner Hawk Beauty, is out of the winner of 2 races in the USA, Lagrimas (by Jacinto) - herself a half-sister to the Eclipse Stakes winner Solford, the American Grade 2 winner No Bias and to the dams of the French Group 2 winner Robertet and the smart American stakes winner Make Change. (Colin Bradford).

PEKAY
Bay colt. Puissance - K-Sera (Lord Gayle).
March 4. 38,000 gns (Newmarket October).
Half-brother to the smart German Group 1 12f and Group 2 German 2,000 gns winner Kornado, to the Belgian listed winner Serasuper (both by Superlative), the minor German 2-y-o winner Kasparow (by Reprimand), the moderate 5f and 6f winner Yukosan (by Absalom), the 2-y-o 5.8f winner Mariecurie Express (by Sizzling Melody) and the 3-y-o 8f winner Willbe Willbe (by Music Boy) - both plating-class. The dam was a fairly useful 2-y-o 7f winner and a half-sister to 7 winners including the Vernons Sprint Cup 2nd Royal Captive, the Yorkshire Cup 2nd Melody Rock and the Prix Gladiateur 2nd Lawrence T. 2nd dam, Deirdre (by Vimy), won once at 3 yrs. (Mr. T. G. Holdcroft)

PLAYMAKER
Bay colt. Primo Dominie - Salacious (Sallust).
March 12. 35,000 gns (Doncaster St Leger).
Half-brother to the fair 2-y-o 6f and 7f winner Highland Spirit (by Scottish Reel), to the minor U.S. winner of 2 races The Auburn Streak (by Melyno) and to the fair 10f placed 3-y-o Palace of Gold (by Slip Anchor). The dam won over 7f and 9f in Ireland including a listed event and is a half-sister to 8 minor winners. 2nd dam, Kalympia (by Kalydon), unplaced on both her outings at 2 yrs, was a half-sister to 7 winners. (Mr Rob Hughes).

WEST AUSTRIA
Bay colt. Tirol - Labwa (Lyphard).
January 24. 6th live foal.
Closely related to the German winner Lamseh (by Thatching) and half-brother to the fairly useful 1994 2-y-o 6f winner Baaderah (by Cadeaux Genereux). The dam is an unraced half-sister to 3 winners including the U.S. Grade 2 Louisiana Derby winner Prince Valiant and the stakes winner Majestic Folly. 2nd dam, Royal Folly (by Tom Fool), was unplaced on her only outing and is a half-sister to the dam of the dual U.S. Grade 1 stakes winner Big Spruce. (Godolphin).

NEVILLE CALLAGHAN

Neville had an average of 11.5% 2-y-o winners to runners over the past two years. That is higher than most trainers, but nonetheless we need to find out which one's are expected to pick up prizes and which aren't. The best four in his yard would appear to the following. **Cadeau**

Elegant - "she won't be very early, but is a very nice looking filly that certainly looks the part," **Sovereign Prince** "well bred, not very big but well made. He has had a slight setback but should be seen out in mid-summer" and **Danehill Dancer** about whom Neville enthuses "he is a very, very nice horse indeed. Quite a big colt, he does everything nicely and we are very hopeful. I wish I owned him myself!" Finally, the promising but backward and unnamed **Rainbow Quest - Racquette** colt is previewed in the premier section of the book. He was bred by Pat Eddery and Neville describes him as a lovely horse and a beautiful mover.

CADEAU ELEGANT
Chestnut filly. Cadeaux Genereux - Wasimah (Caerleon).
February 15. 2nd foal. 22,000 gns (Newmarket October).
Half-sister to the poor 6-8f placed Bedazzle (by Formidable). The dam, a quite useful 2-y-o dual 5f winner, is a half-sister to 8 winners including the very useful 2-y-o 5f winner Penny Blessing. 2nd dam, Pennycuick (by Celtic Ash), was a useful sprinter, a winner of 2 races and a half-sister to Mummy's Pet and the July Cup winner Parsimony. (Mr. T. Foreman).

DANEHILL DANCER
Bay colt. Danehill - Mira Adonde (Sharpen Up).
January 30. 3rd foal. 38,000 Ir gns (Goffs).
Half-sister to the quite useful 1994 Irish 2-y-o 5f winner Fakhira and to the modest 1993 2-y-o 6f placed 2-y-o Gift Box (both by Jareer). The dam ran once, unplaced, at 3 yrs and is a half-sister to the useful listed 7.2f John of Gaunt Stakes winner Swordsmith. 2nd dam, Lettre d'Amour (by Caro), is an unraced half-sister to 7 winners out of the Prix Jacques le Marois and Prix Robert Papin winner Lianga. (Mr. M. Tabor).

SOVEREIGN PRINCE
Bay colt. Bluebird - Everything Nice (Sovereign Path).
April 15. 36, 000 Ir gns (Goffs).
Brother to the 3-y-o Early Peace and half-brother to the very useful 1993 Irish 1,000 gns winner Nicer (by Pennine Walk), to the Italian winner Nice Noble (by Vaguely Noble), the moderate 3-y-o 7f winner Be My Everything (by Be My Guest) and to minor winners in the USA by Big Spruce (2), Spruce Needles and Liloy. He is also a half-brother to the unraced dams of Passing Sale (Group 2 Prix de Conseil de Paris) and the stakes winners Rancher and Family Investment. The dam was a useful winner of the Group 3 Cherry Hinton Stakes and the Group 3 Musidora Stakes and also won twice in the USA. 2nd dam, Emma Canute (by Hardicanute), was a fairly useful 2-y-o 6f and 7f winner. (Mr. M. Tabor).

MICK CHANNON

The Kingsdown stable of Mick Channon is well-known as one of the best producers of two-year-old winners and last year sent out 14% winners to runners in that category. Mick feels that, on the whole, he has a better class of horse this season though he still has a number that will be ready to run in the spring. Amongst those in the latter category he was eager to point out his Brocklesby runner **Dungeon Master** (a neat, compact colt that has won twice since) and three others that should be winning their fair share of races early in the season - **Corniche Quest, Doubly Engaged** and **Maygain**. Others that will be relatively early are **Belzao, Forever Noble** (has done very well and is a nice sort of horse) and the Sporting Life competition horse **Sporting Fantasy** (a tough, compact colt that was ready early). Moving on to his mid-season two-year-olds, **Ciserano, Hencarlam** and **Paris Joelle** are all nice types, whilst he describes **Poly Lad** as "a lovely little horse that will be out around May or June." Looking towards the summer and back-end of the season, some horses Mick feels will do well for him are the colts **Mental Pressure, Poly My Son** and **Warning Reef**. Finally, although May foals and so unlikely to show much until late summer, Mick also assured me that the Anshan colt **Reportory**, the Riverman colt **Riverbourne** and the Polish Patriot filly **CD Super Targeting** are all worth watching out for.

BELZAO
Bay colt. Alzao - Belle Enfant (Beldale Flutter).
March 17. 4th foal. 37,000 gns (Newmarket Highflier).
Half-brother to the fairly useful triple 8f winner Air Commodore (by Elegant Air) and to the modest 2-y-o 7.6f and 3-y-o 10f placed Demurrer (by Dominion). The dam, a quite useful 3-y-o 12f winner, is a half-sister to 6 winners including the Dewhurst Stakes, National Stakes and Gran Premio d'Italia winner (all Group 1 events) Dashing Blade, the useful 2-y-o dual 7f and subsequent French 6-8f winner Navarzato (by Dominion) and the useful 4-y-o dual 7f winner Powerful Edge (by Primo Dominie). 2nd dam, Sharp Castan (by Sharpen Up), a useful 5f winner at 2 yrs and 3rd in the Hoover Fillies Mile, is a half-sister to the smart miler General Vole. (Mr. J. W. Mitchell).

CD SUPER TARGETING (IRE)
Chestnut filly. Polish Patriot - Hazy Bird (Ballymore).
May 6. 3rd foal. 12,000 gns (Newmarket Houghton).
Closely related to the modest 1994 6f placed 2-y-o Kingdom (by Roi Danzig). The dam won 6 races in Ireland including the listed 12f Mooresbridge Stakes and is a half-sister to 2 minor winners. 2nd dam, Pigeon's Nest (by Sovereign Gleam), won 6 races on the flat and 7 over hurdles. (Circular Distributors Ltd).

CISERANO (IRE)
Chestnut filly. Mujtahid - Blue Persian (Majority Blue).
March 22. 19,500 gns (Newmarket October).
Half-sister to the very useful 5f Trafalgar House Sprint Stakes winner Polykratis (by He Loves Me), the 3-y-o 7f winner Iranian (by Indian King), the 2-y-o 5f winner Military Blue (by Sandhurst Prince), the 1994 2-y-o 6f winner Roses Galore (by Gallic League) - all three quite useful - and the fair 3-y-o 5.8f winner Angels Are Blue (by Stanford). The dam was a very useful winner of 3 races including the listed 5f St Hugh's Stakes and was 2nd in the Group 3 5f Prix du Petit Couvert. 2nd dam, Gulf Bird (by Gulf Pearl), won once at 3 yrs over 12f and is a half-sister to the Group 3 Henry II Stakes winner Saronicos. (Mr. K. Dack).

CORNICHE QUEST
Bay filly. Salt Dome - Angel Divine (Ahonoora).
February 22. 2nd foal.
The dam, an unraced twin, is a half-sister to 3 winners including Rock Chanteur (by Ballad Rock), winner of 4 races in Ireland and France and 3rd in the 2-y-o Group 1 7f National Stakes. 2nd dam, Sweet Accord (by Balidar), won twice at 3 years, was 2nd in the listed Azalea Stakes and is a half-sister to 6 winners including the Bessborough Handicap winner Spin of a Coin.

DOUBLY ENGAGED
Bay colt. Two Timing - Daniella Drive (Shelter Half).
March 22. 2nd foal. 11,500 Ir gns.
Half-brother to the fairly useful 1994 2-y-o maiden Blomberg (by Indian Ridge), placed in 4 races from 7-8f. The dam won 12 minor races in the USA and is a half-sister to 2 other minor winners. 2nd dam, De Laroche (by Noble Decree), was placed at 3 yrs in the USA and is a half-sister to 7 winners. (Mr. P. Christey).

DUNGEON MASTER
Chestnut colt. Polish Patriot - Etty (Relkino).
February 23. 14,000 gns (Newmarket October).
Half-brother to the Group 2 12f Ribblesdale Stakes winner and Group 1 Prix de la Salamandre and Grade 1 Selima Stakes placed Miss Boniface (by Tap on Wood), to the moderate 2 mile winner Ellafitzetty, the Belgian winner Night Fighter (both by Ela Mana Mou), the winner of 3 races over hurdles, Crazy River (by Vision) and the 1993 Irish 2-y-o 8.4f winner Paugim (by Danehill). The dam, a quite useful 3-y-o 10f winner, is a half-sister to 8 winners including the Coventry Stakes winner Whip it Quick. 2nd dam, Ma Griffe (by Indian Ruler), was unraced. (Classicstone Partnership).

FOREVER NOBLE (IRE)
Bay colt. Forzando - Pagan Queen (Vaguely Noble).
April 18. 20,000 gns (Newmarket October).
Brother to the fair 1993 8.2f placed 2-y-o Gay Devil - subsequently a winner abroad, closely related to Arcot (by Formidable), a winner of 3 races over hurdles and half-brother to the minor 3-y-o 12f winner La Gracile, the dual hurdles winner Gregoravich (both by Nijinsky), the minor 5-y-o 12f winner Green Steps (by Green Dancer) and the Italian winner Spimpinina (by Be My Guest). The dam won over 12f and 14f at 3 yrs and is a half-sister to 8 winners. 2nd dam, No Relation (by Klairon), a fairly useful filly, won once and stayed 8f. (The Gap Partnership).

HENCARLAM (IRE)
Bay or brown colt. Astronef - War Ballad (Green Dancer).
May 8. 6th foal. 36,000 Ir gns (Goffs).
Half-brother to the fair 1989 2-y-o Trojan Excel, a winner of 4 races from 5-7f and to Sense of Value (both by Trojan Fen), a winner of 5 races over middle distances and 2 races over hurdles. The dam, placed five times in France, is a half-sister to 2 winners abroad out of the placed Kashmirella (by Kashmir), herself a half-sister to 5 winners including the Ascot Gold Cup winner Pardallo. (Mr J. Carey).

MENTAL PRESSURE
Chestnut colt. Polar Falcon - Hysterical (High Top).
February 4. 50,000 Ir gns (Goffs).
Half-sister to 5 winners, namely the useful filly Comic Talent (by Pharly), a winner of 5 races from 7-9f, the fairly useful 7f (at 2 yrs), 8f and 10f winner Green Crusader (by Green Desert), the quite useful 2-y-o 6f winner Bold Amusement (by Never So Bold), the fair 2-y-o 6f winner Rully (by Rousillon) and the fair 3-y-o 8f winner Courageous Bidder (by Known Fact). The dam, a minor 4-y-o 12f winner, is a half-sister to 2 winners out of the very useful 2-y-o Madame's Share (by Major Portion), subsequently winner of the Group 3 8f Prix d'Astarte at 3 yrs. 3rd dam, Night Off (by Narrator), won the 1,000 gns and Cheveley Park Stakes. (Mr P. D. Savill).

PARIS JOELLE (IRE)
Bay filly. Fairy King - Gentle Freedom (Wolver Hollow).
March 6. 6th foal. 15,000 gns (Newmarket Highflyer).
Sister to the fairly useful Irish 2-y-o 7f winner Fairy Fable and to the Irish 3-y-o 8f winner Fairy Lore and half-sister to the quite useful 2-y-o 6f and 7f winner Amoret (by Jareer). The dam is an unraced half-sister to 4 winners and to the dams of Riverina Charm (four Grade 1 wins in Australia and New Zealand), the Australian Grade 2 winner Great Vintage and the Group 3 Van Geest Criterion Stakes winner La Grange Music. 2nd dam, Be Gyrful (by Gyr), won twice at 2 and 3 yrs and is a half-sister to the Nell Gwyn Stakes winner Gently - herself grandam of the Italian Group 1 winner Grease and the Irish Derby 2nd Observation Post. (Mr. R. M. Brehaut).

POLY LAD (IRE)
Bay colt. Alzao - Lady of Shalott (Kings Lake).
January 19. 3rd live foal. 20,000 Ir gns (Goffs).
Half-brother to the fair 3-y-o 7f winner Knight of Shalot (by Don't Forget Me). The dam, a moderate 6f placed 2-y-o and 8f placed 3-y-o, is a half-sister to the Group 2 King Edward VII Stakes winner Head For Heights, the listed Irish Cambridgeshire winner Majestic Star and the listed Italian winner Very Sharp. 2nd dam, Vivante (by Bold Lad, Ire), a quite useful 3-y-o 6f winner, is a half-sister to the dam of the Wokingham Handicap winner Le Johnstan. (Sheet and Roll Convertors Ltd).

POLY MY SON (IRE)
Chestnut colt. Be My Guest - Green Memory (Forli).
March 27. 20,000 Ir gns (Goffs).
Half-brother to the Belgian 2-y-o winner Rock Memory (by Ballad Rock). The dam, a fair winner of 2 races at Catterick over 10.2f at 3 yrs, is a half-sister 4 winners including the Newmarket Pretty Polly Stakes 2nd Fields of Spring. 2nd dam, Memory Lane (by Never Bend),

is a sister to Mill Reef and to the unraced dam of the Group winners Peterhof, Moscow Ballet and Western Symphony. (Sheet and Roll Convertors Ltd).

REPERTORY
Bay colt. Anshan - Susie's Baby (Balidar).
May 4. 19,000 gns (Doncaster St Leger).
Half-brother to the quite useful 2-y-o 5.7f and 3-y-o 6f winner Brockton Dancer (by Fairy King), to the fair sprinter Sir Tasker (by Lidhame) - a winner of ten 5f races including 7 on the all-weather and to the fair 2-y-o 5f winners Kafu Lady and Number One Son (both by Kafu). The dam is an unplaced half-sister to the smart sprinter The Go Between, winner of the Cornwallis Stakes and to 5 other winners. 2nd dam, Game Girl (by Abernant), placed at 2 yrs was a half-sister to the U.S. stakes winner Nervous Position.

RIVERBOURNE (USA)
Bay colt. Riverman - Umaimah (Halo).
May 29. 3rd foal.
Brother to the fair 1993 8f placed 2-y-o Portesham. The dam a fairly useful 2-y-o 7f winner, is a half-sister to 5 winners including the Group 1 Queen Elizabeth II Stakes winner Lahib (by Riverman) and to the U.S. stakes winner and dual Grade 1 placed Maceo. 2nd dam, Lady Cutlass (by Cutlass), won 3 races in the USA from 5-7f, was stakes placed and is a half-sister to 10 winners including the French Group 3 winner and useful sire General Holme and the grandam of Al Bahathri. (Mrs. N. Crook).

SPORTING FANTASY
Bay colt. Primo Dominie - Runelia (Runnett).
February 15. 3rd foal. 13,500 gns (Doncaster St Leger).
Half-brother to the fair 1994 2-y-o 7f winner Rock Foundation (by Rock City). The dam is an unplaced half-sister to 9 winners including the Group 3 Nishapour Curragh Stakes winner Safe Home and the Stewards Cup winner Touch Paper. 2nd dam, Azurn (by Klairon), was placed at 3 yrs in Ireland and is a half-sister to the Oaks and Irish Oaks winner Blue Wind. (Sporting Life).

WARNING REEF
Bay colt. Warning - Horseshoe Reef (Mill Reef).
February 8. 2nd foal. 16,500 gns (Newmarket October).
Half-brother to the fair 1994 6f placed 2-y-o Pumice (by Salse). The dam, a quite useful 3-y-o 10f winner, is a half-sister to 8 winners including the U.S. stakes winner Northeastern and the Yorkshire Oaks 3rd Guilty Secret. 2nd dam, Miss Toshiba (by Sir Ivor), won 7 races including the garde 1 Vanity Handicap and the Group 2 Pretty Polly Stakes and is a half-sister to 8 winners and to the dam of the high class sprinter Committed. (Mr. P. J. Sheehan).

LUCA CUMANI

Last year, the Bedford House Stables sent out 13% 2-y-o winners to runners - a decent enough return - but a significant drop from the previous year when Luca had no less than 25% 2-y-o winners to runners. He has given me three horses which he feels will do well as 2-y-o's, beginning with **Mezzanotte (Ire)** - quite a nice sort that will probably be better this year than next. **Paojiunic** is a horse he likes quite a bit. He bought him at Newmarket in October purely on looks and is described as being "very well-formed, very mature and quite forward." Finally, **Prince of Florence** is "a well-built, good looking 2-y-o that should be racing in May or June."

MEZZANOTTE (IRE)
Bay colt. Midyan - Late Evening (Riverman).
March 22. 5th foal. 26,000 gns.
Half-brother to the fairly useful 2-y-o 7f and 3-y-o 8f listed Heron Stakes winner Joie de Soir (by Caerleon), to the Italian 3-y-o winner Lucio Apuleio (by Nishapour) and the fair 1994 3-y-o 7f winner Deeply Vale (by Pennine Walk). The dam, placed 3 times in France, is a half-sister to 4 winners including the American Grade 3 stakes winner Mrs Cornwallis. 2nd dam, Evening

Off (by Tudor Minstrel), won one in the USA and is out of the champion American 2-y-o filly Evening Out. (Mr. G. Sainaghi).

PAOJIUNIC
Chestnut colt. Mac's Imp - Audenhove (Marduk).
March 24. 31,000 gns.
Half-brother to the fair 1993 2-y-o 6f winner Rooftop Flyer (by Nordico) and to the minor foreign winners Not Too Bad (by Simply Great), Golden Luck (by Indian King), Superb Investment (by Hatim) and Angel of Zurich (by M Double M). The dam won 4 races in Germany and is a half-sister to 5 other winners there. 2nd dam, Academica (by Pantheon), won 3 races in Germany and is a half-sister to the German Derby winner Alpenkonig. (Mr Paulo Riccardi).

PRINCE OF FLORENCE
Chestnut colt. Bluebird - Seme de Lys (Slew O'Gold).
February 26. 1st foal. 22,000 Ir gns.
The dam, a moderate filly, was placed from 6f (at 2 yrs) to 11f in Ireland and is a half-sister to 2 winners. 2nd dam, Blazon (by Ack Ack), a minor winner of 4 races at up to 6f in the USA, is a half-sister to the top class colt Exceller, the dual U.S. 2-y-o Grade 1 winner Capote and to three other good American stakes winners. 3rd dam, Too Bald (by Bald Eagle), was a champion older mare in America. (Mr. G. Sainaghi).

RICHARD HANNON

The East Everleigh Stables of Richard Hannon sent out 58 2-y-o winners last year and 98 in 1993, representing 12% and 17% winners to runners respectively. Among those of his 2-y-o's likely to make their mark early this season are **Ortolan** "2nd at Doncaster first time out and sure to win soon," **Cross the Border** "6f will suit him but he has the speed to win over 5f too," **Decision Maker** "a very nice horse, he goes well and will be early," **Centurion** is "a nice horse that should do well early in the season" and **Lomberto** "a nice colt, he will be out in April, probably at Kempton." Around May or June we should see the following horses winning races - **Paint it Black** - a lengthy colt by Double Schwartz, he will need 6-7f, the Distinctly North colts **Major Dundee** and **North Star** of which Richard says "they are both smashing colts that will need at least 6f," **Wisam** is "working very well and looks a really good colt" and the filly **Prima Volta** "should have the speed to win at around 5-6f." Looking towards the summer, one colt that should earn his keep is **Flying Pennant** (will need 7f).

CENTURION
Chestnut colt. Presidium - Missish (Mummy's Pet).
April 4. 3rd foal. 28,000 gns (Doncaster St Leger).
Brother to the quite useful 2-y-o triple 5f winner Moscow Road. The dam is an unraced half-sister to 3 minor winners out of the fairly useful 6f and 10f winner Miss Kuta Beach (by Bold Lad), herself a half-sister to 8 winners including the very useful miler Bali Dancer. (Mr George E. K. Teo).

CROSS THE BORDER
Bay colt. Statoblest - Brave Advance (Bold Laddie).
January 18. 49,000 gns (Doncaster St Leger).
Half-brother to the fairly useful 1994 5-y-o 6f Wokingham Handicap winner Venture Capitalist (by Never So Bold). The dam a fairly useful 2-y-o 5f winner, is a half-sister to 2 winners in the USA out of the unraced Osculate (by Forli), herself a half-sister to 6 winners including the dam of Robellino. (Mr P. D. Savill).

DECISION MAKER (IRE)
Bay colt. Taufan - Vain Deb (Gay Fandango).
March 14. 20,000 gns (Newmarket October).
Half-brother to the fairly useful 6f Wokingham Handicap winner Red Rosein, the quite useful 7f and 8f (all-weather) winner Gustavia (both by Red Sunset), the modest middle-distance stayer

Vain Prince (by Sandhurst Prince) - a winner of 3 races - and the poor 4-y-o 8f winner Malcessine (by Auction Ring). The dam, a moderate winner of 6 races from 8-9f, is a half-sister to 3 winners out of Saint Mildred (by Gay Fandango), a fairly useful winner of 3 races and herself a half-sister to 7 winners including the dams of 9 stakes winners. (P. W. H. Scott).

FLYING PENNANT (IRE)
Grey colt. Waajib - Flying Beckee (Godswalk).
February 24. 1st foal. 16,000 Ir gns (Goffs).
The dam, unplaced in all her three starts, is a sister to the very useful sprinter A Prayer For Wings and a half-sister to 5 winners. 2nd dam, Late Swallow (by My Swallow), was an unraced half-sister to 6 winners including the Belgian Group 2 winner Hot Valley. (Mrs. L. M. Davies).

HONEYHILL
Bay filly. Thatching - Kentfield (Busted).
January 12. 2nd foal. 15,000 gns (Newmarket October).
Half-sister to the 3-y-o Saleel (by Salse). The dam, unplaced on her only outing, is a half-sister to 4 winners including the Greenlands Stakes winner and useful young sire Puissance. 2nd dam, Girton (by Balidar), a moderate 3-y-o 5f and 6f winner, is a half-sister to 2 winners including the dam of the Flying Childers Stakes and Norfolk Stakes winner Sizzling Melody. (Wyck Hall Stud Ltd).

LOMBERTO
Bay colt. Robellino - Lamees (Lomond).
February 27. 2nd foal 22,000 gns (Newmarket October).
Half-brother to the fair 1994 2-y-o 5f and 6f winner Don Alvaro (by Forzando). The dam is an unraced half-sister to 3 winners out of the French 10f listed stakes winner Vachti (by Crystal Palace), herself a half-sister to the U.S. stakes winner Set Them Free. (Saleh Y. Al Homaizi).

MAJOR DUNDEE (IRE)
Bay colt. Distinctly North - Indigo Blue (Bluebird).
March 21. 1st foal. 30,000 gns (Doncaster St Leger).
The dam, a poor filly, was placed once over 5f at 2 yrs and is a half-sister to the very useful sprinter Mistertopogigo. 2nd dam, Decadence (by Vaigly Great), was unplaced at 2 and 3 yrs and is a sister to the high class sprinter Hallgate. (John Leek).

NORTH STAR (IRE)
Brown colt. Distinctly North - King's Chase (King's Leap).
April 5. 23,000 gns (Doncaster St Leger).
Half-brother to the fair 3-y-o 11f winner Regal Lover (by Alzao) - subsequently a winner of 7 races in Italy, to the moderate 2-y-o 7f winner G.G.Magic (by Strong Gale), the modest 2-y-o 7f winner Shamrock Princess, the Belgian winner Queen's Chase (both by Manado), the moderate 3-y-o 9f and 10f winner Chaste Lady (by Sandford Lad) and the Swedish winner Great Auk (by Auction Ring). The dam ran twice unplaced and is a half-sister to 5 winners out of the placed Hunting Moon (by Tudor Minstrel), herself a half-sister to the Irish 1,000 gns winner Even Star, the Hungerford Stakes winner Lovestone and the listed winner Nato - grandam of the U.S. Grade 1 winners Bundler and Quack. (Mr. I. Peter Sedgwick).

ORTOLAN
Grey colt. Prince Sabo - Kala Rosa (Kalaglow).
April 23. 3rd foal. 11,500 gns (Newmarket October).
Half-brother to the moderate 2-y-o 6f winner Daily Star (by Music Boy). The dam was placed over 6f at 2 yrs and is a half-sister to 6 winners including the useful Cecil Frail Handicap and subsequent U.S. Grade 3 winner Greenwood Star. 2nd dam, Golden Palermo (by Dumbarnie), won a 5f seller at 3 yrs and is a half-sister to 6 minor winners. (Mr. J. A. Lazzari).

PAINT IT BLACK
Chestnut colt. Double Schwartz - Tableaux (Welsh Pageant).
March 7. 34,000 gns (Doncaster St Leger).
Half-sister to the French winner Living Image (by Kenmare), to the Italian 3-y-o winner Captain

Ken (by Vayrann) and the French jumps winner Painting (by Relkino). The dam was placed twice in France including a listed event and is a half-sister to 6 winners including the Italian Group 3 winners King Jay and My Royal Prima and the French listed winner Aborigine. 2nd dam, Prima (by Alcide), won 3 races, was placed in the Pretty Polly Stakes and the Ribblesdale Stakes and is a half-sister to the Falmouth Stakes winner Caprera - herself dam of Group 1 Prix Ganay winner Romildo. (Mr. M. Pescod).

PRIMA VOLTA
Bay filly. Primo Dominie - Femme Formidable (Formidable).
January 24. 3rd foal. 23,000 gns (Newmarket October).
Half-sister to the fairly useful 1994 2-y-o dual 6f winner Femme Savante (by Glenstal). The dam is an unplaced half-sister to the useful middle-distance stayer King of Mercia. 2nd dam, Saint Osyth (by Blakeney), was a useful 12f winner and a half-sister to 4 minor winners. (P. W. H. Scott).

WISAM
Bay colt. Shaadi - Moon Drop (Dominion).
May 7. 4th foal.
Half-brother to the useful 1994 2-y-o 5.2f winner and Coventry Stakes and Gimcrack Stakes placed Moon King (by Cadeaux Genereux) and to the useful 1992 2-y-o 6f winner Mithl Al Hawa (by Salse). The dam, a useful 2-y-o 5f and 3-y-o listed 6f winner, is a half-sister to the very useful 7f and 12f winner Beldale Star. 2nd dam, Little White Star (by Mill Reef), is an unplaced half-sister to the useful sprinter Jukebox Jury out of a fairly useful half-sister to the good miler Saintly Song. (Mr Mohammed Suhail).

PETER HARRIS

At least one of these - **Thai Morning** - will have been out before this publication. Peter indicated to me in mid-March that this colt was the earliest two-year-old he'd ever had and would run in the Brocklesby Stakes. I asked about Mrs Hollis's **Kelly's Kap** and was told he is a classy colt that wouldn't be ready until mid-season at the earliest. **Pride of Kashmir** is a colt Peter is quite keen on. Apparently he is an early sort, shows a lot of speed and should be ready to run in late April. He will be hoping for an even better season than last year when his forty two 2-y-o runners netted six wins - giving a 14% success rate.

KELLY'S KAP (IRE)
Bay colt. Green Desert - Civility (Shirley Heights).
April 11. 6th live foal. 42,000 Ir gns (Goffs).
Half-brother to 4 winners, namely the useful 7-9f winner and Group 2 Falmouth Stakes 2nd Lovealoch (by Lomond), the minor 3-y-o 9f winner Paper Craft (by Formidable), the Italian 2-y-o winner Laura Margaret (by Persian Bold) and the fair 1994 4-y-o 14f and 16f winner Fetes Galantes (by Caerleon). The dam was a useful 3-y-o dual 12f winner and a half-sister to 5 winners including the Group 3 National Stakes winner Piney Ridge. 2nd dam, Makeacurtsey (by Herbager), placed in the USA, was a half-sister to the grandam of the American champion colts Swale and Forty Niner. Being out of a stout daughter of Shirley Heights, this colt won't be out early, but should be watched from mid-season onwards. (Mrs Marlene Hollis).

PRIDE OF KASHMIR (IRE)
Grey colt. Petong - Proper Madam (Mummy's Pet).
February 6. 20,000 gns (Newmarket October).
Half-brother to 3 winners, namely the useful 2-y-o triple 5f winner Madam Millie, the fairly useful dual 2-y-o 5f winner Naive Charm (both by Milford) and the minor 2-y-o 5f winner Madam Tudor (by Blue Cashmere). The dam was a fairly useful winner of 6 races over sprint distances out of the minor 3-y-o winner Old Scandal (by Elopement). (New Recruits Partnership).

THAI MORNING
Grey colt. Petong - Bath (Runnett).
January 27. 15,000 gns (Newmarket October).
The dam was a fair winner of 5 races at 3 and 4 yrs from 7-8f and is a half-sister to 3 other minor winners. 2nd dam, Break of Day (by On Your Mark), was an unraced half-sister to the dam of the smart Premio Roma winner Highland Chieftain. (Thai Connection).

MARK JOHNSTON

The impact Mark Johnston has made on the racing scene in Britain in the past two year's has been quite amazing, to such an extent that the North now houses a number of beautifully bred horses bred by the Maktoum family. They can be found in the main section of this book.
Asked to comment as to which of his two-year-olds I should include as likely 2-y-o winners, Mark was his useful ebullient self - "You could put most of them in! As always, I fully intend to run them as two-year-olds and they are all chosen because of their good pedigrees." Mark probably won't agree with me, but his horses in this section, apart from the cheaply bought **Double O Seven**, don't have quite the same appeal on pedigree as those in the premier section of the book. I have chosen them because, of all those in his yard, the propensity of their sires for producing 2-y-o winners, along with their early foaling dates, make them obvious choices as probable future winners at not necessarily the highest standard. **Boundary Bird** was a horse Mark seemed to like very much, describing him as a very nice colt and very much like his 3-y-o half-brother, the useful Loveyoumillions. He felt that **Branston Jewel** was going well and would be one of his first runners, but that **Bijou B'inde** was very big, typical of his sire, and would take more time to come to hand. **Elfin Queen** was another Mark was pleased with, explaining that she is very sharp and would be out relatively early, as would **Double O Seven**, a big, strong colt. After a muscular problem, **Marie's Crusader** could be fairly early if she comes right, whilst **Bailey's First** and **Delta Tempo** were nice sorts that had yet to do any fast work. No less than 18% of the Kingsley House Stables' two-year-old runners won in 1993 and that figure improved to a very creditable 19% last year.

BAILEY'S FIRST (IRE)
Bay filly. Alzao - Maiden Concert (Condorcet).
February 26. 48,000 Ir gns (Goffs).
Closely related to the moderate 3-y-o 12f winner Green's Van Goyen (by Lyphard's Special) and half-sister to the smart Group 1 Gran Criterium and Group 1 Premio Parioli winner Candy Glen (by Glenstal), to the moderate 2-y-o 5f winner That'll Be The Day (by Thatching), the Italian winner of 3 races at 3 yrs and Group 3 placed Imco Charmer (by Last Tycoon) and the minor 1993 2-y-o winner Ruvolina (by Caerleon). The dam ran once, unplaced, at 2 yrs and is a half-sister to the dams of the Irish 1,000 gns winner More So and the Group 3 Waterford Candelabra Stakes winner Obeah. 2nd dam, Merdemain (by Tamerlane), was a useful winner in Ireland. (Baileys Horse Feeds).

BIJOU B'INDE
Chestnut colt. Cadeaux Genereux - Pushkar (Northfields).
March 9. 20,000 gns (Newmarket October).
Half-brother to the very useful Zetand Gold Cup and John Smiths Magnet Cup winner Eradicate (by Tender King) - subsequently Grade 1 placed in America, to the fairly useful 5-y-o 16f winner Hebridean (by Norwick), the moderate 8f and 10f winner Doctor Roy (by Electric), the minor U.S. 3-y-o winner Gorgeous Traveller (by Hello Gorgeous) and the minor 2-y-o 8f winner Burkes Progress (by Tyrnavos). The dam is an unraced half-sister to the Group 3 Brownstown Stakes winner Red Chip. 2nd dam, Chippings (by Busted), was unraced. (Mr J. S. Morrison).

BOUNDARY BIRD
Bay colt. Tirol - Warning Sound (Red Alert).
April 22. 10,000 gns (Newmarket October).
Half-brother to the useful 1994 2-y-o 6f Tattersalls Breeders Stakes winner Loveyoumillions (by Law Society), the useful 2-y-o 5f and 3-y-o dual 8f winner Remthat Naser (by Sharpo), the Irish

3-y-o 10f winner Second Guess (by Ela Mana Mou), the minor 2-y-o winner Simple Sound (by Simply Great) and the minor 3-y-o winner Siren (by Caerleon). The dam won 3 races in Ireland from 5-10f and is a half-sister to 3 winners including the Italian Group 3 winner Shenable. 2nd dam, Shenachie (by Sheshoon), won once at 3 yrs. (Mrs I. Bird).

BRANSTON JEWEL
Chestnut filly. Prince Sabo - Tuxford Hideaway (Cawston's Clown).
March 14. 5th foal. 21,000 gns (Doncaster St Leger).
Half-sister to the useful multiple sprint winning mare Branston Abby (by Risk Me), to the fairly useful 2-y-o 6f and 7f and subsequent U.S. winner Big Blow and the moderate 2-y-o 6f winner Glowing Dancer (by Glow). The dam, a useful sprinter, won two races at 2 yrs and is a half-sister to 3 winners out of the minor 3-y-o winner Late Idea (by Tumble Wind). (Mr J. David Abell).

DELTA TEMPO (IRE)
Grey filly. Bluebird - Alpine Spring (Head For Heights).
March 8. 2nd foal. 11,000 Ir gns (Goffs).
Half-sister to the fair 1994 3-y-o 8-10f winner Pennine Pink (by Pennine Walk). The dam won over 7f in Ireland at 2 yrs, stayed 10f well and is a half-sister to the very useful 1991 2-y-o Mill Reef Stakes and July Stakes winner Showbrook and the very useful 1993 3-y-o 8-10f winner Smargitano. 2nd dam, Aldern Stream (by Head For Heights), was a useful 2-y-o 7f and 3-y-o 7f winner. (Delta Manufacturing).

DOUBLE O SEVEN
Bay colt. Tirol - Anneli Rose (Superlative).
March 24. 2nd foal. 4,400 gns (Tattersalls October).
Half-brother to the smart 1994 2-y-o Group 1 6f Middle Park Stakes winner Fard (by Reprimand). The dam was a plating class winner of one race, over 6f, on the all-weather at 3 yrs. She is a half-sister to another Middle Park Stakes winner in Gallic League, also winner of the Group 2 Flying Childers Stakes. 2nd dam, Red Rose Bowl (by Dragonara Palace), won one race over 7f at 2 yrs in Ireland and is a half-sister to the French listed winner Dorimant and the Cesarewitch winner Private Audition. An astonishingly cheap yearling, considering his pedigree, his trainer seems in no doubt that he was well worth his purchase price. (Mr R. W. Huggins).

ELFIN QUEEN (IRE)
Bay filly. Fairy King - West of Eden (Crofter).
February 13. 4th foal. 18,000 Ir gns (Goffs).
Sister to the quite useful filly Cindora, a winner of five races over the minimum trip at 2 and 3 yrs. The dam is an unraced half-sister to 9 winners including the listed placed Loughanreagh and Alpine Meadow. 2nd dam, Eden Quay (by King's Bench), was placed as a 2-y-o and is a sister to the Greenlands Stakes winner Victoria Quay. (Mr J. David Abell).

MARIE'S CRUSADER (IRE)
Bay filly. Last Tycoon - Pampala (Bold Lad).
February 26. 10,000 Ir gns (Goffs).
Half-sister to the very useful Group 3 Gordon Richards Stakes winner Noble Patriarch (by Alzao), to the useful 2-y-o 8f and 3-y-o 12f winner Pistol River (by Simply Great), the French 2-y-o and 3-y-o winner My Sin (by High Estate) and the minor Irish 6f and 8f winner Fletcher Christian (by Ahonoora). The dam, an Irish maiden, is a half-sister to 2 winners out of the unraced Pantamerla (by Tamerlane) - herself a half-sister to the Irish 2,000 gns winner Pampapaul. (Express Marie Curie Racing).

GEOFF LEWIS

Geoff feels his horses have more scope this year than they've had for a long time and so he is looking forward to having some decent mid to back end 2-y-o's. Amongst those that he'll be taking his time with are **Civil Liberty** - "a really classy colt who will be introduced at around 6 or 7 furlongs," **Flyfisher** - "a colt by the first season sire Batshoof who I expect to do well at stud, this colt is really nice and worth being patient with" and the two Risk Me colts **Trojan Risk** and **No Cliches** " the best Risk Me's I've ever had." Those likely to be quite early are **Anotheranniversary** "a very nice filly with the speed to win at 5f but the potential to stay a bit further," **Sketchbook** - "a very, very nice horse that shows a lot of pace and would benefit by 6f rather than 5f as would **Arctic Romancer** - a grand type of horse that shows plenty of ability" and finally **Caricature** is "a real neat little horse and a proper 2-y-o. He was a bit cheeky so I had him gelded but he's still a classy fellow and I'll start him over 6f or so."

ANOTHERANNIVERSARY
Grey filly. Emarati - Final Call (Town Crier).
February 21. 30,000 gns (Doncaster St Leger).
Half-sister to Jo Maximus (by Prince Sabo) - placed three times over 5f at 2 yrs in 1994 - and to 5 winners, namely the useful 2-y-o 7f winner and subsequent French 12f winner Stage Hand (by Sagaro), the 2-y-o 5f winner My Anniversary (by Dublin Taxi), the 2-y-o 5f seller winner One Missing (by Comedy Star), the useful 3-y-o 6f winner Night Bell (by Night Shift) and the hurdles winner Deciding Bid (by Valiyar). The dam was a fair 2-y-o 5f winner and a half-sister to the sprinter On Stage, a winner of 10 races and placed in the Prix Morny, July Cup and Kings Stand Stakes. 2nd dam, Last Case (by Firestreak), won 9 races and was placed in the Nassau Stakes. (Mr. D. Barker).

ARCTIC ROMANCER
Bay colt. Distinctly North - Kowalski (Cyrano de Bergerac).
April 4. 1st foal. 19,000 gns (Doncaster St Leger).
The dam ran unplaced twice at 2 yrs and is a half-sister to 5 minor winners out of the minor 2-y-o winner Free Course (by Sandford Lad), herself a half-sister to 5 winners. (Mr Abdulla Al Khalifa).

CARICATURE (IRE)
Brown colt. Cyrano de Bergerac - That's Easy (Swing Easy).
March 10. 23,000 gns (Newmarket October).
Half-brother to the quite useful Irish 2-y-o 5f winner On Display (by Exhibitioner), the fair 2-y-o 6f and 3-y-o 12f winner Maestroso (by Mister Majestic) and the minor Irish 2-y-o 6f winner Flaming Sunset (by Hays). The dam, an Irish 3-y-o 9f winner, is a half-sister to 5 minor winners. 2nd dam, Quoff (by Quorum), won 4 minor races from 2-5 yrs and is a half-sister to 8 winners. (White Bear Ltd).

CIVIL LIBERTY
Bay colt. Warning - Libertine (Hello Gorgeous).
March 8. 4th foal. 58,000 gns - failed to reach reserve - (Newmarket Highflyer).
Brother to the 1994 French 2-y-o winner and Group 3 8f Prix d'Aumale 4th Take Liberties. The dam, a very useful filly, won over 5.5f on her first outing at 2 yrs and the Group 2 Premio Federico Tesio at 3 yrs and was placed in the French 1,000 gns, the Prix Robert Papin, the Premio Lydia Tesio and the Prix Saint-Alary. She is a half-sister to the 2-y-o Group 3 8f Prix des Chenes winner Harmless Albatross and the Group 2 Prix d'Harcourt winner Fortune's Wheel. 2nd dam, North Forland (by Northfields), was a useful 3-y-o 10f winner, was 2nd in the Ribblesdale Stakes and is a half-sister to the Group 1 Prix Ganay winner Infra Green - herself dam of three Group 3 winners. (Midcourts).

FLYFISHER
Bay colt. Batshoof - Inveraven (Alias Smith).
February 22. 5th foal. 24,000 gns (Newmarket October).
Half-sister to the moderate 1993 dual 7f (including one on the all-weather) and 7.5f 2-y-o winner Demi-Plie (by Squill) and to the Belgian winner Inner Storm (by Celestial Storm). The dam, unplaced on all three of her outings, is a half-sister to 7 winners including the Norwegian Group 3 winner Coulstry and the useful 12f winner Rynechra. 2nd dam, Marypark (by Charlottown), a fairly useful stayer, won 3 races and is a half-sister to 6 winners. (Highclere Thoroughbred Racing Ltd).

NO CLICHES
Chestnut colt. Risk Me - Always on a Sunday (Star Appeal).
April 12. 3rd foal. 39,000 gns (Doncaster St Leger).
Brother to the modest 1994 5f to 7.5f placed 2-y-o Fishy Affair and to the 1994 3-y-o Sunday Risk, placed three times abroad. The dam, a useful winner of the listed 10f Newmarket Pretty Polly Stakes, is a sister to the fairly useful 3-y-o 9f winner Sunday Sport Star - herself dam of the listed 2-y-o National Stakes winner Signs (by Risk Me) - and a half-sister to 8 winners. 2nd dam, Justine (by Luciano), won 4 races in Germany. (Mr. M. H. Watt).

SKETCHBOOK
Chestnut colt. Sharpo - Cape Chestnut (Bustino).
March 6. 22,000 gns (Newmarket October).
Half-brother to the useful winner of 4 races here and in France, Dazzling Heights, the fairly useful 12.3f to 16.5f winner Tree of Life, the Italian winner Cape Heights (all by Shirley Heights), the useful 2-y-o dual 6f winner Moogie (by Young Generation) and the Swiss winner Newfangled Tango (by Dance in Time). The dam, a quite useful 8f winner at 3 yrs, is a half-sister to 5 winners including Colway Rally - a winner of 9 races here and in the USA including the Grade 2 Citation Handicap. 2nd dam, Boswelia (by Frankincense), won 4 races including a listed event and was a half-sister to 6 winners including the Italian Group 1 winner Rolle. (Highclere Thoroughbred Racing Ltd).

TROJAN RISK
Chestnut colt. Risk Me - Troyes (Troy).
March 20. 4th foal. 5,000 gns (Newmarket Highflyer).
Brother to the 3-y-o Avranches, unplaced on his only outing at 2 yrs and half-brother to the fairly useful 1994 3-y-o 9f winner Tromond (by Lomond). The dam, a quite useful 3-y-o 12f winner, is a sister to the 2-y-o winner and Group 2 12f King Edward VII Stakes 2nd New Trojan and a half-sister to 4 winners including the Group 1 12f Yorkshire Oaks winner Hellenic. 2nd dam, Grecian Sea (by Homeric), was a useful 2-y-o 6f winner in France. (Mr. J. McCarthy).

TERRY MILLS

Here are three young horses from another trainer who had a good season with his two-year-olds last year. 18% winners to runners is better than most managed and Terry will be hoping for more of the same. **Suparoy** should be out be about May time and although not very big, is well put together, moves well and is a sharp colt who will be started off at 5f. **Brother Roy** needs a bit more time but should be ready by mid-season whilst **Future's Trader** is a nice, rangy type of colt, is bred to get a trip and may not be out until the late-summer.

BROTHER ROY
Bay colt. Prince Sabo - Classic Heights (Shirley Heights).
February 20. 2nd foal. 21,000 gns.
The dam is an unraced half-sister to the high class Group 2 Princess of Wales's Stakes and Group 2 King Edward VII Stakes winner Head For Heights, to the Irish Cambridgeshire winner Majestic Star and to the Italian listed winner Very Sharp. 2nd dam, Vivante (by Bold Lad, Ire), won as a 3-y-o and is a half-sister to the good 5-7f colt Le Johnstan. (Mrs.T. Mills).

SUPAROY
Bay colt. Midyan - Champ d'Avril (Northfields).
February 3. 24,000 gns.
Half-brother to the smart 2-y-o Superpower (by Superlative), winner of the Group 1 Heinz 57 Phoenix Stakes and the Group 3 Norfolk Stakes, to the fairly useful 2-y-o triple 5f winner Zandril (by Forzando), the minor 2-y-o 5f winner Florentynna Bay (by Aragon) and to the minor winner abroad Al Akbar (by Cadeaux Genereux). The dam was a quite useful dual 5f winner and a half-sister to 6 minor winners out of the 2-y-o winner April Twelfth - herself a half-sister to Music Boy. (Mr T. Mills).

100 To Follow

FUTURE'S TRADER
Bay colt. Alzao - Awatef (Ela Mana Mou).
February 24. 5th foal. 25,000 gns.
Brother to the quite useful 1994 2-y-o winner Wot-If-We and half-brother to the 2-y-o 7f winner Daja (by Doulab) - subsequently a winner of 4 races in Italy - and to the 3-y-o 8f winner Maastricht (by Common Grounds). The dam, placed in France at 3 yrs, is a half-sister to 4 winners including the top class broodmare Royal Sister II (dam of Ezzoud and Distant Relative). 2nd dam, Ribasha (by Ribot), is a placed half-sister to the Alabama Stakes winner Natashka - herself dam of the Group winners Gregorian, Truly Bound, Blood Royal, Arkadina and Ivory Wand and grandam of Dark Lomond, Gold and Ivory, Mukaddamah, Tatami and Itsamaza (U.S. Grade 1 winner). (Abdel Hakim).

SIR MARK PRESCOTT

Another trainer with an excellent record in the last two seasons with his two year olds. Sir Mark had 16 juvenile wins last year - representing a winners to runners ratio of 17% - which is 2% better than the previous year. The two-year-olds I fancy from his yard to win races this year are **Just Ice** and **Serious Trust**, both of which look like being useful mid-season types.

JUST ICE
Bay filly. Polar Falcon - Justine (Luciano).
April 13. 20,000 gns (Newmarket Highflyer).
Half-sister to the useful 1988 2-y-o Always on a Sunday, placed in the Lowther Stakes and May Hill Stakes and winner of the 10f listed Pretty Polly Stakes (awarded race) at 3 yrs, to the 3-y-o 9f winner Sunday Sport Star, the 7f and 8f winner All Hell Let Loose - both fairly useful, the Italian winner Justar (all by Star Appeal), the German listed winner Palmetto Express (by Glint of Gold), the German winner and Group 1 placed Junior Lombard (by Lombard) and to minor winners by Good Times (2), Celestial Storm and Julio Mariner. The dam won 4 races in Germany at 2 and 4 yrs and is a half-sister to the German Group 3 winner Justus. 2nd dam, Joie d'Amour (by Birkhahn), won 8 races in Germany. (Canary Thoroughbreds).

SERIOUS TRUST
Bay colt. Alzao - Mill Line (Mill Reef).
March 6. 2nd live foal. 31,000 gns (Newmarket October).
Half-brother to the useful 1994 2-y-o Group 3 7f Prestige Stakes winner Pure Grain (by Polish Precedent). The dam was a fair 3-y-o 14.6f winner at 3 yrs and a half-sister to 5 winners including the useful 2-y-o 8f winner Known Line. 2nd dam, Quay Line (by High Line), was a very useful filly and winner of 6 races including the Group 2 Park Hill Stakes, is a sister to the listed stakes winners High Finale and Trade Line and to the Italian Group 2 winner Ancholia. (Mr G. Moore).

MRS LYNDA RAMSDEN

Jack Ramsden was quite optimistic about the chances of the Breckenborough House 2-y-o's this year. Not surprisingly, after the success they had with the Master Willie colt Chilly Billy last season, he expressed his keenness for **Smarter Charter** - another son of Master Willie - describing him as a nice colt who is quite forward and should be ready by about May. Two colts who are going well and should see the racecourse in April or May are **Privileged** and the American bred **Evening Chime**. Around May or June we should see the introduction of **Annaberg**, a filly bred to get a trip, the nice filly **Polar Refrain** and a colt that Lynda particularly likes - **Arabian Heights** (though middle distances seem to beckon next year). Come mid-summer we will see a colt that should be useful in time, **Alpine Joker**, though Jack warns us that his pedigree suggests soft ground would be ideal. Finally, a colt for the back-end could well be **Known Secret**. Lynda likes him and Jack feels he was a bargain at $25,000 so watch out for him towards the back-end of the season. Over the past two years, 12% of the Ramsden 2-y-o runners won.

ALPINE JOKER
Bay colt. Tirol - Whitstar (Whitstead).
February 8. 16,000 gns (Newmarket Highflyer).
Half-brother to the useful colt Two Left Feet (by Petorius), a winner of 9 races including the listed 8f Ben Marshall Stakes at Newmarket. The dam was a fairly useful 10.2f winner at 2 yrs and is a half-sister to the very useful 6-10f winner Homeboy and to Hill's Pageant, a winner of 10 races on the flat and over hurdles including a Group 3 event in Germany. 2nd dam, Reita (by Gilles de Retz), was a quite useful miler.
(Mr. G. Armitage)

ANNABERG
Bay filly. Tirol - Icecapped (Caerleon).
February 9. 4th foal. 10,000 gns (Newmarket October).
Half-sister to the fair 1994 3-y-o all-weather 7f winner (placed over 9.4f) Racing Brenda (by Faustus). The dam, a fairly useful middle-distance stayer, won twice at 3 yrs and is a half-sister to 2 winners. 2nd dam, Osmunda (by Mill Reef), won in Ireland at 3 yrs over 10f and is a half-sister to the Group 2 Beresford Stakes and Group 2 John Porter Stakes winner Icelandic and to the Group 2 Sun Chariot Stakes winner Snow.

ARABIAN HEIGHTS
Chestnut colt. Persian Heights - Arabian Rose (Lyphard).
February 11. 4th foal. 27,000 gns (Newmarket October).
Half-brother to Moonlight Quest (by Nishapour), a quite useful winner of 5 races at around 12f, to Arabian Storm (by Celestial Storm), a 2-y-o winner in Hungary and to the modest middle distance placed filly Pip's Dream (by Glint of Gold). The dam ran once, unplaced, in France and is a half-sister to 4 minor winners. 2nd dam, Gamalat (by Pretense), won one race in France. (Mr. P. A. Leonard).

EVENING CHIME (USA)
Bay colt. Night Shift - Brattice Cloth (L'Enjoleur).
March 14. 1st foal. $60,000 (Keeneland September).
The dam won 7 races from 2-5 yrs and was stakes-placed in the USA. She is a half-sister to 9 winners including the minor stakes winners Andalante (dam of 2 stakes winners), Button Hook and Meditation (dam of 2 stakes winners). 2nd dam, Allegheny II (by Charlottesville), was placed in the USA and a half-sister to 11 winners. (Mr. P. A. Leonard).

KNOWN SECRET (USA)
Chestnut colt. Known Fact - Loa (Hawaii).
May 15. 3rd foal. $25,000.
The dam won 5 races at 3 and 4 yrs in the USA including a minor stakes event and is a half-sister to 5 winners including the Grade 2 Bold Ruler Stakes winner Pok Ta Pok and the dams of 3 stakes winners. 2nd dam, Tiy (by Nalees Man), was a minor American winner at 3 and 4 yrs and a half-sister to 3 good stakes winners. (Mr. D. McKenzie).

POLAR REFRAIN
Chestnut filly. Polar Falcon - Cut No Ice (Great Nephew).
March 10. 3rd foal. 24,000 gns (Newmarket Highflyer).
Half-sister to the fairly useful 1994 2-y-o 5f winner (awarded race) and to the moderate 8f placed filly Cut Adrift (by Nordico). The dam won a listed event in France, a 7f maiden at Newbury and stayed 10f. She is a half-sister to 4 winners out of the very useful filly Foiled Again (by Bold Lad, Ire), winner of the Sandleford Priory Stakes at Newbury and placed in the Prix Saint Alary, Ribblesdale Stakes and Nassau Stakes. (Mr. P. A. Leonard).

PRIVILEGED
Bay colt. Efisio - Prejudice (Young Generation).
February 12. 3rd foal.
Brother to Al Moulouki, a winner of 5 races at 3 yrs in 1993 from 7-8f and half-brother to Hob Green (by Move Off), a winner of 3 races at 3 and 4 yrs from 6-7f - both quite useful. The dam, a quite useful filly, was placed 5 times from 6-8f and is a half-sister to 4 winners including the

Group 3 Beeswing Stakes winner Casteddu and the listed stakes winner Barbaroja (both by Efisio). 2nd dam, Bias (by Royal Prerogative), was a useful winner of 6 races at 2 and 3 yrs from 7f to 10.4f. (Mrs. A. E. Sigsworth).

SMARTER CHARTER
Brown colt. Master Willie - Irene's Charter (Persian Bold).
March 8. 3rd foal. 15,500 gns. (Newmarket October).
Brother to the unraced Ramsden trained 3-y-o Master Charter. The dam was a fair winner of 4 races from 3-5 yrs and from 7-10f. 2nd dam, Crestia (by Prince Tenderfoot), an Irish 6f winner at 2 yrs, is a half-sister to 6 winners including the smart French stayer El Badr, winner of the Group 1 Prix du Cadran and to the U.S. Grade 3 winner Noble Savage. Master Willie, with his fairly stout pedigree, doesn't get many 2-y-o runners. Of those that do run, however, a good percentage of them win - (50% in the last two years).

JAMIE TOLLER

Another trainer who feels his two-year-olds are a good bunch this year, Jamie is particularly pleased with the colts **Effectual** - looks a tough colt and should be a nice 2-y-o - and **Mellors** who is also going well at the moment. He also felt I should mention the American breds **Bewitching** and **The Dilettanti** - both of which are showing up nicely in their work, and in particular the colt **Verulam** - one he seems very taken with. Two others that should improve as the season progresses are the fillies **Intimation** (a leggy filly - will need time) and **Kidston Lass**. Four of Jamie's 24 two-year-old runners in the past two 2 years won - representing a ratio of just over 16%.

BEWITCHING (USA)
Chestnut filly. Imp Society - Mrs Magnum (Northjet).
March 20. 6th foal. Not sold - bid reached 7,800 gns. (Newmarket October).
Sister to Capote's Imp, Mr Imp and Mrs Society - winners of 8 minor races between them in the USA and half-sister to the minor U.S. stakes placed winner Arizona Irish (by Irish Open). The dam is an unraced half sister to 5 winners. 2nd dam, Mauna Loa (by Hawaii), a minor American winner, is a half-sister to 10 winners including the top class horse Exceller, the Grade 1 Breeders Cup Juvenile winner Capote and three other good American stakes winners. (Mr P. C. J. Dalby).

EFFECTUAL
Bay colt. Efisio - Moharabuiree (Pas de Seul).
March 22. 2nd foal. 42,000 gns (Newmarket October).
Half-brother to the unplaced 1994 2-y-o Risky Rose (by Risk Me). The dam was placed in sellers over 8f and 10f and is a sister to the U.S. Grade 3 winner Baldomero (by Pas de Seul). 2nd dam, Clonavee (by Northern Dancer), is an unraced half-sister to the U.S. stakes winner Lady of Cornwall out of the Grade 1 Frizette Stakes winner Molly Ballantine. (Blandford Thoroughbreds).

INTIMATION
Bay filly. Warning - It's Terrific (Vaguely Noble).
March 2. 17,500 gns (Newmarket October).
Half-sister to the Italian listed winner It's Money (by Faraway Son), the useful 1990 3-y-o 7f and 8f winner Model Village (by Habitat), the quite useful 8-10f winner Beverly Knight (by Be My Guest) and minor winners abroad by Fabulous Dancer, Habitat, Monteverdi and Wassl. The dam won 10 races from 10-13f at 3 yrs in Ireland and is out of the 3-y-o winner Pelerine (by Crepello). (Blandford Thoroughbreds).

KIDSTON LASS (IRE)
Bay filly. Alzao - Anthis (Ela Mana Mou).
April 19. 1st foal. 13,000 Ir gns (Goffs).
The dam was 2nd over 12f in Ireland on her only 3-y-o start and is a half-sister to the useful 3-y-o 10f winner Coryana, herself dam of the very smart miler Waajib, and to the Italian 2,000 gns

3rd Robo Fina. 2nd dam, Rosolini (by Ragusa), was a useful winner of the 10f Lupe Stakes and a half-sister to the high class middle distance stayer Knockroe. (Mr J. Toller).

MELLORS
Bay colt. Common Grounds - Simply Beautiful (Simply Great).
April 15. 1st foal. 14,500 Ir gns (Goffs).
The dam was placed from 7-12f in Ireland at 3 yrs. 2nd dam, Black and Beauty (by African Sky), won at 2 yrs and is a half-sister to 3 winners. 3rd dam, Compliment, is an unraced half-sister to the champion filly Humble Duty. (Blandford Thoroughbreds).

THE DILETTANTI (USA)
Bay colt. Red Ransom - Rich Thought (Rich Cream).
January 17. 1st foal. $40,000 (Keeneland September).
The dam, a minor winner at 4 yrs in the USA, is a half-sister to 7 winners including the Grade 2 San Felipe Handicap winner Stancharry, the Grade 2 Gamely Handicap 2nd Up to Juliet and the stakes placed winner Keep on Dancing - herself dam of a stakes winner. 2nd dam, Good Thought (by On-and-On), is an unraced half-sister to the champion 2-y-o Barbizon and the good American stakes winner Hillsborough. (Duke of Devonshire).

VERULAM (IRE)
Bay colt. Marju - Hot Curry (Sharpen Up).
February 2nd. 3rd foal. 13,000 Ir gns (Goffs).
Half-brother to the minor 1993 6f placed 2-y-o Ewar Empress and to the unplaced (in two starts) 1994 2-y-o Marchant Ming (both by Persian Bold). The dam, an 8f winner at 3 yrs in the USA, is a half-sister to 4 winners including the French listed stakes winner Dinner Out. 2nd dam, Gourmet Dinner (by Raise a Cup), a stakes placed winner of 5 races in the USA, is a half-sister to 10 winners including Golden Pheasant (Arlington Million, Prix Niel, etc), Trial and Error (Dee Stakes) and Seewillo (Grade 3 Queen Charlotte Handicap). (Blandford Thoroughbreds).

STALLION REFERENCE

The index numbers under each sire indicate their two-year-old representatives in the premier section of the book.

AFFIRMED
1975 Exclusive Native - Won't Tell You (Crafty Admiral).
The brilliant triple crown winner Affirmed may not be as good a stallion as he was a racehorse, but nonetheless he is a distinctly useful sire. The best of his runners is surely the champion grass mare and $2.5 million earner Flawlessly. Amongst his other good American and Canadian stakes winners are Peteski (Horse of the Year and three Grade 1 wins in Canada), the Canadian champions Charlie Barley and One From Heaven and the Grade 1 Top Flight Handicap winners Buy the Firm and Firm Stance. He also had a filly in the Experimental Free Handicap for 2-y-o's in America last year - Blond Moment. In Europe, although he hasn't had anything to compare with Flawlessly, his overall record is probably even better with such as - Trusted Partner (Irish 1,000 gns), Bint Pasha (Prix Vermeille and Yorkshire Oaks), Zoman (Prix d'Ispahan and the Budweiser International), Regal State (Prix Morny) and Claude Monet (Dante Stakes) - plus several other Group winners. Affirmed stands at Jonabell Farm in Lexington, Kentucky at a fee of $20,000 (live foal) and his AEI is 3.10.
(340)

ALLEGED
1974 Hoist the Flag - Princess Pout (Prince John).
Successful 1994 performers by Alleged include the Prix Kergorlay and Prix du Cadran winner Molesnes, the Italian Oaks winner Shahmiad, the middle distance stayer Always Earnest, the Ormonde Stakes 2nd Shrewd Idea, the 3-y-o 10f winner Strategic Choice - all very useful and, best of all, the high class Group 1 Premio Presidente della Republica and Prince of Wales's Stakes winner Muhtarram (winner of the Phoenix Champion Stakes the previous season). An outstanding racehorse himself and twice winner of the Prix de l'Arc de Triomphe, Alleged has been responsible for many other good horses over the years. The best of them include the Group/Grade 1 winners Fiesta Gal (Coaching Club American Oaks), Hours After (French Derby), Law Society (Irish Derby), Leading Counsel (Irish St Leger), Legal Case (Champion Stakes), Midway Lady (1,000 gns and Oaks), Milesius (Manhattan Handicap), Miss Alleged (Breeders Cup Turf) and Sir Harry Lewis (Irish Derby). Alleged stands at Walmac International Farm in Lexington, Kentucky at a fee of $25,000 (live foal). His AEI is a commendable 2.89.
(169, 244)

ALZAO
1980 Lyphard - Lady Rebecca (Sir Ivor).
For the first time Alzao has numerous representatives in this book - an indication perhaps that he bagan to receive higher class mares from 1992 as a result of his successful record at stud. Last season he was around the top of the various sires lists yet again, due in part to the smart horses Alpride (Group 2 Premio Lydia Tesio), Bobzao (Group 2 Hardwicke Stakes) and Unblest (Group 3 Prix de la Porte Maillot). He is noted for producing lots of winners - thanks largely to his annual bumper crops of foals - usually at distances of up to 10f. With the well-bred 2-y-o's he has this year, Alzao could well get one or two which prove to be on a par with the best of his offspring which include the Sussex Stakes winner Second Set, the Beverly Hills Handicap winner Alcando and the Group 1 winning 2-y-o fillies Capricciosa and Pass the Peace. Alzao stands, at a fee of 15,000 Ir gns (Oct 1st), at Coolmore Stud in Ireland. His 1994 yearling average was 31,042 gns (43 sold).
(96, 101, 114, 275, 336)

BELMEZ
1987 El Gran Senor - Grace Note (Top Ville).
Belmez is a son of the outstanding 2,000 gns and Irish Derby winner El Gran Senor out of a winning half-sister to the French Oaks winner Lypharita. Despite fertility problems, El Gran Senor has an excellent record of 18% stakes winners to foals and they include the top class colt Rodrigo de Triano. Belmez tasted victory five times, notably in the King George VI and Queen Elizabeth Diamond Stakes, the Great Voltigeur Stakes and the Dalham Chester Vase. His first 2-y-o's ran last year but sadly none of them managed to win a race. Belmez stands at Wolferton Stud in Norfolk at a fee of £6,000 (live foal). His 1994 yearling average was 19,598 gns (12 sold).
(193)

BE MY CHIEF
1987 Chief's Crown - Lady Be Mine (Sir Ivor).
Be My Chief made a fair start to his stud career with 6 individual winners in his first crop of 2-y-o's last year. None were out of the ordinary, although the filly Magongo did promise quite a lot for her second season. A son of Chief's Crown, also sire of Erhaab and Grand Lodge, Be My Chief was the champion 2-y-o colt in 1989 when he was unbeaten in six races, notably the Group 1 Racing Post Trophy. As a three year old he was unplaced on his only outing. Reportedly unsuited by the prevailing firm going, he was unable to be trained sufficiently to enable him to race again that season. Be My Chief stands at Newmarket's National Stud at a fee of £4,500 (1st Oct) and his yearling average was 19,494 gns (29 sold).
(179, 229)

BE MY GUEST
1974 Northern Dancer - What a Treat (Tudor Minstrel).
He may be getting on in years, but Be My Guest again proved himself a decent sire of 2-y-o winners in 1994 with 8 winners in Britain and Ireland and 50% winners to runners. The best of them was probably the Group 3 Anglesey Stakes winner Smart Guest and, among his older horses, the smart 4-y-o My Patriarch won the Henry II Stakes and the Lonsdale Stakes. His most memorable winners over the years have been Go and Go, Luth Enchantee, Invited Guest, Intimate Guest, Most Welcome, Double Bed, Free Guest, Astronef, Media Starguest, Nothern Treat and Anfield. He kicked off this season in fine style though the victories of Pelder in the Group 1 Prix Ganay and Pentire in the three Classic Trials. Be My Guest stands at Coolmore in Ireland at 6,000 Ir gns (Oct 1st). His 1994 yearling average was 20,845 gns (37 sold).
(75, 288)

BLUSHING JOHN
1985 Blushing Groom - La Griffe (Prince John).
A son of the outstanding sire Blushing Groom, Blushing John has sired 25 winners from his first two crops, though only one, the Grade 3 winner Jaggery John, is the winner of a stakes race. That represents a disappointing start for the American sire and his results need to improve. Wins in the Group 3 9f Prix Saint Roman (as a 2-y-o), and the Group 3 8f Prix de Fontainebleau, preceded Blushing John's victory in the French 2,000 gns. A smart colt in Europe, he went on to win 5 more races in America, notably the Grade 1 Hollywood Gold Cup. He stands at Brookside Farms in Kentucky and his AEI is 1.51.
(315, 346)

CADEAUX GENEREUX
1985 Young Generation - Smarten Up (Sharpen Up).
The champion European sprinter of 1989, Cadeaux Genereux won 7 races from 5f to 7f, notably the July Cup and the William Hill Sprint Championship. He was also first past the post, but disqualified, in the Prix de l'Abbaye and seemed to improve with age, being best of all as a 4-y-o. With two crops racing, he has already sired one Group 1 winner in the Prix Morny heroine Hoh Magic, along with such useful winners as Alanees and Ultimo Imperatore. Certainly not the least interesting aspect about the pedigree of Cadeaux Genereux is that it is totally devoid of Northern Dancer blood, thereby providing a ready outcross for mares from that all-powerful line. Standing at Whitsbury Manor Stud at a fee of £7,000 (live foal), his yearling average in

1994 was a distinctly healthy 53,223 gns (17 sold).
(1, 127, 302)

CAERLEON
1980 Nijinsky - Foreseer (Round Table).
Not a sire to be mentioned in the same breath as his illustrious stud companion Sadlers Wells, but nevertheless Caerleon generally manages to make good use of the excellent opportunities he gets. His two sires championships in 1988 and 1991 are the highlights of his career to date, but he has had some terribly disappointing seasons. The two Group 1 winners Moonax (St Leger) and Only Royale (Yorkshire Oaks), along with the smart Earl of Sefton Stakes winner Del Deya made 1994 an excellent year for him regarding quality as well as quantity. The most outstanding Caerleon colt to date is, of course, the Derby, Irish Derby and King George winner Generous. Standing at Coolmore Stud in Ireland, Caerleon's 1994 yearling average was a superb 117,215 gns (15 sold).
(4, 19, 29, 84, 130, 146, 156, 159, 170, 287, 333)

DANCING SPREE
1985 Nijinsky - Blitey (Riva Ridge).
Not a sire that will be instantly recognisable to most Europeans, Dancing Spree did all his racing in America where he ran 35 times from 3-5 yrs for 10 victories including the Breeders Cup Sprint, the Carter Handicap, the Suburban Handicap (all Grade 1 events) and the Grade 2 True North Handicap. He is a full brother to the Grade 2 winning filly Dancing All Night and a half-brother to the Grade 1 winner Fantastic Find. Dancing Spree's first 2-y-o's ran last year when his yearling average was 18,233 gns (10 sold). He stands at the Haras de Meautry near Deauville at a fee of 60,000 FF (Oct 1st).
(283)

DANEHILL
1986 Danzig - Razyana (His Majesty).
Certainly one of the most successful of dual hemisphere sires, the Group 1 Ladbroke Sprint Cup winner Danehill was the champion Australian sire of 2-y-o's in 1993-94. 'Down under' he has sired the top class winners, Danzero, Danewin and Danarani. Back in Ireland, he has sired the Group 1 Coronation Stakes winner Kissing Cousin, the Grade 1 Keeneland Queen Elizabeth II Challenge Cup winner Danish, the Italian Group 2 winner Fred Bongusto, the Group 3 winners Ardana, Hill Hopper and Indian Jones and the very useful 10f winner Alriffa. Inbred 3x3 to Natalma - the dam of Northern Dancer - Danehill stands at Coolmore Stud in Ireland at a fee of 15,000 Ir gns (1st Oct) and the Arrowfield Stud in Australia. His 1994 yearling average in Europe was 33,605 gns (40 sold).
(32, 182, 237)

DANZIG
1977 Northern Dancer - Pas de Nom (Admiral's Voyage).
An absolutely outstanding sire, Danzig had yet another successful year in 1994 with the American Graded stakes winners Dispute (Grade 1 Spinster Stakes), Lure (Grade 1 Caesar's International Handicap), Princess Polonia, Strolling Along and Tribulation, and the European Group winners Emperor Jones, Maroof (Group 1 Queen Elizabeth II Stakes), Petit Loup (Group 1 Gran Premio de Milano) and Zieten. His previous Group/Grade 1 winners are Adjudicating, Chief's Crown, Contredance, Dance Smartly, Danzig Connection, Dove Hunt, Easy Now, Furiously, Lotka, One of a Klein, Pine Bluff, Polish Navy, Stephans's Odyssey, Qualify and Versailles Treaty in the USA and Danehill, Dayjur, Green Desert, Hamas, Polish Patriot, Polish Precedent, Polonia and Shaadi in Europe. Very few of Danzig's stock stay twelve furlongs, though among those that have are Petit Loup and the Belmont Stakes winner Danzig Connection. Standing at Kentucky's Claiborne Farm, where his stud fee is private, Danzig's AEI is a monumental 6.21, the highest in North America in 1994.
(8, 124, 166, 171, 173, 211, 212, 224, 255, 292, 313, 331)

DARSHAAN
1981 Shirley Heights - Delsy (Abdos).
Flying the flag for Darshaan last season were the smart E.P.Taylor Stakes and Prix de

Royaumont winner Truly a Dream and the very useful Group 3 Prix Minerve winner Sharamana (a half-sister to Shergar). Darshaan hasn't really lived up to expectations of him as a sire after a first crop that included the disqualified Oaks winner Aliysa (clearly the winner on merit) and the Greenham Stakes winner Zayyani. However, his son Kotashaan won numerous Grade 1 events in the USA including the Breeders Cup Turf and there has also been Hellenic (Yorkshire Oaks), Arzanni (Yorkshire Cup), Grand Plaisir (Prix Noailles), Narwala, Game Plan and Satin Wood. Darshaan stands at the Gilltown Stud in County Kildare at a fee of Ir£15,000. His 1994 yearling average was 17,720 gns (8 sold).
(269, 286)

DAYJUR
1987 Danzig - Gold Beauty (Mr Prospector).
A leading first season sire last year, Dayjur had 7 winners in Europe and the USA including the useful Cornwallis Stakes winner Millstream, the highly promising Nwaamis and the American colt Jump the Shadow. That was no more than expected and bigger prizes are sure to come Dayjur's way. The outstanding European racehorse of 1990, he won five races in succession, starting with the Sears Temple Stakes and followed by the Kings Stand Stakes, the Keeneland Nunthorpe Stakes, the Ladbroke Sprint Cup and the Ciga Prix de l'Abbaye. His style of racing was characterised by a blistering early pace which totally dominated his opponents. And yet he will probably be best remembered for the final race of his career, a race he ought to have won, but lost in the most amazing fashion. By jumping a shadow that fell across the track at Belmont Park, he was just beaten by the American filly Safely Kept in the Breeders Cup Sprint. Not surprisingly, one of his offspring has already been named Jump the Shadow - a 2-y-o winner last year that was also 2nd in the Group 3 Tremont Breeders Cup Stakes. Being by Danzig and out of a champion mare by Mr Prospector, Dayjur could hardly be better bred and the staff at Shadwell Farm, Kentucky where he now stands, must be hoping for great things from him. I will always remember Dayjur for the fantastic speed he showed at York and Haydock Park, and it really is a pity that he wasn't kept in training as a four year old. His 25 yearlings sold at public auction last year fetched an average of $311,680. 1995 Stallion Fee:- $50,000 live foal.
(46, 90, 102, 104, 158, 223, 250, 251, 256, 301, 335)

DIESIS
1980 Sharpen Up - Doubly Sure (Reliance II).
Although at stud in the United States, Diesis is unquestionably a sire whose stock are overwhelmingly suited by European conditions. The talented filly Diminuendo (Epsom and Irish Oaks) and the Eclipse and Phoenix Champion Stakes winner Elmaamul have proved his best performers, followed by the Prix de l'Abbaye winner Keen Hunter, Rothmans International winner Husband, Juddmonte International 2nd Sabrehill, Premio Roma winner Knifebox, Enharmonic, Kerrera, Marillette, Pollen Count and the American Graded stakes winners Rootentootenwooten (Grade 1 Demoiselle Stakes), Daarik, Suivi and Timely Business. We can add to that list the good 1994 performers Eternal Reve (Coronation Stakes 2nd) and Gneiss (Jersey Stakes winner in a dead-heat). Diesis won both the Middle Park Stakes and the Dewhurst Stakes, is a full brother to the champion miler and sire Kris and has sired Group 1 winners from 5f to 12f. He stands at Mill Ridge Farm in Lexington, Kentucky at a fee of $30,000 (live foal). His AEI currently stands at 2.54.
(36, 52, 60, 184)

DISTANT RELATIVE
1986 Habitat - Royal Sister II (Claude).
As a broodmare sire, Habitat is unquestionably of the highest class. As a sire of sires however, he has been a distinct disappointment. This horse, Distant Relative, may just buck the trend, for his 2-y-o's in 1994 placed him amongst the best in the first season sires list with 9 individual winners including the useful filly Germane, winner of the Rockfel Stakes. Distant Relative won six Group races, most notably the Group 1 Sussex Stakes and the Group 1 Prix du Moulin and was certainly a high class miler. He is a half-brother to the equally talented, if somewhat enigmatic, Ezzoud - winner of the Juddmonte International in both 1993 and 1994. Standing at Whitsbury Manor Stud at a fee of £3,500 (Oct 1st), Distant Relative's 1994 yearling average was 17,248 gns (12 sold).

DOYOUN
1985 Mill Reef - Dumka (Kashmir II).
This is Doyoun's 4th crop of 2-y-o's and he can best be described as a moderately successful sire. His Group 1 2-y-o National Stakes winner Manntari did not reappear after finishing last in the Irish 2,000 gns (reportedly distressed), the very useful fillies Adaika and Dalara won the Prix Chloe and the Prix de Royallieu respectively and Hiwaya was a useful English 1994 2-y-o. Doyoun himself won the 2,000 gns and was 3rd in the Derby, the Waterford Crystal Mile and the Champion Stakes and he is a half-brother to the Hungerford Stakes winner Dalsaan and the Cork and Orrery Stakes winner Dafayna. Standing at Gilltown Stud in Ireland, his fee seems a bit expensive at Ir£10,000, given that his 1994 yearling average was just 13,657 gns (8 sold).
(252, 274)

EASY GOER
1986 Alydar - Relaxing (Buckpasser).
The champion 2-y-o colt of 1988 in America and $4.8 million earner Easy Goer won no less than 9 Grade 1 races including the Belmont, Travers and Wood Memorial Stakes and the Woodward, Suburban and Whitney Handicaps. He was also 2nd, beaten each time by Sunday Silence, in the Kentucky Derby, the Preakness Stakes and the Breeders Cup Classic. His first 2-y-o's ran last year and included 5 individual winners, though none of any consequence.
(95, 177)

EL GRAN SENOR
1981 Northern Dancer - Sex Appeal (Buckpasser).
The 2,000 gns and Irish Derby hero El Gran Senor has never been a particularly fertile stallion and consequently his numbers of foals have been small compared to other top class stallions. What he lacks in quantity however, he certainly makes up for in quality. He has a high percentage of stakes winners to foals, the best of them being the English and Irish 2,000 gns winner Rodrigo de Triano, the King George winner Belmez, the William Hill Futurity winner Al Hareb and the American Grade 1 winners Corrazona, Senor Tomas and Toussaud. Last season his best performers in Europe were George Augustus, Colonel Collins and Lit de Justice. El Gran Senor stands at Ashford Stud in Kentucky, at a fee of $30,000 (live foal). His AEI is an excellent 3.83.
(168)

ELMAAMUL
1987 Diesis - Modena (Roberto).
Elmaamul made a tentative start to his stud career in 1994 with 4 individual winners. However, both his sire and broodmare sire are noted for producing good three year olds, rather than precocious juveniles, so we must wait a year or two before passing judgement on his ability as a sire. On the racecourse he had considerable ability, winning 5 races at 2 and 3 yrs from 7-10f including the Group 1 Coral Eclipse Stakes and the Group 1 Phoenix Champion Stakes. He was also 2nd in the Juddmonte International at York and 3rd in the Derby. A very well bred stallion, Elmaamul is by the 1982 champion 2-y-o Diesis - a high class sire - and out of a half-sister to the dam of Zafonic. He stands, at a fee of £3,500 (Oct 1st), at Newmarket's Eagle Lane Farm and his 1994 yearling average was 14,331 (4 sold).
(2, 271, 278)

FAIRY KING
1982 Northern Dancer - Fairy Bridge (Bold Reason).
For a horse that ran just once, and was unplaced at that, it could well be said that Fairy King's success at stud has been astonishing. That isn't the whole story however, as he happens to be a full brother to the all-conquering Sadlers Wells and a three-parts brother to Nureyev. Since retiring to stud himself in 1986, he has proved himself a most useful sire of winners both numerically and of quality racehorses. His biggest winner to date came last year with the runaway victory of Turtle Island in the Irish 2,000 gns. That win was supported by Group 3 successes for the 2-y-o's Burden of Proof and Ghostly, along with listed wins for four horses including the very useful Eurolink Thunder. In previous years he has had the 2-y-o Group 1 winners Fairy Heights (Fillies Mile) and Pharaoh's Delight (Phoenix Stakes). Fairy King stands at Coolmore in Ireland at 25,000 Ir gns (Oct 1st) - a 25% increase on last year - and his 1994 yearling average

was 38,885 gns (38 sold).
(267, 341)

FORTY NINER
1985 Mr Prospector - File (Tom Rolfe).
The champion American 2-y-o colt of 1987, Forty Niner won 11 of his 19 races at 2 and 3 yrs from 6-10f including the Champagne Stakes, Futurity Stakes, Travers Stakes and Haskell Invitational Stakes (all Grade one events). Having had three crops racing, we can now make a judgement as to his worth as a stallion and with 11 stakes winners, 6 of them Graded, it seems clear he is a very smart sire. The best of them are the Grade 1 Apple Blossom Handicap winner Nine Keys, the highly rated 1994 2-y-o colt On Target and the dual Grade 2 winner Twining. In Britain, his best performers have been the smart dual 10f winner Luhuk, the very useful 9f-10.2f winner Island of Silver and the very promising 1994 2-y-o 7f winner and Dewhurst Stakes 4th Takkatamm. Standing at Kentucky's Claiborne Farm, Forty Niner's AEI is an exceptionally high 4.05.
(37, 64, 89, 157, 280, 339)

GENEROUS
1988 Caerleon - Doff the Derby (Master Derby).
The 2-y-o's of this particular sire are perhaps the most eagerly awaited of all first season stallions. His well documented racing career demands attention. Despite having won twice already as a 2-y-o and been 2nd in the Coventry Stakes, he was allowed to start in the Group 1 Dewhurst Stakes at the odds of 33-1. Even after winning that most prestigious of English 2-y-o races, Generous was hardly expected to carry all before him as a three year old, but by virtue of his wins in the Derby, the Irish Derby and the King George (by an aggregate of 15 lengths), he was worthily dubbed the best of his age in Europe. Perhaps his victory in the Irish Derby, by 3 lengths from the future 'Arc' winner Suave Dancer actually gave him the nod over that fine colt in the final analysis for European Champion 3-y-o. Generous is a half-brother to 2 stakes winners including the Irish Group 3 and U.S. Grade 3 winner Wedding Bouquet. His dam is a half-sister to the high class racemare Trillion - herself dam of the brilliant Triptych. As he is also a son of the dual champion sire Caerleon, the omens look good for a successful stallion career for Generous and his yearling average in 1994 was an exceptional 135,487 gns (8 sold). His stallion fee, at Banstead Manor Stud in Newmarket, is private.
(23, 64, 89, 157, 280, 339)

GREEN DESERT
1983 Danzig - Foreign Courier (Sir Ivor).
Green Desert has been one of the top young sires in Europe since his first crop of 2-y-o's in 1990 made him the champion first-season sire. He gets plenty of horses with speed in abundance, notably the Breeders Cup Sprint, Keeneland Nunthorpe Stakes and Haydock Sprint Cup winner Sheikh Albadou and the July Cup winner Owington. His other good performers are the Group 3 winners Absurde, Ardkinglass, Magic Ring, Mojave, Redden Burn, Sahara Star and, in 1994, Gabr, Mint Crisp and Tropical. He also had the smart 10f gelding Desert Shot, the very useful 2-y-o colt Tatami and the American 2-y-o stakes winner Christmas Gift last year. Green Desert's fee, at Norfolk's Shadwell Stud, is £25,000 (live foal) and his 1994 yearling average was 58,151 gns (17 sold).
(9, 15, 34, 42, 49, 56, 121, 122, 139, 167, 205, 209, 221, 241, 245, 248, 289, 305, 306, 327, 347)

GREEN FOREST
1979 Shecky Greene - Tell Meno Lies (The Axe II).
The dual 7f winner New Capricorn and the dual 8f winner Golden Kabubby - both useful 4-y-o's - were Green Forest's best runners in Europe last year. He began his stud career very well, with the champion 2-y-o filly and Irish 1,000 gns winner Forest Flower in his first crop, but he failed to continue in the same vein and he hasn't sired another Group 1 winner. The decent horses he has sired are Forest Wind (Group 2 Mill Reef Stakes), Made of Gold (Group 2 Royal Lodge Stakes), Ozone Friendly (Group 2 Prix Robert Papin), Somethingdifferent (Group 2 Moet and Chandon Rennen) and the Group/Grade 3 winners Forest Glow, Green Line Express and Indian Forest.
(66)

GULCH
1984 Mr Prospector - Jameela (Rambunctious).
A very successful American stallion, Gulch had a fantastic weekend in early May when his son Thunder Gulch won the Kentucky Derby and his daughter Harayir captured the 1,000 gns. Gulch had two colts and a filly on the American 2-y-o Experimental Free Handicap last season - the filly Sea Breezer running 2nd in the Grade 1 Spinaway Stakes and the colts De Niro and Thunder Gulch both winning stakes events. Along with Thunder Gulch and Harayir, the best performers by Gulch to date - with just three crops racing - are the Grade 1 Super Derby and $1.1 million winner Wallenda and the Grade 1 Hopeful Stakes winner Great Navigator. Gulch himself won over $3 million and 13 of his 32 races from 5f to 9f, notably the Hopeful Stakes, the Futurity Stakes, the Wood Memorial Invitational, the Metropolitan Handicap (twice), the Carter Handicap and the Breeders Cup Sprint - all Grade 1 events. His dam won three Grade 1 races herself, along with over a million dollars, in the States. Gulch stands at Kentucky's Lane's End Farm at a fee of $40,000 (live foal) and his AEI is 2.70.
(22, 314)

HANSEL
1988 Woodman - Count on Bonnie (Dancing Count).
First-season sire Hansel won 7 of his 14 starts from 5f (at 2 yrs) to 12f, notably the Belmont Stakes, Preakness Stakes (both Grade 1), Arlington-Washington Futurity, Jim Beam Stakes, Lexington Stakes (all Grade 2) and the Grade 3 Tremont Breeders' Cup Stakes. No doubt it was the winning of two legs of the Triple Crown which gained him the title of champion 3-y-o colt. Being a son of the extremely successful stallion Woodman helped make Hansel a popular choice of sire at the 1994 yearling sales - the average price for his 4 colts and 6 fillies being $90,900. Standing at Gainsborough Farm in Versailles, Kentucky, Hansel's stallion fee for 1995 is $30,000 (live foal).
(21, 123, 228, 230, 294)

HIGH ESTATE
1986 Shirley Heights - Regal Beauty (Princely Native).
The champion 2-y-o of 1988, High Estate won 5 races, notably the Coventry Stakes, the Lanson Champagne Vintage Stakes, the Imry Solario Stakes and the Royal Lodge Stakes. Unusually for a son of Shirley Heights, he left his best form behind him as a juvenile, for as a 3-y-o he won just one of his four races - and that a three runner affair. However, his drop in form may well have been due to the operation he received on a split pastern. These are High Estate's 3rd crop of 2-y-o's and he has already sired a Group 1 winner in Close Conflict - the Peter Chapple-Hyam trained winner of the Gran Premio d'Italia - along with the Group 2 Lancashire Oaks winner State Crystal. Standing at Coolmore Stud in Ireland, High Estate's fee is 4,000 Ir gns (Oct 1st) and his 1994 yearling average was 19,525 gns (21 sold).
(73)

HIGHEST HONOR
1983 Kenmare - High River (Riverman).
A winner of 4 races in France - notably the Group 1 Prix d'Ispahan - and placed in four other Group 1 races there, Highest Honor is now a sought after stallion and was the champion French sire in 1994 (by numbers of winners). With four crops racing he has sired the U.S. dual Grade 2 winner Gothland, the Group 2 Prix Vicomtesse Vigier winner Dadarissime, the German Group 2 winner Erminius and the French triple Group 3 winner Take Risks. Only four Group or Graded stakes winners then, but last season he had 11 two-year-old winners and the quality of his mares has improved since he first showed his capabilities as a sire. Standing at the Haras du Quesnay in Deauville, at a fee of 100,000 FF, Highest Honor's 1994 yearling average was 23,204 gns (28 sold).
(161)

HOUSEBUSTER
1987 Mt. Livermore - Big Dreams (Great Above).
First season sire Housebuster won 15 of his 22 starts from 6f to a mile, notably the Jerome Handicap, the Vosburgh Stakes and the Carter Handicap - all Grade 1 events in New York and was the champion American sprinter at both 3 and 4 yrs. His dam won four minor stakes events,

whilst his sire, Mt Livermore, won 11 races including three Graded stakes and is a son of Blushing Groom. Mt Livermore is a succesful American stallion himself, being responsible for around 25 stakes winners including the Grade 1 Breeders Cup Juvenile Fillies winner Eliza. This isn't a familiar pedigree to European eyes, and it will be interesting to see if Housebuster can make his mark over here. He stands at Jonabell Farm in Lexington, Kentucky at a fee of $20,000 (live foal) and had no less than 27 yearlings sold at auction last year, bringing an impressive average of $115,000.
(132, 321)

HOUSTON
1986 Seattle Slew - Smart Angle (Quadrangle).
Houston's first 2-y-o's raced last season and he had several minor winners in the States. As a racehorse himself, he won five of his eleven starts from 6-8f furlongs including the Grade 2 Bay Shore Stakes, the Grade 3 Derby Trial Stakes and the Grade 3 King's Bishop Stakes in the USA. His dam, Smart Angle, the champion American 2-y-o filly of 1979, is a sister to the Grade 2 winner Quadratic and a half-sister to the dual Grade 2 winner Smarten. Houston stands at Walmac International Farm in Lexington, Kentucky at a fee of $15,000.
(207)

IN THE WINGS
1986 Sadlers Wells - High Hawk (Shirley Heights).
It will be fascinating to see which stallion sons of Sadlers Wells, if any, become successful sires themselves and In the Wings would appear to have as good a chance as any. His first crop appeared on the racecourse last year with six of them winning - not bad for a sire as stoutly bred as In the Wings clearly is. Although none of them have hit the headlines yet - in the main, his runners should certainly benefit from time and middle-distances - they include the Prix de Fontenoy winner Winged Love and the very promising colt Singspiel. In the Wings was a top class middle-distance racehorse and won 7 of his 11 races, notably the Breeders Cup Turf, the Coronation Cup and the Grand Prix de Saint-Cloud. Group 1 victories in three different countries is a record to be proud of and his pedigree (he is out of the Shirley Heights mare, High Hawk, winner of the Ribblesdale Stakes), also bodes well for his prospects. He stands at Ireland's Ragusa Stud at a fee of Ir£8,000 (Oct 1st) and his yearling average was 50,866 gns (9 sold).
(100, 145, 194, 246, 332)

JAVA GOLD
1984 Key to the Mint - Javamine (Nijinsky).
A winner of 9 races in the USA from 5.5f to 10f, notably the Remsen Stakes, the Travers Stakes, the Marlboro Cup Invitational Handicap and the Whitney Handicap - all Grade one events - Java Gold earned $1.9 million on the track for his owner Paul Mellon. Java Gold's dam, Javamine, won four Graded stakes races, is a half-sister to the dam of the Kings Stand Stakes winner Bluebird and has also bred the Doncaster Cup winner Spicy Story. This is his fourth crop of runners and the only important winner to date has been the dual U.S. Grade 2 winner Grand Jewel. He stands at Kentucky's Lane's End Farm.
(196)

KAHYASI
1985 Ile de Bourbon - Kadissya (Blushing Groom).
With three crops of runners to date, Kahyasi has sired three Group winners, namely the Group 2 Gallinule Stakes winner Massyar, the Prix du Lutece winner Shaiybara and the Prix Berteux winner Bayrika. He began his stud career at a fee of 20,000 Irish gns in 1989, not unusual for a dual Derby winner in a time of high stallion prices. Now, however, his fee is a much more accessible Ir£5,000 and with the support of the Aga Khan's fine broodmare band, he could well get his first Group 1 winner soon. If so, it will very probably come over middle distances. Kahyasi stands at Gilltown Stud in Ireland and his one yearling sold at auction last year fetched just 3,571 gns.
(285)

KEEN
1981 Sharpen Up - Doubly Sure (Reliance II).
A full brother to Kris and Diesis, Keen won the Granville Stakes at 2 yrs and the listed Easter Stakes at 3 yrs before finishing 2nd in the St James's Palace Stakes. He has been a successful sire in Australia with such as the Grade 1 winner Gamine and the Grade 3 winner On With It and his first European crop were 2-y-o's of 1994. Keen stands at the National Stud in Newmarket at a fee of £2,500 (Oct 1st) and his 1994 yearling average was 10,912 gns (18 sold).
(253)

KNOWN FACT
1977 In Reality - Tamerett (Tim Tam).
The very useful colt So Factual, a winner of 3 races in Dubai and 2nd in the Cork and Orrery Stakes at Ascot, was the best of Known Fact's runners in Europe last season when he also had the Canadian Grade 3 winner Nice to Know. A disappointing year for a sire whose record has been inconsistent over the years. The best of his stock have been the outstanding miler and good young sire Warning and the high class miler Markofdistinction. His other 25 stakes winners, many of them being in the USA, have been nothing to write home about, save perhaps for the Group 3 Prix de Porte Maillot winner Nidd and the Breeders Cup Juvenile 2nd Itsali'lknownfact. Known Fact won the 2,000 gns (upon the disqualification of Nureyev) and the Queen Elizabeth II Stakes after a great tussle with Kris. He stands at Juddmonte Farm in Kentucky at a fee of $12,500 (live foal). His AEI last year was 2.24.
(155)

KRIS
1976 Sharpen Up - Doubly Sure (Reliance II).
Kris continues to sire several good horses each year without reaching the heights he scaled in the 80's. His most successful runners in 1994 were the Nassau and Musidora Stakes winner Hawajiss and the Curragh Futurity Stakes and Sweet Solera Stakes winner Jural. Those two are both fillies of course, as are most of Kris's best offspring, such as the Fillies Triple Crown heroine Oh So Sharp, the respective Epsom and French Oaks winners Unite and Rafha, the Prix Saint-Alary winner Fitnah, the E.P.Taylor Stakes winner Sudden Love and other good winners such as Ristna, Divine Danse and Shamshir. His best colts - Flash of Steel, Shavian and Sure Blade - all won Group 1 races over a mile. Another of his sons, the Group 1 Prix de a Salamandre winner Common Grounds, is proving himself a good sire of 2-y-o winners. Kris stands at Newmarket's Plantation Stud at a fee of £17,500 (Oct 1). His 1994 yearling average was 51,502 gns (8 sold).
(7, 31, 35, 70, 109, 140, 249, 290, 304, 307, 328, 329, 345, 349)

LAST TYCOON
1983 Try My Best - Mill Princess (Mill Reef).
A very gifted and versatile racehorse, Last Tycoon won three Group 1 events - the Breeders Cup Mile, the William Hill Sprint Championship and the Kings Stand Stakes. His dam is a half-sister to the Irish Derby winner Irish Ball and to the top class broodmare Irish Bird - dam of the classic winners Assert, Bikala and Eurobird. Last Tycoon's stallion career has been successful both here and in Australia where Tracy's Element, Lady Jakeo and Mahogany - all Australian bred - have won Grade 1 races. His Group 1 winners in Europe are Marju (St James's Palace Stakes), Ezzoud (Juddmonte International - twice), Bigstone (Sussex Stakes, Queen Elizabeth II Stakes, Prix de la Foret and Prix d'Ispahan), Poliuto (Premio Parioli) and Lost World (Grand Criterium). Last Tycoon stands at Coolmore in Ireland and his 1994 yearling average was 22,783 gns (31 sold).
(303)

LEAR FAN
1981 Roberto - Wac (Lt. Stevens).
Lear Fan is certainly not a top class stallion, and 1994 was a poor year for him, but he has built up a perfectly respectable record nonetheless. His best performers include the multiple Italian Group 1 winner Sikeston, the French Group 1 Criterium de Saint-Cloud winner Glaieul, the Group 2 winners Corrupt, Run Don't Fly and Verveine, the Champion Stakes 2nd Cruachan, the Kentucky Derby 2nd Casual Lies and the Grade 2 Arlington Handicap winner Fanmore. Lear

Fan was a good miler and winner of the Group 1 Prix Jacques le Marois, the Group 2 Laurent Perrier Champagne Stakes and the Group 3 Craven Stakes. His dam is a full sister to the dam of Alysheba. Lear Fan stands at Gainesway Farm in Lexington, Kentucky at a fee of $17,500 (live foal). His AEI is 2.24
(348)

LOMOND
1980 Northern Dancer - My Charmer (Poker).
Not a sire one hears much of these days, although in 1994 his smart son, the gelding River North, won the Group 1 Aral-Pokal in Germany, Lomond is a half-brother to Seattle Slew and won the 2,000 gns in 1983. He was the champion first season sire in 1987 when his 2-y-o's included the good fillies Ashayer (Group 1 Prix Marcel Boussac), Flutter Away (Group 1 Moyglare Stud Stakes), Lomond Blossom, Inchmurrin (Group 2 Child Stakes) and Dark Lomond (Group 1 Irish St Leger). That was quite amazing by any standards, but since then his record has been poor. From his extremely large crops, the only good performers to have emerged have been Oczy Czarnie, Citidancer, Duck and Dive, Once In My Life, Julie La Rousse, Chicmond, the aforementioned River North and the champion filly Marling. Lomond now stands in Italy.
(201)

LYCIUS
1988 Mr Prospector - Lypatia (Lyphard).
First-season sire Lycius was a high-class colt but only managed to win 2 races, the Group 1 6f Middle Park Stakes and a listed 7f event at Deauville. He ran very well in most of his other races though and was unlucky not to win another Group 1 event - being placed in six races at the highest level. Those placings came in the 2,000 gns, the July Cup, the Prix Jacques le Marois, the Prix de la Salamandre (2nd each time), the Irish 2,000 gns and the Prix du Moulin. As a son of the top class stallion Mr Prospector, a full-brother to the Group winner Tereshkova and a half-brother to the Graded stakes winner Akabir, Lycius should prove to be a successful stallion. He stands in Ireland at the Ragusa Stud at a fee of Ir£6,000 (Oct 1st) and his 1994 yearling average was 23,030 gns (11 sold).
(153, 247)

LYPHARD
1969 Northern Dancer - Goofed (Court Martial).
Lyphard seems to churn out good winners every year and has built up a formidable reputation as one of the foremost thoroughbred sires in the world. His best European 2-y-o's in 1994 were the Group 1 8f Grand Criterium winner Goldmark and the promising 6f and 7f winner Muhab. His 3-y-o's were led by the very useful French listed 8f winner Beccari and the Group 3 10f Sandown Classic Trial winner Linney Head. Best of all though, was the 4-y-o filly Ski Paradise, a high class winner of the Group 1 8f Prix du Moulin and a Grade 2 event in Japan. He's already had one Grade 1 winner in the States this year with Queens Court Queen, winner of the Santa Margarita Invitational. Among the best of Lyphard's previous 18 crops were the European Group 1 winners Three Troikas (Prix de l'Arc de Triomphe), Riviere d'Or (Prix Saint-Alary), Dancing Maid (French 1,000 gns), Ensconse (Irish 1,000 gns), Pearl Bracelet (French 1,000 gns), Monteverdi (Dewhurst Stakes), Durtal (Cheveley Park Stakes), Jolypha (Prix Vermeille), Reine de Saba (Prix Saint-Alary), Pharly (Prix du Moulin), the good French racehorses and sires Al Nasr and Esprit du Nord and the American Grade 1 winners Au Point, Dahar, Ends Well, Lyphard's Wish, Rainbows For Life, Sabin and Sangue. Best of all are the 1986 3-y-o colts Dancing Brave (European champion) and Manila (champion U.S. turf horse). Lyphard stands at Gainesway Farm in Lexington, Kentucky at a fee of $50,000 (live foal). His AEI, one of the best, is an excellent 4.83.
(91, 279)

MACHIAVELLIAN
1987 Mr Prospector - Coup de Folie (Halo).
The champion European 2-y-o of 1989, Machiavellian began his stud career really well with 9 individual winners last year including the three listed stakes winners Art of War (Sirenia Stakes), Luminoso and Vitellozzi (both in France). Machiavellian himself won the Group 1 Prix de la Salamandre and the Group 1 Prix Morny and was 2nd to Tirol in the 2,000 gns. He is a son of

the outstanding sire Mr Prospector (whose successful stallion sons include Fappiano, Miswaki and Woodman), a brother to one Group 1 winner in Coup de Genie and a half-brother to another in Exit to Nowhere. Standing at Dalham Hall Stud in Newmarket, Machiavellian's stud fee is private - in 1994 it was £20,000 - and his 1994 yearling average was 91,399 gns (9 sold).
(39, 61, 63, 99, 107, 148, 185, 324)

MANILA
1983 Lyphard - Dona Ysidra (Le Fabuleux).
The Italian Derby winner Timestar, the Prix de Psyche winner Agathe and the Chesham Stakes winner Montjoy were three very useful winners in Europe last year for the successful American stallion Manila. Although his stakes winners at the end of 1994 (with four crops racing) numbered only eight, they include the multiple Grade 1 winner and $2.33 million earner Bien Bien and the English trained Italian Group 1 winner Great Palm. Manila himself won 12 of his 18 races - including five Grade 1 stakes - and was the champion grass horse in the USA. He put up a superb performance when winning the Breeders Cup Turf from Theatrical, Estrapade and Dancing Brave and beat Theatrical again the following year when winning the Budweiser-Arlington Million. Manila stands at Kentucky's Lane's End Farm and his AEI is 3.26 - helped enormously by Bien Bien's considerable prize money.
(213)

MARJU
1988 Last Tycoon - Flame of Tara (Artaius).
Certainly one of the most interesting of first-season sires, Marju is by the highly successful stallion Last Tycoon (sire of Bigstone and Ezzoud) and is a half-brother to the Oaks, 1,000 gns and Irish Derby winner Salsabil. Marju himself was a high class miler and won the St James's Palace Stakes after finishing runner-up to Generous in the Derby. Standing at Derrinstown Stud in Ireland at a fee of 5,000 Ir gns (Oct 1st), his 1994 yearling average was 21,039 gns (26 sold).
(16, 133)

MIDYAN
1984 Miswaki - Country Dream (Ribot).
A very smart colt and winner of 3 races including the Group 3 7f Jersey Stakes, Midyan was placed in his other 7 races including the 2,000 gns. He is a son of the highly successful sire Miswaki and is himself a noted sire of plenty of winners. It has to be said, however, that the class of his winners is not particularly high. In fact, there have been just three Group winners in his first four crops, namely the multiple Italian Group 1 and Group 2 Gardner Merchant Mile winner Alhijaz, the Group 3 Goodwood Cup winner Tioman Island and the Group 3 Prix de Saint-et-Oise winner Central City. Midyan stands, at a fee of £4,000 (Oct 1st), at Whitsbury Manor Stud and his 1994 yearling average was 12,274 gns (36 sold).
(227)

MISWAKI
1978 Mr Prospector - Hopespringseternal (Buckpasser).
Since retiring to stud in 1982, the Prix de la Salamandre winner Miswaki has sired over 50 stakes winners. In Europe they include the Prix de l'Arc de Triomphe winner Urban Sea, other French Group winners such as Aliocha, Waki River, Grafin, Balawaki and Whakilyric (the dam of Hernando), the Italian Group winners Misil, Miscrown and Miswaki Tern and the Group 3 Jersey Stakes winner Midyan - now a useful sire himself. In America, the $3.37 million earner and Breeders Cup Classic winner Black Tie Affair has been his chief standard bearer, followed by the Canadian Grade 1 winners In My Heart and Playlist and the U.S. Graded stakes winners Now Listen, Mistaurian, Papal Power and Le Belvedere. Miswaki stands at Walmac International Farm in Kentucky at a fee of $30,000 (live foal) and his AEI is 2.77.
(24)

MOST WELCOME
1984 Be My Guest - Topsy (Habitat).
A top class racehorse from 8-12f, Most Welcome won twice as a 2-y-o, the Select Stakes at Goodwood at 3 yrs and the Juddmonte Lockinge Stakes at 5 yrs. He was also placed in the Derby, the Champion Stakes, the Sussex Stakes and the Breeders Cup Mile. His 2-y-o's this

season are his 3rd crop and to date he has sired several useful horses but none out of the ordinary. Flying Dream won a Group 3 race in Germany whilst Kissair won three 10f races on the flat and this year's Triumph Hurdle. His dam, Topsy, won the Group 2 10f Sun Chariot Stakes and is a half-sister to Teenoso. Most Welcome stands, at a fee of £3,500 (Oct 1st), at Meddler Stud in Newmarket. His 1994 yearling average was only 5,288 gns (18 sold).
(351)

MR PROSPECTOR
1970 Raise a Native - Gold Digger (Nashua).
The legendary stallion Mr Prospector had another good year on both sides of the Atlantic last year. In Europe, his son Distant View, winner of the Group 1 8f Sussex Stakes, was named champion 3-y-o miler, the fillies Macoumba (Group 1 Prix Marcel Boussac), Red Carnival (Group 3 Cherry Hinton Stakes) and Tereshkova (Group 3 Prix de Cabourg) showed much promise for 1995 and Coup de Genie was a very useful winner of the 7f Prix Imprudence. In Canada, the 2-y-o Always a Rainbow won the Grade 1 Cup and Saucer Stakes and in the United States, the 4-y-o filly Educated Risk won the Grade 1 8f Top Flight Handicap and Numerous took the Grade 3 8f Churchill Downs Derby Trial Stakes. Mr Prospector has proved an exceptional sire of sires, particularly through his sons Conquistador Cielo, Fappiano, Forty Niner, Gone West, Gulch, Jade Hunter, Miswaki, Seeking the Gold and Woodman. Quite apart from those already mentioned, Mr Prospector has sired a multitude of top class horses including the Group/Grade 1 winners Ravinella (1,000 gns, French 1,000 gns), Rhythm (Breeders Cup Juvenile Stakes, Travers Stakes), Machiavellian (Prix de la Salamandre), It's in the Air (Vanity Handicap, Alabama Stakes), Eillo (Breeders Cup Sprint), Queena (Maskette Stakes, Ballerina Stakes), Kingmambo (French 2,000 gns, St James's Palace Stakes) and Tank's Prospect (Preakness Stakes). Altogether his tally of Group or Grade 1 winners stands at 36 - a magnificent total. He stands at Kentucky's Claiborne Farm with an AEI of 4.84.
(14, 74, 118, 126, 131, 172, 208, 215, 218, 257, 298, 311, 322, 325, 326)

MTOTO
1983 Busted - Amazer (Mincio).
The promising 2-y-o colt Presenting, a listed 8f winner, was the one shining light in an otherwise dull 1994, quality-wise, for Mtoto. He gets plenty of winners alright and, surprisingly for a top class middle distance son of Busted, he had 8 individual 2-y-o winners in Europe last year. What he really needs however, is a top class winner or two in 1995 and, on his racing career at least, it would be thoroughly deserved. Mtoto won 8 races from 3-5 yrs including the King George, the Eclipse Stakes (twice) and the Prince of Wales's Stakes (twice). He also made two gallant attempts to win the Arc, finishing 2nd to Tony Bin and 4th to Trempolino. A very popular racehorse, Mtoto stands at Aston Upthorpe Stud in Oxfordshire, at a fee of £5,000 (Oct 1st). His 1994 yearling average was 14,757 gns (16 sold).
(68, 125)

MUJTAHID
1988 Woodman - Mesmerize (Mill Reef)
The champion British 2-y-o of 1990, Mujtahid won three of his four races including the Group 2 Gimcrack Stakes and the Group 3 July Stakes and was weighted only below the French colt Hector Protector - also a son of Woodman - in the Free Handicap. Unfortunately, after fracturing a cannon bone in the winter, he wasn't able to race as a three year old when he would have been one of the favourites for the 2,000 gns. These are Mujtahid's first 2-y-o's and he stands, at a fee of 5,000 Ir gns (Oct 1st), at Derrinstown Stud, along with three other young stallions owned by Hamdan Al-Maktoum - Hamas, Lahib and Marju. Mujtahid's 1994 yearling average was 38,972 gns (22 sold).
(299)

NASHWAN
1986 Blushing Groom - Height of Fashion (Bustino).
An outstanding racehorse, Nashwan is the only horse to have won the 2,000 gns, the Derby, the 'King George and the Eclipse Stakes in the same year. He was also a racehorse that could move with a beauty and grace to match his ability, for his magnificent action was like poetry in motion. After a slow start to his stud career, Nashwan seems to be proving his worth, though all his best

winners to date have been fillies. They are the 1995 classic contenders Myself - winner of the Nell Gwyn Stakes - and Aqaarid - winner of the Fillies Mile and the Fred Darling Stakes, the smart listed winner Wandesta and the very useful Irish Oaks 3rd Gothic Dream. The 1994 2-y-o Prix de la Salamandre 3rd Bin Nashwan seems to be his best colt up to now. Standing at the Nunnery Stud in Norfolk, Nashwan's 1994 yearling average was an outstanding 148,468 gns (4 sold) - which includes a 320,000 gns buy.
(43, 78, 81, 128, 129, 134, 163, 174, 189, 219, 225, 226, 231, 238, 261, 272, 273, 343)

NIGHT SHIFT
1980 Northern Dancer - Ciboulette (Chop Chop).
1994 was quite a good year for Night Shift. His very useful son Just Happy won the Group 2 Prix Guillaume d'Ornano and he had a number of listed stakes winners including the very useful Tote Gold Trophy and March Stakes winner Midnight Legend and the useful sprinter Eveningperformance. His Group winners in past seasons have been the top class Juddmonte International, Champion Stakes, Irish 1,000 gns and Coronation Stakes winner In the Groove, the U.S. Grade 1 Starlet Stakes winner Creaking Board, the Group 2 Mill Reef Stakes winner Time Gentlemen and the Group 3 Phoenix Sprint winner Northern Goddess. Particularly adept at siring plenty of 2-y-o winners, Night Shift stands at Coolmore Stud in Ireland at a fee of 12,500 Ir gns (Oct 1st). His 1994 yearling average was 19,750 (2 sold).
(88)

NIJINSKY
1967 Northern Dancer - Flaming Page (Bull Page).
This year sees the final crop of foals by Nijinsky who died in April 1992. He has left a legacy of numerous top class sons and daughters that make his influence on the breed immeasurable. Due to diminishing numbers of mares over his last few years - brought on by advancing age - he hasn't been the force he was, but he was the leading broodmare sire in America last year with earnings of around 7 million dollars. His top class sons and daughters over the years have included the Derby winners Golden Fleece and Shahrastani, the Kentucky Derby and Breeders Cup Classic winner Ferdinand, the Breeders Cup Mile winner Royal Academy, the King George winner Ile de Bourbon, the French Derby winner Caerleon and the 2,000 gns winner Shadeed. A fair number of his sons, of course, including Caerleon, Green Dancer, Niniski and Shadeed, have bred top class horses themselves. It would be nice if his 3-y-o son, Lammtarra, could make a name for himself this season - he certainly seems a high class prospect.
(135, 147, 342)

NINISKI
1976 Nijinsky - Virginia Hills ((Tom Rolfe).
After a commndable racing career when he won both the French and the Irish St Legers, Niniski has built up a creditable record as a sire. Surprisingly, for a horse endowed with so much stamina, he became the champion first season sire in 1984 due largely to the exploits of his champion 2-y-o Kala Dancer. Despite the precocity of some of his stock, however, he is primarily regarded as a sire of middle-distance stayers. Since his first crop, Niniski's best performers have been Petoski (King George VI and Queen Elizabeth Diamond Stakes), Hernando (French Derby), Minster Son (St Leger), Assessor (Prix Royal-Oak), Lomitas (Geno-Europe Preis), Louis Cyphre (Mervyn LeRoy Handicap) - all Group or Grade 1 performers - and the Group 2 winners Sapience and Alflora. In 1994, the filly Coigach won the Group 2 Park Hill Stakes, Hernando only just got beaten in the Prix de l'Arc de Triomphe, Vialli won a Group 2 event in Germany and Alflora won two more Group 2 races. Standing at Newmarket's Lanwades Stud at a fee of 8,000 gns (Oct 1st), Niniski's 1994 yearling average was 24,926 gns (10 sold).
(20)

NUREYEV
1977 Northern Dancer - Special (Forli).
A perenially successful stallion at the highest level, Nureyev's standard bearers last season were the Irish 1,000 gns winner Mehthaaf, the Sun Chariot Stakes winner La Confederation, the French Group winners Jeune Homme, Fadeyev, Flagbird and Trishyde, the smart Prix de la Foret 3rd Neverneyev and the very useful English colts Loyalize and Opera Score. Any list of his best performers in the past would have to include the great Miesque, the brilliant Zilzal, the

popular and very talented Sonic Lady - all milers, the high class sprinters Great Commotion, Polar Falcon, Soviet Star and Vilikaia, and the American Grade 1 stakes winners Alwuhush, Annoconnor, Pattern Step, Stately Don and Theatrical. Nureyev stands at Walmac International Farm in Lexington, Kentucky at a stud fee of $125,000 (live foal) - one of the highest in the world. His AEI, at 4.83, puts him among the top American sires.
(26, 92, 136, 141, 165, 175, 186, 198, 268)

OLD VIC
1986 Sadlers Wells - Cockade (Derring Do).
With just one 2-y-o winner in Britain and Ireland as a first-season sire in 1994, Old Vic will hopefully be judged on what his offspring are like as three and four year olds. Although he won over 8f at 2 yrs himself, it was the following year, when he won all five of his races, that he really came good and proved himself an outstanding racehorse. Having won the Derby Trials at Sandown and Chester, Old Vic annihilated his opponents in the French Derby, becoming the first English trained horse to win the race this century. His final race of the season was the Irish Derby which again he took in facile fashion from Observation Post and Ile de Nisky. Quite often when a stallion is sent abroad, things start to happen for him at home and in his case, Old Vic has been leased to a Japanese stud. Here's wishing Old Vic all the best as a stallion and let's hope we see him back at Dalham Hall soon. His 1994 yearling average was only 12,858 gns (5 sold).
(46, 117, 353)

POLAR FALCON
1987 Nureyev - Marie d'Argonne (Jefferson).
First-season sire Polar Falcon is a welcome addition to the stallion ranks in England. His sire, of course, is famous for the high numbers of classy performers he has produced - notably Miesque, Zilzal, Theatrical, Sonic Lady and Soviet Star, whilst his dam is a winning half-sister to the Group 2 Prix de Pomone winer Marie de Litz. Polar Falcon won the Group 1 6f Ladbroke Sprint Cup in impressive fashion from Sheikh Albadou and also won the Group 2 Lockinge Stakes at Newbury. He stands, at a fee of £6,500 (Oct 1st), at Newmarket's Cheveley Park Stud and his 1994 yearling average was 35,316 gns (18 sold).
(262)

POLISH PRECEDENT
1986 Danzig - Past Example (Buckpasser).
Only a moderately successful sire in terms of both the quality and quantity of his mares, particularly when one considers the classy broodmares he has received, Polish Precedent's best performers to date (these are his 3rd crop of 2-y-o's), are the Group 2 Geoffrey Freer Stakes winner Red Route and the French Oaks 2nd Her Ladyship. It is still early days for him though and he may yet prove himself a good sire. One of the leading European milers of 1989 when rated 2nd behind Zilzal in the mile category of the Free Handicap, he was retired to stud after winning 7 of his 8 races, notably the Prix Jacques le Marois and the Prix du Moulin. He proved himself a top class miler and although put firmly in his place in the Queen Elizabeth II Stakes, he came up against an exceptional miler that day in the shape of Zilzal. Indeed they are quite closely related, being by different stallion sons of Northern Dancer (Zilzal is by Nureyev) and out of mares that are half-sisters. Standing at Dalham Hall Stud at a fee of £15,000 (Oct 1), Polish Precedent's 1994 yearling average was 42,179 gns (6 sold).
(18, 33, 144, 150, 154, 191, 214, 234, 297, 308, 317)

POSEN
1985 Danzig - Michelle Mon Amour (Best Turn).
A winner of 6 races in the USA, including the Grade 2 Saranac Stakes, the Grade 2 Rutgers Handicap and the Grade 3 Forerunner Stakes, Posen has had two crops to race which have included just the one listed winner in Diligent Dodger (in Ireland at 3 yrs in 1994). He stands, at Ireland's Ballylinch Stud, for a fee of Ir£3,000 (Oct 1st) and his 1994 yearling average was 8189 gns (14 sold).
(243)

PRECOCIOUS
1981 Mummy's Pet - Mrs Moss (Reform).
Unbeaten in all his five 2-y-o races, including the Group 2 Gimcrack Stakes, the Group 3 Molecomb Stakes and the Group 3 Norfolk Stakes, Precocious certainly lived up to his name and was a high class colt. As a sire he's been only moderately successful - his best winner being the Group 2 Kings Stand Stakes and Group 2 Temple Stakes winner Elbio. Standing at Yorkshire's Stockwell Stud at a fee of £1,500 (Oct 1st), his 1994 yearling average was just 4,317 gns (5 sold).
(5)

PRINCE SABO
1982 Young Generation - Jubilee Song (Song).
The champion British and Irish sire of 2-y-o's (prize money won) in 1994 was Prince Sabo, thanks largely to the huge sum won by his filly Maid For Walking, winner of the Tote 2-y-o Trophy at Redcar. With the winners of 16 races, Prince Sabo was also high on the 2-y-o sires list based on the number of races won. His two other good horses last year were the Group 2 Mill Reef Stakes winner Princely Hush and the listed St Hugh's Stakes winner Easy Option. Up to now, they're just about as good as any he has sired since his first crop which ran in 1989 and that just about sums Prince Sabo up as a stallion. He gets plenty of winners, no doubt about that, though he has yet to sire anything that might be termed high class. Prince Sabo himself won four races over five furlongs including the Group 2 Flying Childers Stakes and the Group 3 Palace House Stakes. He stands at Newmarket's Cheveley Park Stud at a fee of £4,500 (Oct 1st) and his 1994 yearling average was 11,925 gns (25 sold).
(263)

PRIVATE ACCOUNT
1976 Damascus - Numbered Account (Buckpasser).
A high class stallion with 15 Group or Graded stakes winners to his credit, the highlights for Private Account last season were the French 1,000 gns and French Oaks victories of his daughter East of the Moon and the Acorn Stakes and Ashland Stakes wins of his American filly Inside Information. His best 2-y-o in America last year was the useful filly Pretty Discreet. Previously his best American horses have been the million dollar earners Corporate Report, Personal Flag, Private Terms, Valley Crossing and the unbeaten top class filly Personal Ensign, the triple Grade 1 winner Classy Cathy and the Grade 1 Arlington-Washington Futurity winner Secret Hello. In Europe, his best performers before East of the Moon came along were the Group 1 Coronation Stakes winner Chimes of Freedom, the Group 1 Criterium de Saint Cloud winner Miserden and the Group 3 winners Graecia Magna and Zindari. Private Account himself won the Widener and Gulfstream Park Handicaps (both Grade 1 10f events) and he is a half-brother to the dams of Assatis, Warrshan and the champion American 2-y-o colt Rhythm. Private Account stands at Claiborne Farm, Kentucky and his AEI is 3.74.
(53, 55, 97)

RAINBOW QUEST
1981 Blushing Groom - I Will Follow (Herbager).
Rainbow Quest had a successful 1994 with the Group winners Sunshack (Group 2 Prix du Conseil de Paris), Bonash (Group 2 Prix de Malleret), Wagon Master (Group 2 Princess of Wales's Stakes), Bin Ajwaad, Chatoyant, Richard of York and Urgent Request - subsequently winner of the Grade 1 Santa Anita Handicap. No Group 1 winners this time however, whereas in previous years his winners at the highest level have been the aforementioned Sunshack (Criterium de Saint-Cloud), Raintrap (Prix Royal- Oak), Bright Generation (Italian Oaks), Knight's Baroness (Irish Oaks), Sought Out (Prix du Cadran), Armiger (Racing Post Trophy), Quest For Fame (Derby) and Saumarez (Prix de l'Arc de Triomphe). An impressive list for one of the very best thoroughbred sires in Europe, Rainbow Quest stands at Banstead Manor Stud at a fee of £30,000 (live foal). His 1994 yearling average was an exceptional 105,844 gns (6 sold).
(50, 54, 87, 94, 111, 192, 203, 232, 293, 350)

ROCK CITY
1987 Ballad Rock - Rimosa's Pet (Petingo).
Rock City made a relatively slow start to his stud career with four 2-y-o winners in Britain and

Ireland from his first crop last year. As a son of the speedy Ballad Rock and being a smart sprinter/miler himself, one would expect plenty more 2-y-o winners to come. Not only was he a smart colt, but Rock City's record of never being unplaced in any of his 15 races speaks volumes for his consistency. In all, he won 6 races from 5-7 furlongs including the Group 2 Gimcrack Stakes and the Coventry, July, Greenham and Criterion Stakes (all Group 3 events). He was also 4th in five Group 1 races, notably when 2nd in the St James's Palace Stakes. Rock City stands at the National Stud at a fee of £2,500 (Oct 1st) and his 1994 yearling average was 6,291 gns (23 sold).
(62)

ROYAL ACADEMY
1987 Nijinsky - Crimson Saint (Crimson Satan).
The most expensive yearling of 1988 at a cool $3.5 million, Royal Academy actually went on to prove he was worth it. After losing out by a neck to Tirol in the Irish 2,000 gns, his trainer Vincent O'Brien reverted him to sprinting and his decision was vindicated by the colt's victory in the Group 1 July Cup. He was a high class sprinter alright, but Dick Hern had a better one in Dayjur, as was made plain in the Group 1 Ladbroke Sprint Cup. Royal Academy's finest hour though, came when winning the Grade 1 Breeders Cup Mile from Itsallgreektome and Priolo in a tremendously exciting finish, made all the more so beacause the man on board Royal Academy was none other than Lester Piggott, returning after a five year absence. Royal Academy's two year olds last year gave him the first season sires championship. Painter's Row, winner of the Horris Hill Stakes in convincing fashion, was the best of them although the Irish winners Sharp Point and Oscar Schindler (apparently already a massive 17.2 hands as a 2-y-o), look very promising sorts. Royal Academy stands at Coolmore Stud in Ireland at a fee of 15,000 Ir gns (1st Oct) and his 1994 yearling average was 34,689 gns (35 sold). The Coolmore policy of sending large numbers of mares to their stallions will ensure they retain a high profile in the various sires championships.
(45, 151, 190, 266)

RIVERMAN
1969 Never Bend - River Lady (Prince John).
The very useful 3-y-o 7f winners Mur Taasha and River Deep were the best of Riverman's representatives in Europe last season, whilst the 4-y-o Virginia Rapids - winner of the Grade 1 7f Carter Handicap - was his best performer in America. Consistently, Riverman has proved himself one of the world's best stallions. In Europe the best of his winners over the years have been All at Sea, Detroit, Gold River, Houseproud, Irish River, River Lady, Policeman, Treble, Triptych and the English trained colts Dowsing, Half a Year, Lahib and Rousillon. His top American horses have included Latin American, Pillaster, Rivlia, River Memories and River Special - all Grade 1 winners. His sons Dowsing and, in particular, Irish River, have proved themselves very good stallions too and Riverman is also the broodmare sire of the Group 1 winners Carnegie, Hector Protector, Helen Street and Saint Cyrien. Riverman stands at Gainesway Farm, Lexington, Kentucky at a fee of $75,000 (live foal) and his AEI is 2.87.
(142, 202, 291)

SADLERS WELLS
1981 Northern Dancer - Fairy Bridge (Bold Reason).
It remains to be seen whether he will prove to be an outstanding sire of sires, but one thing is for certain, in terms of siring top class winners, Sadlers Wells is a truly great thoroughbred stallion. Last year his son Barathea captured the Grade 1 Breeders Cup Mile and in Europe he had three Group 1 winners - Poliglote (Criterium de Saint-Cloud), King's Theatre (King George), and Carnegie (Prix de l'Arc de Triomphe). His Group 2 and Group 3 winners in 1994 were Dancing Bloom, Foyer, Hawker's News, Northern Spur, Royal Ballerina and Scribe. The best of Sadlers Wells' offspring in previous seasons include In the Wings, Intrepidity, Opera House, Old Vic and Salsabil, though one could fill a page with his stakes winners which currently number over 12% of his extremely large crops of foals. Standing at Ireland's Coolmore Stud and servicing well over a hundred mares each year at 100,000 Irish gns a time, Sadlers Wells is a positive gold mine - is income being approximately equivalent to someone winning the national lottery twice each year. His yearling average for 1994 was 141,584 gns (43 sold) and once again he has

considerably more 2-y-o's in this book - an amazing 44 - than any other sire.
(3, 12, 13, 25, 38, 41, 51, 57, 71, 77, 79, 80, 82, 83, 85, 86, 98, 103, 108, 110, 143, 152, 162, 164, 176, 180, 181, 183, 187, 199, 200, 210, 239, 259, 265, 282, 284, 296, 310, 316, 320, 334, 338)

SANGLAMORE
1987 Sharpen Up - Ballinderry (Irish River).
Having initially retired to stud in Kentucky in 1992 - and thus these are his first 2-y-o's - Sanglamore moved to France next year to stand at the Haras du Quesnay in Deauville. A high class racehorse, he finished 2nd in his only race as a 2-y-o and won three of his four races next season including the French Derby and the William Hill Dante Stakes. He reappeared as a 4-y-o to win the Group 1 9f Prix d'Ispahan and be placed in the Eclipse Stakes and the King George at Ascot. By the champion sire Sharpen Up and out of the Ribblesdale Stakes winner Ballinderry (a half-sister to the Group winners Lydian, Mot D'Or and Sharpman), Sanglamore's stud fee for 1995 is 75,000FF and his four yearlings sold at auction last year fetched an average of 28,717 gns.
(27, 160, 222)

SAUMAREZ
1987 Rainbow Quest - Fiesta Fun (Welsh Pageant).
Charting the racing career of this horse must be somewhat irksome to Henry Cecil who trained him to win twice over 8f at the start of his 3-y-o career. He was taken to Chester and after being beaten in the Dee Stakes by Blue Stag (rec 4lb), was sold by his owner Charles St George. The lucky trainer to receive the horse was the then relatively obscure Frenchman N.Clement. Saumarez went on to win the Grand Prix de Paris, the Prix du Prince d'Orange and, of course, the Prix de l'Arc de Triomphe from Epervier Bleu and Snurge. Quite a transformation! His first crop were 2-y-o's in 1994 and, truth to tell, made no impact at all. With his middle distance pedigree, his stock will clearly be much better three-year-olds. Saumarez stands at the Haras du Quesnay in France at a fee of 150,000FF. His 1994 yearling average was 39,349 gns (13 sold).
(220)

SCENIC
1986 Sadlers Wells - Idyllic (Foolish Pleasure).
A son of Sadlers Wells out of a half-sister to the dams of Rainbow Quest, Commander in Chief, Warning and Deploy, Scenic won't surprise many people if he proves to be a successful stallion. As a 2-y-o, Scenic dead-heated with Prince of Dance for the Group 1 Dewhurst Stakes and although he trained on well enough, he only managed one more win, in the 10f William Hill Scottish Classic, in the next two seasons. These are his 2nd crop of European 2-y-o's and last year his 4 winners included the listed winner Viaticum. As a dual hemisphere sire, he has had the chance to prove himself in Australia too and his first crop yielded the Grade 1 winner Blevic. Standing at Coolmore Stud (when in Ireland), Scenic's fee is 3,000 Ir gns (Oct 1st). His 1994 yearling average was 11,016 gns (17 sold).
(254)

SEATTLE DANCER
1984 Nijinsky - My Charmer (Poker).
The world-record priced yearling, at $13,100,000, Seattle Dancer went on to prove himself a smart racehorse and won the Derrinstown Stud Derby Trial and the Windfields Gallinule Stakes (both over 10f). In the last of his five races he finished 2nd in the Group 1 Grand Prix de Paris, again over 10f, to Risk Me. He started his stud career off very well with the Group 1 Racing Post Trophy winner Seattle Rhyme in his first crop. Since then however, he has failed to live up to expectations - (he is closely related to Lomond and a half-brother to Seattle Slew) - with his best performers being the Grade 1 Australian Derby winner Dance the Night Away, the Group 3 Desmond Stakes winner Via Borghese, the Grade 3 American winner Seattle Rob and the Chesham Stakes winner State Performer.
(44, 240)

SEATTLE SLEW
1974 Bold Reasoning - My Charmer (Poker).
Not all the great racehorses of the past 25 years have made the transgression to join the world's

stallion elite. Brigadier Gerard, Dancing Brave and Spectacular Bid (ten Grade 1 wins) are cases in point. This fellow though, has been almost as successful at stud as he was a phenomenon on the American racetracks in the 1970's. From 2-4 yrs, Seattle Slew ran 17 times, winning on 14 occasions, notably the Kentucky Derby, the Preakness Stakes, the Belmont Stakes and five other Grade one stakes races. At stud his 19 Grade/Group one winners include the champion American colts A.P.Indy, Slew O'Gold, Swale and Capote, the champion American 2-y-o filly Landaluce, the good French colts Seattle Song and Septieme Ciel and the Coronation Stakes winner Magic of Life. His best performer in 1994 was undoubtedly Lakeway, a winner of four Grade 1 stakes events in the USA, though he also had two representatives on the Experimental Free Handicap for 2-y-o's in Cyrano and Mackenzie Slew. A half-brother to the good sires Lomond and Seattle Dancer, Seattle Slew stands at Three Chimneys Farm in Kentucky at a fee $80,000 (live foal). His AEI, at 5.05, is one of the very best of all American sires.
(106, 216)

SHAADI
1986 Danzig - Unfurled (Hoist the Flag).
The sire of 18 winners of 26 races in 1994, including eight 2-y-o winners, Shaadi's best offspring to date is the Group 3 6f Lowther Stakes and listed 3-y-o 10f winner Velvet Moon. Shaadi won 5 of his 8 races from 7-8f, notably the Irish 2,000 gns, the St James's Palace Stakes and the Craven Stakes. A son of the outstanding sire Danzig, he is also a half-brother to the dual U.S. Grade 3 winner Pleasure Cay and has had 2 crops racing so far. His 1994 yearlings at the sales brought an average of 88,938 gns (6 sold).
(115, 281, 295)

SHADEED
1982 Nijinsky - Continual (Damascus).
From 1987 to 1992 Shadeed averaged 36 foals per year - not particularly large by today's standards - and not surprisingly his total number of stakes winners is just nine. However, they include the 1,000 gns, Prix Jacques le Marois Stakes, Cheveley Park Stakes and Moyglare Stud Stakes winner Sayyedati, the 1,000 gns and Prix Marcel Boussac winner Shadayid, the Canadian dual Grade 1 winner Alydeed and the Brazilian Grade 1 winner Indian Hope. Moreover, two useful English winners of his are Satin Flower (Jersey Stakes) and Splendent (Gimcrack Stakes), whilst Infamous Deed has won a Grade 3 stakes race in the USA. Shadeed himself won the 2,000 gns and the Queen Elizabeth II Stakes and he now stands at Gainesborough Farm in Kentucky. His 1995 stallion fee is $10,000 and his AEI is 2.27.
(11)

SHAREEF DANCER
1981 Northern Dancer - Sweet Alliance (Sir Ivor).
Shareef Dancer's best runners have been the Irish Oaks winner Possessive Dancer, the Hardwicke and Princess of Wales's Stakes winner Rock Hopper, the Prix de Pomone winner Colorado Dancer and the Long Island Handicap winner Shaima. Despite these high class horses, Shareef Dancer is more correctly regarded as a sire of plenty of ordinary winners. He stands at Dalham Hall Stud in Newmarket at a fee of £5,000 (Oct 1st) and his 1994 yearling average was 17,526 gns (16 sold).
(236, 312)

SHERNAZAR
1981 Busted - Sharmeen (Val de Loir).
A half-brother to Shergar, Shernazar was a high class colt himself and won the Group 2 Geoffrey Freer Stakes and the Group 3 September Stakes. As a sire, he hasn't really lived up to expectations - his only Group 1 winners being Kartajana (Prix Ganay) and the Italian Derby winner Houmayoun. In 1994, his best performers were the useful dual 8f listed stakes winner Kayfa and the French listed winner Zafarana. Shernazar stands in Ireland at the Aga Khan's Gilltown Stud at 2,500 Ir gns (Oct 1st). His 1994 yearling average of 15,460 gns (5 sold) was exaggerated by a 55,000 Ir gns colt sold at Goffs in Ireland.
(270, 276)

SHIRLEY HEIGHTS
1975 Mill Reef - Hardiemma (Hardicanute).
Still siring good horses after 16 years at stud, Shirley Heights' best performers in 1994 were the Ascot Gold Cup winner Arcadian Heights and the Great Voltigeur Stakes winner Sacrament - both very useful. Previously, his best colts have been the top class French Derby winner Darshaan and the equally talented Epsom Derby winner Slip Anchor, followed by Elegant Air, Head For Heights, High Estate, Perpendicular and Shady Heights. His best fillies have been nowhere near so good, but they include the Group 1 winners High Hawk (the dam of In the Wings) and Infamy. Shirley Heights stands at the Sandringham Stud in Norfolk at a fee of £15,000 (Oct 1st) and his 1994 yearling average was 122,200 gns (5 sold) - a figure grossly exaggerated by the 390,000 gns paid for his filly out of Brocade. Named National Treasure, she can be found in this book under her trainer Michael Stoute.
(6, 93, 112, 113, 138, 260, 309, 337)

SILVER HAWK
1979 Ribot - Gris Vitesse (Amerigo).
One of a number of highly successful stallion sons of Roberto - the others include Red Ransom, Kris S and Lear Fan - Silver Hawk has sired five Group or Grade 1 winners. They are Lady in Silver (Prix de Diane), Magnificent Star (Yorkshire Oaks), Hawkster (Secretariat Stakes, Oak Tree Invitational and Norfolk Stakes), Silver Ending (Pegasus Handicap) and Zoonaqua (Oak Leaf Stakes). Other good American performers of his include the Graded stakes winners Silver Medallion, Dansil, Silver Ray and the useful 1994 2-y-o filly Comstock Queen. In Europe, quite apart from Magnificent Star and Lady in Silver, he is the sire of Red Bishop (Brigadier Gerard Stakes), Silver Wisp (Jockey Club Stakes), Silver Wedge (Queens Vase) and Silver Lane (Prix de la Grotte). Silver Hawk himself won the Solario Stakes and the Craven Stakes and was placed in the Derby and the Irish Derby. He stands at Airdrie Stud in Kentucky and his AEI is 2.66.
(67, 105, 178)

SLIP ANCHOR
1982 Shirley Heights - Sayonara (Birkhahn).
The Oaks, Irish Oaks and St Leger winner User Friendly stands out as easily the best of Slip Anchor's stock up to now. He has also sired quite a few other smart horses, in particular the Prix Gladiateur winner Safety in Numbers, the Ribblesdale Stakes winner Third Watch and the St Simon Stakes winner Up Anchor, but all in all I feel he has been slightly disappointing. Perhaps I've been expecting too much, but when a stallion sires a filly like User Friendly early in his stud career, one tends to expect great things from him. His winners to foals ratio however, at 51%, is excellent. Slip Anchor stands at Newmarket's Plantation Stud, at a fee of £10,000 (Oct 1st) and his 1994 yearling average was 19,696 gns (Oct 1st).
(10)

SOVIET STAR
1984 Nureyev - Veruschka (Venture VII).
Despite having had the benefit of being bred to many high class mares, Soviet Star has proved to be just a moderately successful stallion. With three crops racing, he has produced just three Group 3 winners - the very smart 1994 4-y-o Supreme Stakes winner Soviet Line, the Prix Quincey winner Bon Point and the smart 1994 3-y-o Prix de la Jonchere winner Freedom Cry. Soviet Star was a top class sprinter-miler and won 8 races, notably the Sussex Stakes, the French 2,000 gns, the Prix de la Foret the Prix du Moulin and the July Cup - all Group 1 events. His 1994 yearling average was 24,242 gns (9 sold).
(30, 217, 242, 258, 319, 352)

STEINLEN
1983 Habitat - Southern Seas (Jim French).
One glance at Steinlen's immediate breeding is enough to suggest that, nicely bred though he is, it is hardly a stallion's pedigree. That statement is based on the fact that Habitat - a great broodmare sire - has been a relative failure as a sire of sires. Hopefully that won't stop Steinlen bucking the trend. After winning four races as a 4-y-o in France, he crossed the Atlantic to score 16 more victories until retiring to stud as an eight year old. Those American wins included four in Grade 1 company - the Breeders Cup Mile, the Arlington Million, the Bernard Baruch

Handicap (all as a 6-y-o when he was voted the champion turf male) and the Hollywood Turf Handicap. He carried top-weight, or equal top-weight, for all four of those wins. Steinlen's first crop of 2-y-o's last year included only one winner - Miss Union Avenue - but she was highly rated on the Experimental Free Handicap at just 10 lbs below the top filly Flanders. Standing at Lane's End Farm in Lexington, Kentucky, Steinlen's fee is private.
(233)

STORM BIRD
1978 Northern Dancer - South Ocean (New Providence).
The champion two-year-old of 1980 and now a high class stallion, Storm Bird had the brilliant filly Balanchine, winner of the Oaks and the Irish Derby, representing him last year, along with the American Graded stakes winners Ocean Crest and Islefaxyou and the useful two-year olds Squadron Leader (in America), Done Well and Missel. Since his first runners appeared in 1985, Storm Bird's Group or Grade 1 winners have been the marvellous French Oaks and Champion Stakes winner Indian Skimmer, the Preakness Stakes winner Summer Squall, the Irish-trained colts Bluebird and Prince of Birds, the Prix Jean Prat winner Magical Wonder, the Santa Anita Derby winner Personal Hope, the Hollywood Oaks winner Pacific Squall and the Young America Stakes winner Storm Cat - now a top American stallion. Standing at Kentucky's Ashford Stud, Storm Bird's AEI is 3.18.
(40, 59)

STORM CAT
1983 Storm Bird - Terlingua (Secretariat).
The very smart, John Gosden trained, 6-7 furlong colt Catrail, the German Group 2 winner Munaaji and the very useful winners Mistle Cat and Elrafa Ah were the best representatives of the American stallion Storm Cat in Europe last year. Across the Atlantic, he had two fillies on the Experimental Free Handicap for 2-y-o's - Cat Appeal and Musical Cat, but it was his 3-y-o's that gave him a tremendous 1994. Thay included the Preakness and Belmont Stakes winner Tabasco Cat, the Kentucky Oaks winner Sardula and the Graded stakes winners Delineator, Stellar Cat and Cat Attack. With just four crops racing he has had a marvellous start to his stud career, for he's also had the Grade 1 winners Harlan, Missed the Storm and November Snow, along with the Grade 2 winner and $1.47 million earner Mountain Cat. Storm Cat stands at Overbrook Farm in Lexington, Kentucky and his AEI is an exceptional 5.09.
(48)

UNFUWAIN
1985 Northern Dancer - Height of Fashion (Bustino).
At the beginning of his stud career it seemed highly unlikely that Unfuwain would outshine his half-brother Nashwan at stud, given the better class of mares that the Derby winner would receive. At the moment however, he is doing just that, for his first crop of 3-y-o's last season included the Irish Oaks winner Bolas, the promising May Hill Stakes winner Mamlakah and the useful Italian listed winner Streisand. A very talented colt himself, Unfuwain won 6 races, notably the Group 2 Princess of Wales's Stakes and the Jockey Club Stakes and was 2nd in the King George to Mtoto. It was unfortunate that he never won a Group 1 race, for he was clearly superior to many that have done so. The firm ground that was prevalent for much of his 4-y-o season prevented him from running more than twice and he won both those races. Unfuwain stands at the Nunnery Stud in Norfolk at a fee of £8,000 (Oct 1st) and his 1994 yearling average was 21,687 gns (10 sold).
(116, 277, 330)

WARNING
1985 Known Fact - Slightly Dangerous (Roberto).
Third crop sire Warning has proved himself a sire of considerable merit already with winners such as Piccolo (Group 1 Keeneland Nunthorpe Stakes), Prophecy (Group 1 Cheveley Park Stakes), the Group 2 winners Torch Rouge and Bishop of Castel and the very promising 1994 2-y-o colt Annus Mirabilis. As a racehorse himself, Warning was right out of the top drawer. He won 8 races including the Queen Elizabeth II Stakes, the Sussex Stakes, the Queen Anne Stakes and, at 2 yrs, the Richmond Stakes and the Laurent Perrier Champagne Stakes. The distaff side of his pedigree includes his half-brothers, the Derby winner Commander in Chief and the Irish

Derby 2nd Deploy. His dam is also a half-sister to the dam of the top class sire Rainbow Quest. The champion first-season sire of 1993, Warning stands at Banstead Manor Stud at a fee of £12,000 (live foal). His 1994 yearling average was 22,175 gns (16 sold) and I expect him to go from strength to strength.
(137)

WOODMAN
1983 Mr Prospector - Playmate (Buckpasser).
A high class Irish 2-y-o in 1985, Woodman won two Group 3 races - the 6.3f Anglesey Stakes and the 8f Ferrans Futurity Stakes - but failed to train on. He had a sensational start as a sire, being responsible for the champion European 2-y-o and subsequent French 2,000 gns and Prix Jacques le Marois winner Hector Protector, the smart July Stakes and Gimcrack Stakes winner Mujtahid and the Belmont Stakes and Preakness Stakes winner Hansel. There followed three dismal seasons when the best of his measly four Group/Graded stakes winners was probably the Group 2 Prix de l'Opera winner Andromaque. Last year however, on the strength of the high class mares he received in 1992, Woodman was all the rage yet again. In America his son Timber Country proved himself the champion two-year-old after wins in the Grade 1 Breeders Cup Juvenile and the Grade 1 Champagne Stakes. In Britain, the filly Gay Gallanta won the Group 1 Cheveley Park Stakes and the Queen Mary Stakes at Royal Ascot. His 1994 sales-topping yearlings at Tattersalls Highflyer and Goffs can be found in this book under their respective trainers, Henry Cecil and John Gosden. Woodman stands at the Ashford Stud in Kentucky and his AEI is 2.75.
(28, 69, 72, 76, 120, 188, 195, 197, 206, 264, 323, 344)

ZALAZL
1986 Roberto - Salpinx (Northern Dancer).
One swallow doesn't make a summer and the fact that Zalazl's daughter Epagris looks a high class prospect for 1995 doesn't necessarily mean that his sale to Japan was a big mistake. He had other minor 2-y-o winners abroad in his first crop last year, but he gets into this book on the strength of his 2-y-o full sister to Epagris. As a racehorse, Zalazl was a high class winner of six of his nine races including the Group 2 Great Voltigeur Stakes. A $300,000 yearling, Zalazl was a game and consistent horse, if not out of the top drawer. His yearling average in 1994 was just 9,009 gns (4 sold).
(58)

ZILZAL
1986 Nureyev - French Charmer (Le Fabuleux).
With only 39 foals in his first two crops and just 25 runners, Zilzal was clearly not going to break any records in his early years as a stallion. To date, he has sired 14 winners including the 6-10f filly Monaassabaat, the very promising French filly Shaanxi and the middle distance colt Zilzal Zamaan - all very useful. Zilzal's record as a racehorse was an exceptional if dismally short one, of five wins from six races. His efforts in winning the Sussex Stakes, Queen Elizabeth II Stakes and Jersey Stakes were superb and his only disappointing performance came in the Breeders Cup Mile where his name was added to the long list of defeated British hopes. The champion European miler of 1989, Zilzal is closely related to another top class miler of his generation, Polish Precedent and stands at Gainsborough Farm in Kentucky. His stallion fee is private.
(119, 300, 318)

RACING TRENDS

TWO YEAR OLD RACE TRENDS - A STATISTICAL ANALYSIS

In the continuous quest for horses to follow, I have researched scores of two year old races to discover those that have proved most fruitful in pinpointing future three year old stars.

Logging second season form for each winner of these races since 1980 unearths a select number of juvenile events that regularly provide us with subsequent Group race winners.

All these statistics may not mean a great deal on their own, but with the invaluable aid of the form book and a knowledge of their pedigrees, one ought to be able to predict a significant number of the very best of the classic generation.

Similar exercises over the past three years selected the classic winners Rodrigo de Triano, Zafonic and Mister Baileys (all 2,000 gns), Sayyedati (1,000 gns), Marling (Irish 1,000 gns), Culture Vulture (French 1,000 gns), Dr Devious (Derby) and Bob's Return (St Leger), along with 13 other Group race winners.

We begin with the Lowther Stakes, an event which has produced no less than eight individual 3-y-o Group winners in the past fourteen years. The figures in the third column indicate the number of wins recorded as a 3-y-o and GW indicates a Group race winner at that age.

These then, are the winners of the featured races (Aqaarid and Sri Pekan actually won two each) and anyone looking for horses to follow in the Group/classic events of 1995 might well want to bear them in mind. Those that have been highlighted are, I feel, particularly worthy of attention.

Aqaarid	Marha
Celtic Swing	Musetta
Definite Article	**Painter's Row**
Double Eclipse	**Pennekamp**
Dreamer	Pipe Major
Eltish	**Red Carnival**
Gay Gallanta	Signs
Harayir	**Smart Alec**
Jumilla	**Sri Pekan**
Lammtarra	Tajannub
Mamlakah	Wijara

National 2-y-o Stakes
Sandown, 5 furlongs, May

1980	NO RACE	
1981	ABANDONED	
1982	Krayyan	0
1983	Precocious	Non-Runner
1984	Primo Dominie	1 GW
1985	Bakharoff	1 GW
1986	Risk Me	3 GW
1987	Tricky Note	0
1988	Superpower	0
1989	Princess Taufan	0
1990	NO RACE	
1991	Marling	3 GW
1992	Lyric Fantasy	1
1993	Redoubtable	0
1994	Signs	

The nine runnings of this race from 1984 to 1993 have produced a very respectable four individual Group winners for this early two-year-old event. Richard Hannon has trained the last three winners of this event and although the very useful 1993 winner, Redoubtable, was tried in Group company last year, he failed to win. The filly, Signs, seems a long way short of top class and cannot be recommended as one to follow in Group races this season.

Coventry Stakes
Royal Ascot, 6 furlongs, June.

1980	Recitation	2 GW
1981	Red Sunset	0
1982	Horage	1 GW
1983	Chief Singer	3 GW
1984	Primo Dominie	1 GW
1985	Sure Blade	3 GW
1986	Cutting Blade	1
1987	Always Fair	1 GW
1988	High Estate	1
1989	Rock City	2 GW
1990	Mac's Imp	0
1991	Dilum	2 GW
1992	Petardia	1
1993	Stonehatch	Non-Runner
1994	Sri Pekan	

Nearly always an excellent race for throwing up high class horses, perhaps the best among those in the list above is the marvellous sprinter/miler Chief Singer. Sri Pekan has a lot to do to emulate Chief Singer's racing record this year, but as a 2-y-o he could hardly be faulted. Given normal improvement, he's bound to pick up a good race or two at distances up to 8f.

Cherry Hinton Stakes
Newmarket, 6 furlongs, July

1980	Nasseem	1
1981	Travel On	0
1982	Crime of Passion	0
1983	Chapel Cottage	0
1984	Top Socialite	1 GW
1985	Storm Star	0
1986	Forest Flower	1 GW
1987	Diminuendo	4 GW
1988	Kerrera	1
1989	Chimes of Freedom	2 GW
1990	Chicarica	0
1991	Musicale	1 GW
1992	Sayyedati	2 GW
1993	Lemon Souffle	1 GW
1994	Red Carnival	

With seven of the previous ten winners of this race going on to Group race victories at 3 yrs, Red Carnival has a lot to live up to, but I expect her to be up to the task. She certainly needs to improve a good deal in order to be mentioned in the same breath as Sayyedati and Diminuendo, but don't dismiss her in the Group races at around a mile this season.

Lanson Champagne Stakes
Goodwood, 7 furlongs, July.

1980	Church Parade	1
1981	Treboro	0
1982	All Systems Go	0
1983	Trojan Fen	2 GW
1984	Petoski	2 GW
1985	Faustus	2 GW
1986	Don't Forget Me	2 GW
1987	Undercut	0
1988	High Estate	1
1989	Be My Chief	0
1990	Mukaddamah	1 GW
1991	Dr Devious	2 GW
1992	Maroof	1
1993	Mister Baileys	1 GW
1994	Eltish	

The above statistics don't tell all the story as Maroof, winner of this race in 1992, went on to win the Group 1 Queen Elizabeth II Stakes as a 4-y-o. All in all, this event looks pretty important in terms of trying to predict future stars, with the recent classic winning colts Dr Devious and Mister Baileys standing out. Eltish was being trained with the Kentucky Derby speciifically in mind, but hopefully his races won't be confined to the United States as he looks a particularly exciting prospect, especially with his commendable 2nd in the Breeders Cup Juvenile behind Timber Country.

Virginia Water Stakes
Ascot, 6 furlongs, July.

1980	Silken Knot	0
1981	Johara	0
1982	Habibti	4 GW
1983	Rusticello	Non-Runner
1984	Helen Street	1 GW
1985	Maysoon	1 GW
1986	Gayane	2
1987	Ashayer	1 GW
1988	Musical Bliss	1 GW
1989	Gharam	0
1990	Dangora	0
1991	Sun and Shade	Non-Runner
1992	Dancing Bloom	0
1993	Glatisant	0
1994	Aqaarid	

In the spring of 1994, trainer John Dunlop expressed his concern that Aqaarid would prove difficult to train in the long term due to her poor front legs. However, she went on to win the Group 1 Fillies Mile, and subsequently the Fred Darling Stakes before finishing 2nd in the 1,000 gns. She should certainly win further races as a three-year-old, particularly over 10 furlongs or more.

Princess Maiden Stakes
Newmarket, 6 furlongs, July

1980	Tolmi	1 GW
1981	DIV 1 Corsky	0
	DIV 2 Circus Ring	0
1982	Royal Heroine	4 GW
1983	Desirable	0
1984	Al Bahathri	3 GW
1985	Lady Brideshead	Non-Runner
1986	Canadian Mill	0
1987	Bluebook	1 GW
1988	Didicoy	1
1989	Ozone Friendly	0
1990	Only Yours	2 GW
1991	Harvest Girl	1
1992	Lake Pleasant	Non-Runner
1993	Prophecy	0
1994	DIV 1Tajannub	
	DIV 2 Jumilla	

Of the fillies to have won the two divisions of this race last year, Tajannub was rated by far the highest at the end of the season and she may be good enough to win a Group 3 event at 3 yrs, probably at around 7 or 8 furlongs.

Washington Singer Stakes
Newbury, 6 furlongs, August

1980	Poldhu	1
1981	Custer	0
1982	Horage	1 GW
1983	Trojan Fen	2 GW
1984	Khozaam	0
1985	Faustus	2 GW
1986	Deputy Governor	0
1987	Emmson	0
1988	Prince of Dance	1 (DISQ)
1989	Karinga Bay	1 GW
1990	Heart of Darkness	0
1991	Rodrigo de Triano	4 GW
1992	Tenby	2 GW
1993	Colonel Collins	0
1994	Lammtarra	

A beautifully bred colt, being by the Triple Crown hero Nijinsky and out of the Oaks winner (albeit on the disqualification of Aliysa) Snow Bride, Lammtarra will be suited by ten furlongs or more and is a most interesting prospect. Having overwintered in Dubai, he should be well forward when he does come back to Britain and he could be anything.

Lowther Stakes
York. 6 furlongs. August.

1980	Kittyhawk	1.00
1981	Circus Ring	0.00
1982	Habibti	4 GW
1983	Prickle	0.00
1984	Al Bahathri	3 GW
1985	Kingscote	0.00
1986	Polonia	3 GW
1987	Ela Romara	1 GW
1988	Miss Demure	0.00
1989	Dead Certain	1 GW
1990	Only Yours	2 GW
1991	Culture Vulture	1 GW
1992	Niche	2 GW
1993	Velvet Moon	1.00
1994	Harayir	

Harayir beat Gay Gallanta comprehensively in the Lowther and although the tables were turned in the Cheveley Park Stakes, Harayir subsequently won the 1,000 gns from Aqaarid and Moonshell with Gay Gallanta well behind. The list of good fillies that have won the Lowther Stakes is impressive, including as it does the French and Irish 1,000 gns winners Culture Vulture and Al Bahathri, along with the top class sprinters Habibti and Polonia.

May Hill Stakes
Doncaster, 8 furlongs, September

1980	Exclusively Raised	0
1981	Height of Fashion	2 GW
1982	Bright Crocus	Non-Runner
1983	Satinette	0
1984	Ever Genial	2 GW
1985	Midway Lady	2 GW
1986	Laluche	0
1987	Intimate Guest	1
1988	Tessla	0
1989	Rafha	3 GW
1990	Majmu	0
1991	Midnight Air	0
1992	Marillette	1 GW
1993	Hawajiss	2 GW
1994	Mamlakah	

By the Group 2 12f winner Unfuwain and out of a 2-y-o 5f winner, Mamlakah would seem to be taking after her sire, stamina-wise, and will stay at least 10f this year. She could easily pick up another Group event or two and should be watched closely.

Fillies Conditions Stakes
Newbury 7 furlongs September

1980	NO RACE	
1981	NO RACE	
1982	Salvinia	1
1983	Mahogany	1 GW
1984	Dubian	1
1985	Mill on the Floss	1
1986	Milligram	3 GW
1987	Andaleeb	1 GW
1988	Samaza	0
1989	Free at Last	1 (IN USA)
1990	Fragrant Hill	1
1991	Freewheel	1
1992	Sueboog	1 GW
1993	Balanchine	2 GW
1994	Musetta	

The brilliant fillies Balanchine and Milligram stand out in this Group. Although not even Musetta's greatest fan could expect her to improve to their standard, she is a useful filly, though perhaps of listed, rather than class. She will stay a mile, perhaps ten furlongs, at 3 yrs.

Laurent Perrier Champage Stakes
Doncaster, 7 furlongs, September.

1980	Gielgud	Non-Runner
1981	Acheived	1 GW
1982	Gorytus	0
1983	Lear Fan	2 GW
1984	Young Runaway	2 GW
1985	Sure Blade	3 GW
1986	Don't Forget Me	2 GW
1987	Warning	3 GW
1988	Prince of Dance	0
1989	ABANDONED	
1990	Bog Trotter	2 GW
1991	Rodrigo de Triano	4 GW
1992	Petardia	1
1993	Unblest	1 GW
1994	Sri Pekan	

One of last season's best and most consistent 2-y-o's, Sri Pekan may seem up against it with Pennekamp and Celtic Swing around, but he shouldn't be underestimated. There are surely one or two good prizes to be won by this son of the successful young American sire Red Ransom. In the last 14 runnings of this race, 11 of the winners have gone on to win 21 races between tham as three-year-olds. Notice the two English and Irish 2,000 gns winners Rodrigo de Triano and Don't Forget Me! Prince of Dance would surely have been another big race winner but for his early death and Warning was arguably the most talented of them all on his day.

Woodchester Credit Lyonnais Futurity Conditions Stakes
(formerly the Reference Pointer Stakes)
Sandown 8 furlongs September.

1980	Obrovac	0
1981	ABANDONED	
1982	Magic Rarity	Non-Runner
1983	Forest of Dean	2
1984	Lord Grundy	1
1985	Dancing Brave	6 GW
1986	Reference Point	5 GW
1987	Albadr	1
1988	Mired	0
1989	Elmaamul	3 GW
1990	Generous	3 GW
1991	King's Loch	1
1992	Geisway	1
1993	Overbury	1 GW
1994	Dreamer	

Not within 30 lbs of some of the previous winners of this event, notably Dancing Brave, Generous and Reference Point, Dreamer would do well to win a Group 3 event this term, though he is a nicely bred colt, being by Zilzal out of a half-sister to the dam of Zoman.

Blue Seal Stakes
Ascot, 6 furlongs, September.

1980	Petroleuse	1 GW
1981	Dancing Rocks	1 GW
1982	Khaizaraan	0
1983	Rappa Tap Tap	1
1984	Dafayna	2 GW
1985	Sonic Lady	6 GW
1986	White Mischief	0
1987	New Trends	0
1988	Ensconse	2 GW
1989	Alwathba	0
1990	Crystal Gazing	1 GW
1991	Misterioso	0
1992	Queens View	1
1993	Tablah	0
1994	Marha	

This race always threatens to highlight a lively prospect for the following season's top fillies' races and although Ensconse won the Irish 1,000 gns, the brilliant Sonic Lady is out on her own among this Group. Sadly, last year's winner of this race, Marha, doesn't appear to be in the same league as most of her predecessors and will do extremely well to win a Group event this year.

National Stakes
Curragh, 7 furlongs, September.

1980	Storm Bird	0
1981	Day is Done	0
1982	Glenstal	1 GW
1983	El Gran Senor	3 GW
1984	Law Society	2 GW
1985	Tate Gallery	0
1986	Lockton	3
1987	Caerwent	2
1988	Classic Fame	1 GW
1989	Dashing Blade	2 GW
1990	Heart of Darkness	0
1991	El Prado	0
1992	Fatherland	0
1993	Manntari	1
1994	Definite Article	

This race has had its ups and downs and at the moment is very much on the latter. Manntari failed to turn out again after finishing distressed in the Irish 2,000 gns and both El Prado and Fatherland disappointed their trainer Vincent O'Brien. Definite Article is trained by Dermot Weld and, although unbeaten in his two races last year, needs to improve significantly to enter the classic picture.

Mornington Stakes
Ascot 7 furlongs September

1980	Centurius	1 GW
1981	General Anders	0
1982	By Decree	0
1983	Donzel	0
1984	Tour D'Or	0
1985	Zahdam	1 GW
1986	Ajdal	4 GW
1987	Sheriff's Star	2 GW
1988	Shaadi	3 GW
1989	Shavian	2 GW
1990	Big Blow	Non-Runner
1991	Assessor	2 GW
1992	Inchinor	3 GW
1993	Mutakddim	3
1994	Wijara	

The very useful 1993 winner, Mutakddim, may have failed to win a Group event last season, but he may well put that right this year. The success of the previous 7 winners of this race to run as three-year-olds is quite amazing. They include the champion sprinter Ajdal and the high class colts Inchinor, Sheriff's Star, Shaadi and Shavian. Wijara won both his two-year-old races last season, but needs to improve considerably to be considered in Group events in Britain this year.

Dewhurst Stakes
Newmarket, 7 furlongs, October.

1980	Storm Bird	0
1981	Wind and Wuthering	0 (2,000 gns 2nd)
1982	Diesis	
1983	El Gran Senor	2 GW
1984	Kala Dancer	0
1985	Huntingdale	0
1986	Ajdal	4 GW
1987	ABANDONED	
1988	Prince of Dance & Scenic (dead heat)	1 (DISQ) 1
1989	Dashing Blade	2 GW
1990	Generous	3 GW
1991	Dr Devious	2 GW
1992	Zafonic	1 GW
1993	Grand Lodge	1 GW
1994	Pennekamp	

A mighty list indeed! Derby winners Generous and Dr Devious, champion sprinter Ajdal and the 2,000 gns winners El Gran Senor and Zafonic stand out. Having won the 2,000 gns, Pennekamp will now try to prove he's the best, and certainly the most versatile, of all these by winning the Epsom Derby.

Westley Maiden Stakes
(In 1994, the Port of Felixtowe Maiden)
Newmarket, 7 furlongs, October.

1980	Kings Glory	1
1981	Simply Great	1 GW
1982	DIV 1 Tolomeo	1 GW (In USA)
	DIV 2 Mandelstam	0
1983	Chelkov	0
1984	Profess	0
1985	DIV 1 Cromwell Park	1
	DIV 2 Illumineux	0
1986	DIV 1 Pollenate	0
	DIV 2 Tweeter	0
1987	DIV 1 Doyoun	2GW
	DIV 2 Charmer	0 (2nd in 2,000 gns)
1988	DIV 1 Pirate Army	1
	DIV 2 Observation Post	0
1989	DIV 1 Mukddaam	1
	DIV 2 Cutting Note	0
1990	DIV 1 Environment Friend	2GW
	DIV 2 Sapieha	0
1991	DIV 1 Modernise	0
	DIV 2 Pursuit of Love	3
1992	DIV1 Placerville	2GW
	DIV 2 Barathea	1GW
1993	Darnay	0
1994	DIV 1 Painter's Row	
	DIV 2 Smart Alec	

Usually run in two divisions due to the large number of entries, this race really came into its own in 1987 when Doyoun went on to capture the 2,000 gns at the expense of Charmer. Painter's Row went on from this race to win the Horris Hill Stakes last year and so ended the season rated higher than Smart Alec. For 1995 though, it's too early too say which one will end up the better colt. They are both high class prospects that should be suited by at least 10 furlongs as three-year-olds.

Soham House Stakes
Newmarket, 8 furlongs, October.

1980	Video Tape	0
1981	Dudley Wood	4
1982	Coming and Going	0
1983	Sassagras	0
1984	Verdance	2
1985	Dancing Brave	6 GW
1986	Pillar of Wisdom	0
1987	Kahyasi	4 GW
1988	Warrshan	2 GW
1989	Belmez (Carlsburg Stakes)	4 GW
1990	Polish King	0
1991	Hill Glitter	0
1992	Shaiba	1
1993	King of Naples	1
1994	Pipe Major	

Somewhat disappointing since 1990, this race has nevertheless pinpointed the great Dancing Brave, the top class colts Kahyasi and Belmez, and the dual Group winner Warrshan. Pipe Major is surely not in their league, but he is a very promising sort and can win more races this season if not tried too highly.

Zetland Stakes
Newmarket, 10 furlongs, October.

1980	Krug	0
1981	Paternoster Row	0
1982	John French	1 GW
1983	High Debate	0
1984	Ulterior Motive	2 GW
1985	Highland Chieftain	2 GW
1986	Grand Tour	0
1987	Upper Strata	Non-Runner
1988	Mamaluna	1 GW
1989	Rock Hopper	1 GW
1990	Matahif	0
1991	Bonny Scot	2 GW
1992	Bob's Return	3 GW
1993	Double Trigger	1 GW
1994	Double Eclipse	

Bob's Return, hero of the St Leger, became the first English classic winner to emerge from this race during the period in review, whilst Rock Hopper improved with age to become a high class four-year-old. Double Eclipse is a full-brother to the previous year's winner, Double Trigger, who ran well in both the Great Voltigeur Stakes and the St Leger before winning the Italian St Leger in Turin. Double Eclipse will be an equally smart 3-y-o and will stay just as well as his brother does.

Cheveley Park Stakes
Newmarket, 6 furlongs, October.

1980	Marwell	5 GW
1981	Woodstream	0
1982	Ma Biche	3
1983	Desirable	0
1984	Park Appeal	0
1985	Embla	1
1986	Forest Flower	(DISQ) 1 GW
1987	Ravinella	4 GW
1988	Pass the Peace	0
1989	Dead Certain	1 GW
1990	Capricciosa	Non-Runner
1991	Marling	3 GW
1992	Sayyedati	2 GW
1993	Prophecy	0
1994	Gay Gallanta	

There appear to be plenty of decent mile fillies around this year and Gay Gallanta has stronger claims than most for future Group 1 success, particularly due to her win in this race, the Cheveley Park Stakes. Previous 1,000 gns winners Ma Biche, Ravinella and Sayyedati all won this event and although Gay Gallanta does not yet seem to be in their league, one would certainly expect her to win another nice prize this season.

Racing Post Trophy
Doncaster, 8 furlongs, October.

1980	Beldale Flutter	2 GW
1981	Count Pahlen	1 GW
1982	Dunbeath	0
1983	Alphabatim	3 GW
1984	Lanfranco	2 GW
1985	Bakharoff	1 GW
1986	Reference Point	5 GW
1987	Emmson	0
1988	Al Hareb	0
1989	Be My Chief	0
1990	Peter Davies	0
1991	Seattle Rhyme	0
1992	Armiger	1 GW
1993	King's Theatre	2 GW
1994	Celtic Swing	

No surprises here, as Celtic Swing was expected to carry all before him this year. King's Theatre managed to break a disappointing run for this race by winning the King George VI and Queen Elizabeth Diamond Stakes last year and, to say the least, a great deal is expected of Celtic Swing. Although narrowly beaten in the 2,000 gns, he will remain a very difficult horse to beat this season.

INDEX

Absolute Utopia	118	Bush Rose	293
Ailesbury Hill	69	Buttermere	191
Air Quest	87		
Alamo Bay	141	Caer Melyn	333
Alfahaal	327	Callaloo	68
Alhalal	1	Candle Smoke	206
All For Show	208	Canyon Creek	172
Allied Forces	24	Caribbean Quest	203
Alpine	101	Carniola	192
Altamura	168	Casting For Gold	294
Alyshadeed	11	Catalyst	13
Ambassadress	169	Caxton Star	30
Ameer Jumairah	170	Celtic Wing	227
Ambassador	230	Censor	31
Amfortas	19	Chalamont	70
Amusing Aside	332	Charlock	268
Anasazi	143	Charlotte Corday	349
Angel Face	119	Chief Contender	71
Answered Prayer	209	Chirico	173
Antonella Bin	12	Clash Of Swords	295
Arabeski	25	Classic Colours	346
Arutua	142	Classic Jenny	347
Ashbal	278	Classic Mix	212
Ashjar	328	Classic Vintage	348
Aspen Snow	279	Clerkenwell	296
Azwah	331	Clever Cliche'	32
		Color Precedent	297
Balalaika	108	Coronation Gold	322
Balladur	26		
Ballet High	3	Dance Design	334
Balsam	329	Dance Sequence	298
Basood	120	Dancing Shoes	239
Beacontree	247	Darazari	284
Behariya	282	Darkness At Noon	88
Bereg	292	Decrescendo	33
Berry Rose	283	Delta Dancer	4
Bint Salsabil	128	Desert Serenade	122
Bint Shadayid	129	Devil's Dance	299
Birdlip	27	Diali	335
Blue Duster	255	Dimakya	256
Bold Bold	210	Dismissed	102
Bosra Sham	28	Distant Oasis	34
Braidwood	171	Divine Quest	35
Bravalma	211	Doctor Green	241
Bright Desert	121	Don Vito	89
Bright Water	29	Dosthill	36

Double Niner	37	Helicon	43
Dream Bay	14	Helsinki	148
Duel At Dawn	174	Hidden Oasis	305
Dunaysir	285	High Baroque	73
Durrah Green	15	High Priority	16
Dushyamtor	38	High Summer	92
Dusty Gems	124	Hook Line	281
		House of Riches	113
Earth Shaker	300	How Long	114
Easy Definition	336		
Eben Naas	301	Iberian	193
Ecoute	213	Incarvillea	257
Ela-Yie-Mou	109	Inchyre	93
Elmswood	72	In Generosity	339
El Opera	103	Insiyabi	131
Epigram	266		
Et Frem	243	Jarah	204
Exemplaire	214	Johnny Jones	74
Expensive Taste	302		
Extremely Friendly	280	Karamzin	175
		Karanpour	286
Faateq	130	Kasora	269
Fairlight Down	104	Kebili	306
Filly Mi Gnonne	231	Kerenza	44
First Flame	144	Kerry Ring	176
Flamada	20	Kilvine	115
Flamands	110	King Alex	94
Flame Of Athens	190	King's Academy	45
Flamineo	39	King's Flame	307
Flaming Feather	337	Kinlochewe	46
Flaming June	40	Kissing Gate	95
Flying Pegasus	145	Kota	345
Forest Hills	323		
Freequent	111	Lafitte The Pirate	149
		L'Ami Louis	177
Gain Line	90	Land Of Heroes	178
Generosa	23	La Papaya	244
Get Away With It	303	La Pellegrina	75
Grace And Glory	41	Lavanda	258
Grand Concerto	265	Legal Opinion	150
Grape Tree Road	146	Light Reflections	232
Green Barries	248	Like A Hawk	105
Green Charter	42	Lippi	151
Green Planet	9	Lochspring	5
Gretna Green	228	Lothlorian	76
Guest Of Anchor	10	Luna Wells	152
		Lydenburg	153
Haleakala	249		
Hamad	338	Machaera	99
Hammerstein	304	Madame Steinlen	233
Hanbitooh	123	Magellan	21
Handsome Dancer	147	Mamdooh	223
Happy Medium	267	Mansab	132
Hard News	91	Marcomir	250
Height of Secrecy	112	Masafiya	270

Index

Mask Flower	251	Pricket	52
Mawwal	2	Private Audience	53
Mazamet	271	Private Song	97
Mazurek	77	Proud Fact	155
Medsee	96		
Meribel	78	Questing Star	350
Metal Badge	252	Questonia	54
Midday Cowboy	207	Quota	55
Midnight Oasis	196		
Mighty Keen	253	Raheen	313
Migwar	116	Regal Eagle	6
Min Elreeh	224	Restless Carl	156
Mithali	330	Reticent	180
Modern Day	47	Reveuse De Jour	98
Mohawk River	308	Ring Of Music	181
Moonfire	259	Rocky Oasis	314
Moon Is Up	197	Rossel	315
Moon Mischief	229	Royal Court	82
Mountain Holly	260	Royal Hostess	288
Movie Legend	340	Run For Me	182
Mudallel	324	Ruznama	235
Muhtadi	133		
Mukeed	179	Sabaah Elfull	290
Musick House	79	Sacho	183
		Samim	136
Najiya	134	Sandy Floss	56
Namouna	80	Sasura	351
Nanda	261	Scarlet Plume	137
Naseem El Fajr	289	Scarpetta	240
Nash House	81	Scenic Spirit	254
National Treasure	309	Scherma	245
Natural Gold	215	Sea Hill	216
Night Spell	341	Sensation	217
Ninotchka	135	Serif	184
No-Aman	225	Set In Motion	218
North Cyclone	22	Setting Sun	157
		Sevres Rose	287
Old Irish	117	Shady Wells	57
Omara	48	Shahrur	291
Ood Ya Zamann	125	Sharaf Kabeer	185
Opal Jewel	310	Shawanni	236
Oriane	272	Shawkey	226
		Sheraka	274
Papaha	49	Silver Border	7
Patria	311	Silverstorm	220
Phantom Creek	325	Silwana	219
Phantom Quest	50	Ski For Gold	138
Pigeon Hole	205	Skillington	8
Pink Cashmere	262	Socialite	275
Place De L'Opera	51	Sonhos	107
Polent	154	Sourire	158
Polinesso	234	Soviet Dreamer	17
Possessive Artiste	312	Spinning World	198
Power Play	273	Stage Manner	194
Prancing	263	Star And Garter	352

State Circus	242	Wybara	189
State Theatre	83		
Storm Card	58	Xaymara	222
Storm Shelter	59		
Storm Trooper	60	Yahni	166
Subterfuge	61	Yamuna	65
Sulawesi	246	Yogya	202
Supamova	106		
Swan Princess	186	Zaynal	276
Tamatete	159	Not Named	66
Ta Rib	126	Not Named	67
Tarquinia	100		
Tassili	353		
Thracian	139		
Three Hills	237		
Three More	160		
Tillyard	84		
Time Allowed	316		
Touch Judge	342		
Treason	317		
Tria Kemata	140		
Triple Leap	187		
True Joy	318		
Trust Ball	161		
Trust In Luck	343		
Trying Times	162		
Understood	221		
Unitus	319		
Unreal City	62		
Unsold	167		
Upper Gallery	85		
Vaguely Regal	320		
Vautour Rouge	199		
Vice President	18		
Vilayet	63		
Vingt Et Une	200		
Vivat Regina	163		
Vivonne	277		
Wall Street	326		
Water Poet	164		
Wedgewood	344		
Wee Hope	321		
Welcome Parade	64		
Wilawander	238		
Wild Rumour	86		
Willstar	165		
Wind Of Roses	201		
Winter Romance	127		
Woodbury	264		
Woodspell	195		
Wood Vine	188		